ACT® for Busy Students

Related Titles for College-Bound Students

Big Book of ACT Practice Tests
ACT English, Reading, adn Writing Prep
ACT Math & Science Prep
ACT Strategies, Practice & Review
AP Biology
AP Calculus AB & BC
AP Chemistry
AP English Language & Composition
AP English Literature & Composition
AP Environmental Science
AP European History
AP Human Geography
AP Macroeconomics/Microeconomics
AP Physics B & C
AP Psychology
AP Statistics
AP U.S. Government & Politics
AP U.S. History
AP World History
New SAT Premier
New SAT Strategies, Practice & Review
8 Practice Tests for the SAT
Evidence-Based Reading, Writing, and Essay Workbook for the New SAT
Math Workbook for the New SAT
SAT Subject Test: Biology E/M
SAT Subject Test: Chemistry
SAT Subject Test: Literature
SAT Subject Test: Mathematics Level 1
SAT Subject Test: Mathematics Level 2
SAT Subject Test: Physics
SAT Subject Test: Spanish
SAT Subject Test: U.S. History
SAT Subject Test: World History

ACT
for
Busy Students

Fifth Edition

15 Simple Steps to Tackle the ACT

New York

ACT® is a registered trademark of ACT, Inc., which neither sponsors nor endorses this product.

ACT® is a registered trademark of ACT, Inc., which neither sponsors nor endorses this product.

This publication is designed to provide accurate and authoritative information in regard to the subject matter covered. It is sold with the understanding that the publisher is not engaged in rendering legal, accounting, or other professional service. If legal advice or other expert assistance is required, the services of a competent professional should be sought.

© 2016 by Kaplan, Inc.

Published by Kaplan Publishing, a division of Kaplan, Inc.
750 Third Avenue, 7th floor
New York, NY 10017

All rights reserved. The text of this publication, or any part thereof, may not be reproduced in any manner whatsoever without written permission from the publisher.

Excerpt from *A History of Women Artists*, copyright © 1975 by Hugo Munsterberg; Clarkson N. Potter, Inc. (a division of Random House, Inc.), publisher. Reprinted by permission of the author's family.

Excerpt from *Invitation to the Theatre*, Third Edition, copyright © 1985 by George Kernodle. Reprinted by permission of Wadsworth, a division of Thomson Learning: www.thomsonlearning.com
Fax 1-800-730-2212.

Cover and interior illustrations designed by Aaron Meshon.

10 9 8 7 6 5 4 3 2 1

ISBN-13: 978-1-5062-2918-8

Table of Contents

Available Online..xii
How to Use This Book..xiii
Customized ACT Study Schedules...xiv

Part 1: Preparing for the ACT...1

  Step One: Introduction to the ACT....................................3

    Introduction...4
      The Test Format..4
      The Test Strategies..4
      The Concepts Tested...4
    What Is the ACT?...5
    What Is the ACT Writing Test?....................................5
    How Is the ACT Scored?...6
    How Many ACT Scores Will You Get?..........................7
    How Do Colleges Use Your ACT Scores?......................7
    Should You Guess on the ACT?...................................8
    Can You Retake the Test?...8

  Step Two: The Subject Tests...11

    Introduction...12
    English..12
      Standard Format Questions..................................13
      Directions..14
      To Omit or Not to Omit.......................................15
      Nonstandard Format Questions............................15
    Math...16
      Format..16
      Directions..17
      Diagram Questions...17
      Story Questions...18
      Concept Questions...19
    Reading..19
      Format..19
      Directions..20
      Reading Passages...20

Specific Detail Questions 21
  Inference Questions. 21
  Big Picture Questions 22
 Science. 22
  Format. 23
  Directions 23
  Data Representation Questions 23
  Experiment Questions 24
  Principle Questions. 25
 Writing. 25
  Format and Directions 25

Step Three: General Test-Taking Strategies. 27
 Introduction 28
 Do Question Triage 28
 Put the Material into a Form You Can Understand. 29
  Mark Up Your Test Booklet 29
  Reword the Questions 30
  Draw Diagrams 31
 Ignore Irrelevant Issues 32
 Check Back 32
 Answer the Right Question 33
 Look for the Hidden Answer 34
 Guess Intelligently 35
 Be Careful with the Answer Grid 35
 Use the Letters of the Answer Choices to Stay on Track. 36
 Keep Track of Time 37
 Take Control of Your Test 37

Part 2: The ACT English Test 39

Step Four: English Question Types and Strategies 41
 Kaplan's Three-Step Method for ACT English 42
  Step 1. Read Until You Have Enough Information to Identify the Issue. 42
  Step 2. Eliminate Choices That Do NOT Address the Issue. 42
  Step 3. Plug in the Remaining Choices, and Choose the One That Is Most Correct,
  Concise, and Relevant.. 42
 Economy Questions 42
  Redundancy, Verbosity, Irrelevance. 44

Table of Contents

    When in Doubt... 45
  Sense Questions.. 45
    Make It Make Sense 46
    Good Grammar Makes Good Sense................................... 50
  Nonstandard Format Questions 56
    Judging the Passage 56
    Reading-Type Questions... 57

Step Five: Twelve Classic Grammar Errors............................... 59

  Introduction... 60
  Trusting Your Ear 60
    Formal or Informal?... 60
  "Listening" Carefully: Practice Passage.. 61
  Twelve Classic Grammar Errors... 64
    Error 1: *It* and *They* (Singulars and Plurals)............................ 64
    Error 2: Commas or Dashes (Parenthetical Phrases)..................... 65
    Error 3: Run-Ons and Comma Splices 65
    Error 4: Fragments... 66
    Error 5: Misunderstood Punctuation Marks 66
    Error 6: *-ly* Endings (Adverbs and Adjectives) 66
    Error 7: *Its* and *It's* (Apostrophe Use) 67
    Error 8: *There, Their, They're* and *Are, Our* (Proper Word Usage)........ 68
    Error 9: *Sang, Sung, Brang, Brung,* etc. (Verb Forms).................... 68
    Error 10: *-er* and *-est, More* and *Most* (Comparatives and Superlatives).... 68
    Error 11: Confusing *Between* and *Among* 69
    Error 12: Confusing *Less* and *Fewer*................................. 69

Part 3: The ACT Math Test... 71

Step Six: Math Question Types and Strategies 73

  Introduction... 74
  Question Breakdown 74
  Be a Thinker—Not a Number Cruncher 74
  Kaplan's Four-Step Method for ACT Math 76
    Step 1. What Is the Question?... 76
    Step 2. What Information Am I Given? 76
    Step 3. What Can I Do with the Information? 77
    Step 4. Am I Finished?.. 77

Important Math Concepts	80
Kaplan's Two-Pass Plan for ACT Math	81
Know When to Skip a Question	81
What to Do When You're Stuck	82
Guesstimating	82
Eyeballing	83

Step Seven: Calculator Techniques **87**

Introduction	88
Using Calculators	88
Think Before You Calculate	89
Using the Calculator to Save Time	90
Calculators: The Game Plan	90
Know Your Calculator	91
Backsolving and Picking Numbers	92

Step Eight: Algebra, Coordinate Geometry, Percents, and Averages **93**

Introduction	94
Textbook Algebra and Coordinate Geometry Questions	94
Complex Algebra and Coordinate Geometry Questions	95
Restate the Problem	95
Remove the Disguise	97
Pick Numbers	99
Backsolve	100
Story Questions	101
Percent Problems	101
Average Questions	103
Probability Questions	105

Step Nine: Geometry **107**

Introduction	108
Textbook Geometry Questions	108
Complex Geometry Questions	108
Find the Hidden Information	108
Figureless Questions	112
Multistep Questions	113

Part 4: The ACT Reading Test **117**

Step Ten: Skills Reading **119**

Table of Contents

Introduction 120
Know Where You're Going 120
    Common Structural Clues 121
Kaplan's Three-Step Method for ACT Reading 121
    Step 1. Actively Read the Passage, Taking Notes as You Go. 122
    Step 2. Examine the Question Stem, Looking for Clues.. 122
    Step 3. Predict the Answer and Select the Choice That Best Matches
    Your Prediction. 123
Creating a Road Map. 123
    Practice Making a Passage Map. 123
    The General Outline. 125
Special Passages: Prose Fiction, Natural Science, and Paired Passages. 126
    The Prose Fiction Passage. 126
    The Natural Science Passage 127

Step Eleven: Reading Question Types and Strategies 129
Introduction. 130
Detail Questions 133
Inference Questions 134
Big Picture Questions 135
Proven Reading Strategies 136
    Find and Paraphrase 136
    Skipping Questions 137

Part 5: The ACT Science Test 139

Step Twelve: Science Skills and Strategies 141
Reading Skills for Science Reasoning 142
Kaplan's Three-Step Method for ACT Science. 142
    Step 1. Map the Passage, Identifying and Marking the Purpose,
    Method, and Results of the Experiment. 143
    Step 2. Scan Figures, Identifying Variables and Patterns. 143
    Step 3. Find Support for the Answer in the Passage. 143
Reading Tables and Graphs 144
    Look for Patterns and Trends. 146
What to Do When You're Running Out of Time. 148

Step Thirteen: Experiment Questions 149
Introduction. 150
How Scientists Think 150

    General-to-Specific Thinking 150

    Specific-to-General Thinking 150

  How Experiments Work 151

    A Controlled Situation 152

    Find What Varies 152

  Handling Experiment Questions: Practice Passage 153

    Approaching the Passage 155

Step Fourteen: The Conflicting Viewpoints Passage 159

  Introduction 160

  Prereading the Conflicting Viewpoints Passage 160

  The Real Thing: Practice Passage and Key Strategies 162

    Identifying the Conflict 164

    Attacking the Questions 165

Part 6: The ACT Writing Test 169

Step Fifteen: Writing Skills and Strategies 171

  Introduction 172

  Just the Facts 172

    How Will Schools Use the Writing Test? 172

    Who Should Take the Writing Test? 172

  How the ACT Essay Is Scored 173

    What Skills Are Tested? 173

    Do You Need to Prepare for the Essay? 173

  Kaplan's Four-Step Method for the ACT Essay 174

    Step 1. Prompt 176

    Step 2. Plan 177

    Step 3. Produce 180

    Step 4. Proofread 181

  Know the Score: Sample Essays 182

    Turning a 4 into a 6 185

Part 7: Practice Test and Explanations 189

  Answer Key 248

  Answers and Explanations 249

Part 8: Busy Resources ... 281

Busy Summaries ... 283
Last-Minute Tips ... 297
- The Night before the Test ... 298
- The Morning of the Test ... 298
- During the Test ... 299
- After the Test ... 299

Stress Management ... 301
- Managing Your Stress ... 301
- Identify the Sources of Stress ... 301
- My Strengths and Weaknesses ... 302
- Imagine Yourself Succeeding ... 304
- Exercise Your Frustrations Away ... 306
- Take a Deep Breath ... 306
- . . . and Keep Breathing ... 307
- Quick Tips for the Days Just before the Exam ... 307
- Study Tips ... 308
- Handling Stress during the Test ... 309

100 Essential Math Concepts ... 311
Building Your Vocabulary ... 341
- Tough ACT Words ... 341
- Kaplan's Three-Step Method for Vocabulary Building ... 341
- Decoding Strange Words on the Test ... 342

Word Root List ... 345

Available Online

kaptest.com/publishing

The material in this book is up-to-date at the time of publication. However, ACT Inc. may have instituted changes in the test after this book was published. Be sure to read carefully the materials you receive when you register for the test. If there are any important late-breaking developments—or any changes or corrections to the Kaplan test preparation materials in this book—we will post that information online at kaptest.com/publishing.

kaplansurveys.com/books

We'd love to hear your comments and suggestions about this book. We invite you to fill out our online survey form at kaplansurveys.com/books. Your feedback is extremely helpful as we continue to develop high-quality resources to meet your needs.

How to Use This Book

This is the perfect ACT prep book for the overextended high-schooler with a hyperactive lifestyle. *ACT for Busy Students Fifth Edition* crunches Kaplan's years of test-prep know-how into a book that's fast, easy to read, and effective.

Here's how. Studying for the ACT is pretty straightforward:

- You learn overall test-taking skills and strategies.
- You learn Reading and English skills and strategies.
- You learn Math and Science skills and strategies.
- You learn the optional Writing skills and strategies.
- You apply these skills and strategies on a full-length practice ACT.

ACT for Busy Students Fifth Edition teaches the **most important** skills and strategies in 15 super organized steps. Each **Busy** step helps you:

- Know the details of each ACT subject test
- Learn the specific skills that help you with that subject test
- Master Kaplan's proven strategies for answering ACT questions on that subject test

ACT for Busy Students Fifth Edition covers general ACT information and strategies. Each step covers its subject in detail. At the end of the book is a timed, full-length practice ACT. Take it, score it, and you're ready for the real deal.

Okay, you're busy, so let's start.

Customized ACT Study Schedules

Kaplan understands that super busy students like you need to maximize your time and fit your studies into an already crowded schedule. To help you plan, we've created four customized study schedules, depending on how much time you have before test day. Use one of these schedules to make the most of your time, or use the blank schedule provided to create your own.

If You Only Have Six Weeks to Test Day

Though it's a good idea to begin preparing for the ACT as early as possible, if you only have six weeks to study, here's the schedule for you.

Days before the ACT	What to Study
42 Days before the ACT	Read Step One: Introduction to the ACT. This will be your introduction to the ACT. Learning about the ACT is one of the most important things you can do when you are getting ready for test day.
41 Days before the ACT	Read Step Two: The Subject Tests. Here you will learn more about each of the subject tests that make up the ACT.
40 Days before the ACT	Read Step Three: General Test-Taking Strategies. These will apply to every part of the test, so you should focus on these early on.
39 Days before the ACT	Take a day off. You're just getting warmed up in your ACT preparation.
38 Days before the ACT	Move on to Part 2. Read Step Four: English Question Types and Strategies. Start with a review of the Kaplan Three-Step Method for ACT English and learn about a few of the kinds of English questions you will see on test day.
37 Days before the ACT	Read Step Five: Twelve Classic Grammar Errors. You will have the chance to practice some questions and will learn about some classic grammar errors.
36 Days before the ACT	If there is anything that you didn't understand in Part 2, go back and study it today.
35 Days before the ACT	Take a day off. Let your mind and body recover.

34 Days before the ACT	Jump back into the ACT groove with Part 3: The ACT Math Test. Read Step Six: Math Question Types and Strategies. You'll learn both the Kaplan Three-Step Method for ACT and Kaplan's Two-Pass Plan for ACT Math.
33 Days before the ACT	Read Step Seven: Calculator Techniques. Remember, you can use a calculator on ACT math.
32 Days before the ACT	Read Step Eight: Algebra, Coordinate Geometry, Percents, and Averages. Review the question samples.
31 Days before the ACT	Read Step Nine: Geometry.
30 Days before the ACT	Turn to the Busy Resources and read the first 50 of the 100 Essential Math Concepts. Make sure you're clear on all of these concepts.
29 Days before the ACT	Read the second 50 of the 100 Essential Math Concepts. Make sure you're clear on all of these concepts.
28 Days before the ACT	Take a day off. Let your mind and body recover.
27 Days before the ACT	Now you're ready to tackle ACT Reading. Read Step Ten: Reading Skills.
26 Days before the ACT	Read Step Eleven: Reading Question Types and Strategies.
25 Days before the ACT	Because you might be tested on vocabulary in context, read Building Your Vocabulary in the Busy Resources.
24 Days before the ACT	Read the Word Roots List in the Busy Resources.
23 Days before the ACT	Take a day off. Let your mind and body recover.
22 Days before the ACT	It's time for ACT Science. Read Step Twelve: Science Skills and Strategies to learn the Kaplan Three-Step Method for ACT Science.
21 Days before the ACT	Read Step Thirteen: Experiment Questions to familiarize yourself with Experiment questions.
20 Days before the ACT	Read Step Fourteen: The Conflicting Viewpoints Passage. You should complete the practice passage found in this step.
19 Days before the ACT	With less than three weeks left until the test, it's time to forge ahead and read Step Fifteen: Writing Skills and Strategies. This step will prepare you for the optional ACT Writing test.

18 Days before the ACT	Go back and review one of the steps you feel you haven't mastered yet.
17 Days before the ACT	Go back and review one of the steps you feel you haven't mastered yet.
16 Days before the ACT	Go back and review one of the steps you feel you haven't mastered yet.
15 Days before the ACT	Go back and review the Busy Summaries in the Busy Resources. This resource synthesizes all the information from this book into a condensed review you can complete in under an hour.
14 Days before the ACT	Take the full-length practice test in Part 7. Use the answer key to calculate a raw score.
13 Days before the ACT	Read the answer explanations for every question on the practice test. Be sure to read the explanations not only for questions you got wrong, but also for questions you got right. Kaplan's detailed answer explanations include strategies and tips for answering similar questions on test day.
12 Days before the ACT	Go back and review Part 1: Preparing for the ACT.
11 Days before the ACT	Go back and review Part 2: The ACT English Test.
10 Days before the ACT	Go back and review Steps Six and Seven.
9 Days before the ACT	Go back and review Steps Eight and Nine.
8 Days before the ACT	Go back and review the 100 Essential Math Concepts.
7 Days before the ACT	Go back and review Steps Ten and Eleven.
6 Days before the ACT	Go back and review Building Your Vocabulary and the Word Root List.
5 Days before the ACT	Read Stress Management in the Busy Resources.
4 Days before the ACT	Go back and review Steps Twelve through Fourteen.
3 Days before the ACT	Go back and review Step Fifteen.

1 Day before the Test	Early in the day, go back and review the Busy Summaries in the Busy Resources section. After that, do nothing. Resist the temptation to cram. Put together everything you will need for test day.
Test Day	Go into the test room confident that you are well prepared and ace the ACT!

If You Only Have Four Weeks to Test Day

A month is not a lot of time, but this schedule makes the best use of the time you do have before test day.

Days before the ACT	What to Study
28 Days before the ACT	Read Step One: Introduction to the ACT and Step Two: The Subject Tests. This will be your introduction to the ACT. Learning about the ACT is one of the most important things you can do when you are getting ready for test day.
27 Days before the ACT	Read Step Three: General Test-Taking Strategies. These will apply to every part of the test, so you should focus on these early on.
26 Days before the ACT	Take a day off. You're just getting warmed up in your ACT preparation.
25 Days before the ACT	Move on to Part 2. Read Step Four: English Question Types and Strategies. Start with a review of the Kaplan Three-Step Method for ACT English and learn about a few of the kinds of English questions you will see on test day.
24 Days before the ACT	Read Step Five: Twelve Classic Grammar Errors. You will have the chance to practice some questions and will learn about some classic grammar errors.
23 Days before the ACT	Read Step Six: Math Question Types and Strategies. You'll learn both the Kaplan Three-Step Method for ACT Math and Kaplan's Two-Pass Plan for ACT Math.
22 Days before the ACT	Read Step Seven: Calculator Techniques. Remember, you can use a calculator on ACT math.
21 Days before the ACT	Read Step Eight: Algebra, Coordinate Geometry, Percents, and Averages. Review the question samples.
20 Days before the ACT	Read Step Nine: Geometry.

19 Days before the ACT	Turn to the Busy Resources and read the 100 Essential Math Concepts. Make sure you're clear on all of these concepts.
18 Days before the ACT	Take a day off. Don't burn out on your ACT preparation.
17 Days before the ACT	Now you're ready to tackle ACT Reading. Read Step Ten: Reading Skills.
16 Days before the ACT	Read Step Eleven: Reading Question Types and Strategies.
15 Days before the ACT	Because you might be tested on vocabulary in context, read the Busy Resources: Building Your Vocabulary and Word Root List.
14 Days before the ACT	It's time for ACT Science. Read Step Twelve: Science Skills and Strategies to learn the Kaplan Five-Step Method for ACT Science.
13 Days before the ACT	Read Step Thirteen: Experiment Questions to familiarize yourself with Experiment questions.
12 Days before the ACT	Read Step Fourteen: The Conflicting Viewpoints Passage. You should complete the practice passage found in this step.
11 Days before the ACT	Read Step Fifteen: Writing Skills and Strategies. This step will prepare you for the optional ACT Writing test.
10 Days before the ACT	Go back and review one of the steps you feel you haven't mastered yet.
9 Days before the ACT	Go back and review one of the steps you feel you haven't mastered yet.
8 Days before the ACT	Read Stress Management in the Busy Resources.
7 Days before the ACT	Take the full-length practice test in Part 7. Use the answer key to calculate a raw score.
6 Days before the ACT	Read the answer explanations for every question on the practice test. Be sure to read the explanations not only for questions you got wrong, but also for questions you got right. Kaplan's detailed answer explanations include strategies and tips for answering similar questions on test day.
5 Days before the ACT	Go back and review one of the steps you feel you haven't mastered yet.
4 Days before the ACT	Go back and review one of the steps you feel you haven't mastered yet.

Customized ACT Study Schedules

3 Days before the ACT	Go back and review one of the steps you feel you haven't mastered yet.
1 Day before the Test	Early in the day, go back and review the Busy Summaries in the Busy Resources. After that, do nothing. Resist the temptation to cram. Put together everything you will need for test day.
Test Day	Go into the test room confident that you are well prepared and ace the ACT!

If You Only Have Two Weeks to Test Day

Make the most of your time by following this schedule to prepare for test day.

Days before the ACT	What to Study
14 Days before the ACT	Read Part 1: Preparing for the ACT.
13 Days before the ACT	Read Part 2: The ACT English Test.
12 Days before the ACT	Read Part 3: The ACT Math Test.
11 Days before the ACT	Read the 100 Essential Math Concepts in the Busy Resources.
10 Days before the ACT	Read Part 4: The ACT Reading Test.
9 Days before the ACT	Read Building Your Vocabulary and the Word Root List in the Busy Resources.
8 Days before the ACT	Read Part 5: The ACT Science Test.
7 Days before the ACT	Read Part 6: The ACT Writing Test
6 Days before the ACT	Pick one of the parts (English, Math, Reading, Science, Writing) that you feel the weakest in and review that part until your confidence improves.
5 Days before the ACT	Take the full-length practice test in Part 7. Use the answer key to calculate a raw score. Read the answer explanations for every question on the practice test. Be sure to read the explanations not only for questions you got wrong, but also for questions you got right. Kaplan's detailed answer explanations include strategies and tips for answering similar questions on test day.

4 Days before the ACT	Pick one of the parts (English, Math, Reading, Science, Writing) that you feel the weakest in and review that part until your confidence improves.
3 Days before the ACT	Pick one of the parts (English, Math, Reading, Science, Writing) that you feel the weakest in and review that part until your confidence improves.
1 Day before the Test	Early in the day, go back and review the Busy Summaries in the Busy Resources. After that, do nothing. Resist the temptation to cram. Put together everything you will need for test day.
Test Day	Go into the test room confident that you are prepared to take the ACT!

If You Only Have One Week to Test Day

You'll have to give it everything you've got in order to prepare, but this is the best way to get as much as you can get done before you take the ACT.

Days before the ACT	What to Study
7 Days before the ACT	Read Part 1: Preparing for the ACT.
6 Days before the ACT	Take the full-length practice test in Part 7. Use the answer key to calculate a raw score. Read the answer explanations for every question on the practice test. Be sure to read the explanations not only for questions you got wrong, but also for questions you got right. Kaplan's detailed answer explanations include strategies and tips for answering similar questions on test day.
5 Days before the ACT	Pick one of the parts (English, Math, Reading, Science, Writing) that you feel the weakest in and review that part until your confidence improves.
4 Days before the ACT	Pick one of the parts (English, Math, Reading, Science, Writing) that you feel the weakest in and review that part until your confidence improves.
3 Days before the ACT	Pick one of the parts (English, Math, Reading, Science, Writing) that you feel the weakest in and review that part until your confidence improves.
1 Day before the Test	Early in the day, go back and review the Busy Summaries in the Busy Resources section. After that, do nothing. Resist the temptation to cram. Put together everything you will need for test day.
Test Day	Go into the test room confident that you are prepared to take the ACT!

Create Your Own Schedule

If you prefer to make your own schedule, based on your own time constraints and test preparation needs, use this to map out your plan of attack.

Days before the ACT	What to Study
1 Day before the Test	
Test Day	

Part 1

Preparing for the ACT

Step One

Introduction to the ACT

STEP 1 PREVIEW

Introduction
- The Test Format
- The Test Strategies
- The Concepts Tested

What Is the ACT?

What Is the ACT Writing Test?

How Is the ACT Scored?

How Many ACT Scores Will You Get?

How Do Colleges Use Your ACT Scores?

Should You Guess on the ACT?

Can You Retake the Test?

INTRODUCTION

You've probably heard rumors to the effect that the ACT is a tough exam. Well, the rumors are true. Nevertheless, just because this is a challenging test, does not mean you can't earn a great score. If you follow the steps in this book, you'll have done more preparation for the ACT than most other people sitting with you on test day. You'll learn three things that will enable you to take control of the ACT: the test format, test strategies, and the concepts tested.

The Test Format

The ACT is very predictable. You'd think the test makers would get bored after a while, but they don't. The same kinds of questions, testing the same skills and concepts, appear every time the ACT is given.

Because the test specifications rarely change, you should know in advance what to expect on every subject test. Just a little familiarity with the directions and common question types can make an enormous difference.

The Test Strategies

The ACT isn't a normal exam. Normal exams test mostly your memory. But the ACT tests problem-solving skills as well as memory, and it does so in a standardized test format. That makes the test highly vulnerable to test-smart strategies and techniques.

Most students miss a lot of ACT questions for no good reason. They see a tough-looking question, say to themselves, "Uh-oh, I don't remember how to do that," and start to gnaw on their No. 2 pencils.

But many ACT questions can be answered without complete knowledge of the material being tested. Often, all you need to do to succeed is to think strategically and creatively.

The Concepts Tested

The ACT is designed to test skills and concepts learned in high school and needed for college. Familiarity with the test, coupled with smart test-taking strategies, will take you only so far. For your best score, you need to sharpen the skills and knowledge that the ACT rewards.

The good news is that most ACT content is pretty basic. You've probably already learned in high school most of what the ACT expects you to know. But you may need help remembering.

In short, follow these three principles:
- Learn the test format.
- Learn test strategies.
- Learn the concepts tested.

If you do, you'll find yourself in full command of your ACT test-taking experience.

WHAT IS THE ACT?

Okay, let's start with the basics. The ACT is a three-hour exam (two hours and 55 minutes, to be precise) taken by high school juniors and seniors for admission to college. It's a test of problem-solving skills—which means that you can improve your performance by preparing for it.

All students who take the ACT complete four subject tests: English, Math, Reading, and Science. All four subject tests are designed primarily to test skills rather than knowledge, though some knowledge is required—particularly in English, for which knowledge of grammar and writing mechanics is important, and in Math, for which you need to know the basic math concepts taught in a regular high school curriculum.

The ACT:
- **Is about three hours long**
- **Includes a short break** (between the second and third subtests)
- **Consists of a total of 215 scored questions**
- **Has four subject tests:**
    —English (45 minutes, 75 questions)
    —Math (60 minutes, 60 questions)
    —Reading (35 minutes, 40 questions)
    —Science (35 minutes, 40 questions)
- **Includes an optional Writing test:**
    —Writing (40 minutes, 1 essay question)

WHAT IS THE ACT WRITING TEST?

The ACT Writing test is a 40-minute, optional section of the ACT that measures your writing skills. Colleges and universities have the option to make the Writing test a requirement for admission or to use the results to determine course placement. Students who are applying to college can decide whether to take the Writing test based on the requirements of the schools to which they plan to apply. For this optional test, students write an essay in response to a prompt that asks them to take a stand on an issue. The ACT Assessment plus Writing takes approximately three hours and 40 minutes to complete. You must decide when you sign up to take the ACT whether or not you will be taking the Writing portion. The registration fee for the ACT plus Writing is $56.50; the fee for the basic ACT without the Writing test is $39.50. A list of the schools that require or recommend scores from the ACT Writing test are available at: https://actapps.act.org/writPrefRM.

Should You Take the Writing Test?

Find out the requirements of the schools to which you're applying so you can determine whether to complete the essay on test day.

HOW IS THE ACT SCORED?

Your ACT score is not merely the sum total of questions you get right. That would be too simple. Instead, the test makers add up all of your correct answers to get what they call a "raw" score. Then they put that raw score into a very large computer, which proceeds to shake, rattle, smoke, and wheeze before spitting out an official score at the other end. That score—which has been put through what they call a scoring formula—is your "scaled" score.

ACT scaled scores range from 1 to 36. Nearly half of all test takers score within a much narrower range: 17 to 23. Tests at different dates vary slightly, but the following data are based on a recent administration of the test and can be considered typical:

Percentile Rank*	Scaled (or Composite) Score	Approximate Percentage Correct
99%	33	93%
84%	26	75%
69%	23	63%
55%	21	53%
27%	17	43%

*Percentage of ACT takers scoring at or below given score from www.actstudent.org.

To earn a score of 21 (the 2014 national average), you need to answer only about 53 percent of the questions correctly. On most tests, getting only a bit more than half the questions right would be terrible. Not so on the ACT. That fact alone should ease some of your anxiety about how hard this test is. You can miss several ACT questions and still get a good score. Nobody expects you to get all of the questions right.

HOW MANY ACT SCORES WILL YOU GET?

The ACT scaled score we've talked about so far is technically called the composite score. It's the really important one. But when you take the ACT, you actually receive more than that: the composite score, four (or five) subject scores, and seven (or eleven) subscores.

If you take the Writing test, you will receive a combined ELA score in addition to the four regular subject scores. You will also receive Writing subscores (2–12) for your essay. The English-Writing Score will not be factored into the overall composite score, unlike the other four subject test scores.

Following is a breakdown of the subject scores and subscores. Though the subject scores can play a role in decisions at some schools, the subscores usually aren't important for most people.

1. English score (1–36)
   - Usage/Mechanics subscore (1–18)
   - Rhetorical Skills subscore (1–18)
2. Math score (1–36)
   - Pre-Algebra/Elementary Algebra subscore (1–18)
   - Algebra/Coordinate Geometry subscore (1–18)
   - Plane Geometry/Trigonometry subscore (1–18)
3. Reading score (1–36)
   - Social Sciences/Sciences subscore (1–18)
   - Arts/Literature subscore (1–18)
4. Science score (1–36)
   (There are no subscores in Science.)
5. (Optional) Writing score (1–36)
   - Ideas and Analysis (2-12)
   - Development and Support (2-12)
   - Organization (2-12)
   - Language Use and Conventions (2-12)

HOW DO COLLEGES USE YOUR ACT SCORES?

You may have heard that the ACT is really the only thing colleges look at when deciding whether to admit you. Untrue. Most admissions officers say the ACT is only one of several factors they take into consideration. But let's be realistic. Here's this neat and easy way of comparing all students numerically, no matter what their academic backgrounds and no matter how much grade inflation exists at their high schools. You know the admissions people are going to take a serious look at your scores.

The most important score, naturally, is the composite score (which is an average of the four subject scores). This is the score used by most colleges and universities in the admissions process. The four subject scores and seven subscores on the regular ACT may be used for advanced placement or occasionally for scholarships, but are primarily used by college advisors to help students select majors and first-year courses. Colleges that require the Writing test may use the Writing subscore as part of the admissions process or to determine course placement.

Although many schools deny that they use benchmark scores as cutoffs, we're not sure we really believe them. Most students who are accepted into Big Ten universities and colleges with similarly competitive admissions processes will have ACT scores above 22 or 23. Some schools are less concerned with standardized test scores than others are, but this gives you an idea of what competitive universities want, and for the colleges that do care more about standardized test scores, a strong ACT score will only help your application.

To be fair, no school uses the ACT score as an absolute bar to admission, no matter how low it is. But for most applicants, a low ACT score is decisive. As a rule, only students whose backgrounds are extremely unusual or who have overcome enormous disadvantages are accepted if their ACT scores are below the benchmark.

SHOULD YOU GUESS ON THE ACT?

The short answer? Yes! The long answer? Yes, of course!

As we said, ACT scores are based on the number of correct answers only. This means that questions left blank and questions answered incorrectly simply don't count. Unlike some other standardized tests, the ACT has no wrong-answer penalty. That's why you should always guess on every ACT question you can't answer, even if you don't have time to read it. Though the questions vary enormously in difficulty, harder questions are worth exactly the same as easier ones, so it pays to guess on the really hard questions and spend your time breezing through the really easy ones. We'll show you just how to do this in Step Three: General Test-Taking Strategies.

CAN YOU RETAKE THE TEST?

You can take the ACT as many times as you like. You can then select whichever test score you prefer to be sent to colleges when you apply.

When you sign up for the ACT, you have the option of designating colleges to receive your score. Think twice before you do it. Wait until you receive your score, then send it along if you're happy. This may cost you a few extra dollars (since you won't get to take advantage of the three free reports you get if you designate schools on the registration form before the test), but we think it's worth the extra expense. If you hate your score, you can take the test again and send only the new, improved score. (Seniors, beware! Make sure there is enough time to get your scores in by the application deadline.)

•••

Important Note

Don't automatically designate colleges to receive score reports at the time of registration. If you have time, wait until you're sure you've gotten a score you're proud of.

•••

What this means, of course, is that even if you blow the ACT once, you can give yourself another shot without the schools of your choice knowing about it. The ACT is one of the few areas of your academic life in which you get a second chance.

Step Two
The Subject Tests

Step 2 Preview

Introduction

English
- Standard Format Questions
- Directions
- To Omit or Not to Omit
- Nonstandard Format Questions

Math
- Format
- Directions
- Diagram Questions
- Story Questions
- Concept Questions

Reading
- Format
- Directions
- Reading Passages
- Specific Detail Questions
- Inference Questions
- Big Picture Questions

Science
- Format
- Directions
- Data Representation Questions
- Experiment Questions
- Principle Questions

Writing
- Format and Directions

INTRODUCTION

Okay, you've seen how the ACT is set up. But to really know the test, you've got to know something about the ACT subject tests (which, by the way, always appear in the following order):

- English
- Math
- Reading
- Science
- Writing (optional)

As you'll see, the questions in every subject test vary widely in difficulty. Some are so easy that most elementary school students could answer them. Others might give even college students a little trouble. But, again, the questions are not arranged in order of difficulty. That's different from some other tests, in which easier questions come first. Skipping past hard questions is important, because otherwise you may never reach easier ones.

Don't Get Bogged Down
Skip past hard questions so that you can quickly rack up points on easier questions.

Here's a preview of the types of questions you'll encounter on the subject tests. We'll keep the questions toward the easy end of the difficulty scale here, since you're just becoming familiar with the ACT. Later, we'll be less kind.

Statistic
The English test is 45 minutes long and includes 75 questions. This works out to about 30 seconds per question. The test is divided into five passages, each with about 15 questions.

ENGLISH

Students nearly always get more questions correct in English than in any other subject test. That tends to make them think that English is a lot easier than the rest of the ACT. But, alas, it's not that simple. Because most students do well, the test makers have much higher expectations for English than for other parts of the test. That's why, to earn an average English subscore (a 20, say), you have to get almost two-thirds of the questions right, while on the rest of the test you need to get only about half right.

Note, too, that you have less time per question on the English test than on any of the other three tests. You'll have to move fast.

• •
Keep Moving
Never spend more than 45 seconds or so on an English question.
• •

Standard Format Questions

Almost all of the English questions follow a standard format. A word, phrase, or sentence in a passage is underlined. You're given four options: to leave the underlined portion alone ("NO CHANGE," which is always the first choice) or to replace it with one of three alternatives. For example:

... Pike's Peak in Southwest

Colorado is named <u>before Zebulon</u>
                        37
<u>Pike, an early explorer.</u> He traveled
              37
through the area, exploring . . .

37. **A.** NO CHANGE
    B. before Zebulon Pike became an explorer,
    C. after Zebulon Pike, when,
    D. after Zebulon Pike.

The best answer choice is (D). The other choices all have various problems—grammatical, stylistic, logical.

• •
How Does That Sound?
In English, trust your ears. The right answer is usually the one that "sounds right" to you.
• •

Notice that a single question can test different kinds of writing errors. We find that about one-third of the English questions test writing economy (we call them Economy questions), about another third test for logic and sense (Sense questions), and the remaining third test hard-and-fast rules of grammar (Technicality questions). There's overlap between these question types, so don't worry too much about categories. We provide them to give you an idea of the kinds of errors you'll be expected to correct.

Directions

The directions on the English test illustrate why there's an advantage to knowing the directions before test day. We're going to show you what they look like, but take our advice: don't bother reading them on test day. We'll show you exactly what you need to do. Then, while everyone else is reading the directions on the day of the test, you'll be racking up points.

Directions: In the five passages that follow, certain words and phrases are underlined and numbered. In the right-hand column, you will find alternatives for the underlined parts. In most cases, you are to choose the one that best expresses the idea, makes the statement appropriate for standard written English, or is worded most consistently with the style and tone of the passage as a whole. If you think the original version is best, choose "NO CHANGE." In some cases, you will find in the right-hand column a question about the underlined part. You are to choose the best answer to the question.

You will also find the questions about a section of the passage or about the passage as a whole. These questions do not refer to an underlined portion of the passage, but rather are identified by a number or numbers in a box.

For each question, choose the alternative you consider best and fill in the corresponding oval on your answer document. Read each passage through once before you begin to answer the questions that accompany it. For many of the questions, you must read several sentences beyond the question to determine the answer. Be sure that you have read enough ahead each time you choose an alternative.

You read the directions anyway, didn't you? Well, that's okay. You'll never have to do it again.

Know the Directions
Don't waste time reading directions on test day.

To Omit or Not to Omit

Some English questions offer, as one alternative, the chance to completely omit, or delete, the underlined portion, usually as the last of the four choices. For example:

... Later, Pike fell while valiantly

defending America in the War

of 1812. It goes without saying
            40
that this took place after he
            40
discovered Pike's Peak. He
            40
actually died near York

(now called Toronto). . . .

40. F. NO CHANGE
　　G. Clearly, this must have occurred subsequent to his discovering Pike's Peak.
　　H. This was after he found Pike's Peak.
　　J. OMIT the underlined portion.

Nonstandard Format Questions

Some English questions—usually about ten per exam—don't follow the standard format. These items pose a question and offer four possible responses. In many cases, the responses are either "yes" or "no," with an explanation. Pay attention to the reasoning.

... Later, Pike fell while valiantly

defending America in the War

of 1812. ⎣40⎦ He actually died

40. Suppose the author considered adding the following sentence at this point:

"It goes without saying that this occurred after he discovered Pike's Peak."

Given the overall purpose of the passage, would this sentence be appropriate?

　　F. No, because the sentence adds nothing to the meaning of the passage.
　　G. No, because the passage is not concerned with Pike's achievements.
　　H. Yes, because otherwise the sequence of events would be unclear.
　　J. Yes; though the sentence is not needed, the author recognizes this fact by using the phrase "it goes without saying."

The correct answer is (F). Though (G) correctly indicates that the sentence doesn't belong in the passage, it offers a pretty inappropriate reason. Choices (H) and (J), meanwhile, are wrong because they recommend including a sentence that's clearly redundant.

Many of the Nonstandard Format questions occur at the end of a passage. Some ask about the meaning, purpose, or tone of the text. Others ask you to evaluate it, and still others ask you to determine the proper order of words, sentences, or paragraphs that have been scrambled.

We'll cover strategies for the question types in the two English steps later.

MATH

Time Tip

The Math test is 60 minutes long and includes 60 questions. This works out to a minute a question, but some will take more time than that, some less.

Format

All of the Math questions have the same multiple-choice format. They ask a question and offer five possible choices (unlike questions on the other three subject tests, which have only *four* choices each).

The questions cover a full range of math topics, from pre-algebra and elementary algebra through intermediate algebra, coordinate geometry, plane geometry, and even trigonometry.

Although the Math questions, like those in other subject tests, aren't ordered in terms of difficulty, questions drawn from the elementary school or junior high curricula tend to come earlier in the test, while those from high school curricula tend to come later. But this doesn't mean that the easy questions come first and the hardest ones come later. We've found that high school subjects tend to be fresher in most students' minds than things they were taught years ago, so you may actually find the later questions easier.

Directions

Here's what the Math directions will look like:

Directions: Solve each of the following problems, select the correct answer, and then fill in the corresponding space on your answer sheet.

Don't linger over problems that are too time-consuming. Do as many as you can, then come back to the others in the time you have remaining.

Calculator use is allowed, but some problems may best be done without a calculator.

Note: Unless otherwise noted, all of the following should be assumed.

1. Illustrative figures are NOT necessarily drawn to scale.
2. All geometric figures lie in a plane.
3. The term *line* indicates a straight line.
4. The term *average* indicates arithmetic mean.

Again, when it comes to directions on the ACT, the golden rule is: don't read them on test day. You'll already know what they say by the time you take the test.

Of the four special notes at the end of the Math directions, numbers 2, 3, and 4 almost go without saying. Note 1—that figures are not necessarily drawn to scale—seems pretty scary, but in fact the vast majority of ACT figures are drawn to scale (a fact that, as we'll see, has significant implications for how to guess on geometry questions).

Diagram Questions

About one-third of the Math questions either give you a diagram or describe a situation that should be diagrammed. For these questions, the diagrams are crucial. For example:

1. The figure below contains five congruent triangles. The longest side of each triangle is 4 meters long. What is the area of the whole figure?

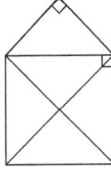

   A. 12.5 square meters
   B. 15 square meters
   C. 20 square meters
   D. 30 square meters
   E. Cannot be determined from the given information.

• •

Don't Get Bogged Down

Let the diagram tell you what you need to know.

• •

The Key to Diagram Questions

The key to this question is to let the diagram tell you what you need to know. Each congruent triangle represents one-quarter of the area of the square, and the sides of the square are 4 meters (you can figure this out because the top side of the square is the hypotenuse—or longest side—of the triangle that makes the "roof"). Since the area of a square can be found by squaring the side, the area of the square is 16 square meters. Thus, each triangle has an area one-fourth as much—4 square meters. Since the whole figure consists of five triangles, each with area 4, the total area is 5 × 4 = 20. The answer is (C).

Story Questions

About another third of the Math questions are Story questions like the following:

2. Evan drove halfway home at 20 miles per hour, then sped up and drove the rest of the way at 30 miles per hour. What was his average speed for the entire trip?

    F. 20 miles per hour
    G. 22 miles per hour
    H. 24 miles per hour
    J. 25 miles per hour
    K. 28 miles per hour

A good way to comprehend—and resolve—a Story question like this is to think of a real situation that's similar. What if Evan had 120 miles to drive? (It helps to pick a distance that's easily divisible by both rates.) He would go 60 miles at 30 mph, then 60 miles at 20 mph. How long would it take? 60 miles at 30 mph is 2 hours; 60 miles at 20 mph is 3 hours. That's a total of 120 miles in 5 hours; 120 divided by 5 gives an average speed of 24 mph. Thus, the answer is (H). (Note: We'll show you alternative ways to answer questions like this later.)

Concept Questions

Finally, about one-third of the math questions directly ask you to demonstrate your knowledge of specific math concepts.

3. If angles *A* and *B* are supplementary, and the measure of angle *A* is 57°, what is the measure, in degrees, of angle *B* ?

    A. 33
    B. 43
    C. 47
    D. 123
    E. 147

This question simply requires that you know the concept of "supplementary angles." Two angles are supplementary when they form a straight line—in other words, when they add up to 180°. So the question boils down to this: what number, added to 57, equals 180? The answer is (D).

READING

Time Tip

The Reading test is 35 minutes long and includes 40 questions. The test contains four passages, or passage sets, each of which is followed by 10 questions. When you factor out the amount of time you'll initially spend on the passages, this works out to about 30 seconds per question—again, more for some, less for others.

Format

There are four categories of Reading passages: Social Science, Natural Science, Humanities, and Prose Fiction. You'll get one passage, or set of passage pairs, in each category. The passages are about 1,000 words long and are written at about the same difficulty level as college textbooks and readings.

The Social Science, Natural Science, and Humanities passages are usually well-organized essays. Each has a very specific theme. Questions expect you to recognize this theme, to comprehend specific facts contained in the passage, and to understand the structure of the essay. Prose Fiction passages require you to understand the thoughts, feelings, and motivations of fictional characters, even when these are not explicitly stated in the passage.

Whatever the type of passage, it's important that you skim it quickly rather than read it carefully. It's crucial not to get bogged down. You can always deal with the details later, if and when they become relevant.

Save Time by Skimming
Skim the passages; do not read them carefully!

After each passage, you'll find ten questions. There are really only three different types of Reading questions:

- Detail questions
- Inference questions
- Big Picture questions

Directions

Here's what the Reading directions will look like:

> **Directions:** This test contains four passages, each followed by several questions. After reading a passage, select the best answer to each question and fill in the corresponding oval on your answer sheet. You are allowed to refer to the passages while answering the questions.

Nothing stupefying here. But nothing very substantive, either. We'll be a little more specific and strategic than the test makers are when we suggest a plan of attack in the two Reading steps.

Reading Passages

What follows is a sample mini-passage. Note that this passage is much shorter than the ones you'll see on the test. We provide it here to give you an idea of the kind of material you'll see and to generate material for the three sample reading questions that follow. In the two Reading steps later on, we'll give you a full-length Reading passage with questions.

> Recent geological studies have demonstrated the existence of huge deposits of gas hydrate, a frozen compound consisting of flammable methane gas trapped in ice, on continental shelves around the globe. These deposits, which exist under extreme pressure at a depth of 1,500 feet under the ocean floor, are believed to contain twice as much potential carbon energy as all fossil fuels combined. Efforts to mine this "burnable ice," however, will pose one of the great engineering problems of this century. Ocean floor avalanches, set off by mining activity, could conceivably release vast amounts of methane into the atmosphere, setting off an intensified "greenhouse effect" that could significantly alter the world's climate.

Specific Detail Questions

Here's a Detail question that might come after the mini-passage you just read:

1. According to the passage, a major obstacle to the successful mining of gas hydrate is:
   A. the inaccessibility of the deposits.
   B. recent climatic changes caused by the "greenhouse effect."
   C. the potential of mining accidents to cause environmental harm.
   D. the danger posed by methane gas to the health of miners.

Detail questions ask about things stated explicitly in the passage. The challenge with them is, first, finding the proper place in the passage where the answer can be found (sometimes you'll be given a line reference, sometimes not), and second, being able to match up what you see in the passage with the correct answer, which will probably be worded differently.

The mention of the "major obstacle" in the question stem should have led you to the last sentence in the passage, where the potential problems of gas hydrate mining are specified: avalanches (mining accidents) could release methane into the atmosphere (environmental harm). That's why (C) is correct here.

Notice how some wrong choices are designed to trip you up by including details from other parts of the passage, or by using the same wording that the passage uses while distorting the meaning.

Inference Questions

Most Reading passages also include a large number of Inference questions, which require you to make an inference from the passage (to "read between the lines"). They differ somewhat from Detail questions. For one thing, students usually consider them harder.

2. It can be inferred that gas hydrate can be used for energy because it:
   F. is under great pressure.
   G. contains gas that can be burned.
   H. will contribute to the greenhouse effect.
   J. is frozen.

Here you have to put two and two together. You're told that gas hydrate contains "flammable methane gas." Later, the gas hydrate is referred to as "burnable ice." Since ice is not normally burnable, it must be the methane in the ice that allows it to be burned, creating energy. (G) is correct.

Big Picture Questions

Although the majority of Reading questions are Detail and Inference questions, some will be what we call Big Picture questions. Some Big Picture questions require you to find the theme, tone, or structure of the passage. Others ask you to evaluate the writing.

3. The author's main purpose in the passage above is to do which of the following?
    A. Advocate the mining of gas hydrate deposits
    B. Show how scientists are looking for alternatives to fossil fuels
    C. Argue that the risks of deep-sea mining are too great
    D. Describe a potential new energy source

The best choice here is (D), since it is general enough to describe the full passage (the potential new energy source being gas hydrate), but it's not overly general or broad (like (B)), and it doesn't introduce value judgments that are not really present in the passage (as (A) and (C) do, by implying that the author either advocates or condemns gas hydrate mining).

We'll discuss strategies for all passage types and question types in the two Reading steps.

SCIENCE

Time Tip

The Science test is 35 minutes long and includes 40 questions. The test contains six passages, each followed by six to seven questions. Factoring out the amount of time you'll initially spend on the passage leaves you a little more than 30 seconds for each question.

No, you don't have to be a scientist to succeed on this test. All that's required is common sense (though a knowledge of standard scientific processes and procedures sure does help).

Science Background

You'll be given passages containing various kinds of scientific information—drawn from the fields of biology, chemistry, physics, geology, astronomy, and meteorology—that you'll have to understand and use as a basis for inferences.

Format

Two (or so) passages will present scientific data, and three passages will discuss specific experiments. There's also usually one passage in which two scientists state opposing views on the same issue. Each passage will generate six to seven questions. A warning: some of these passages will be very difficult to understand, but to make up for that fact, there will be easy questions attached to them. The test makers do show a little mercy once in a while.

Directions

Here's what the Science directions will look like:

> **Directions:** Each of the following passages is followed by several questions. After reading each passage, decide on the best answer to each question and fill in the corresponding oval on your answer sheet. You are allowed to refer to the passages while answering the questions. Calculator use is not allowed on this test.

Sounds a lot like the set of directions for Reading, doesn't it? Not much substance here, either. But don't worry. We'll show you the best strategic way to attack the Science Reasoning test in the three Science steps.

Data Representation Questions

About one-third of the questions on the Science test require you to read data from graphs or tables. In easier questions, you'll need only to report the information. In harder questions, you may need to draw inferences or note patterns in the data. For example:

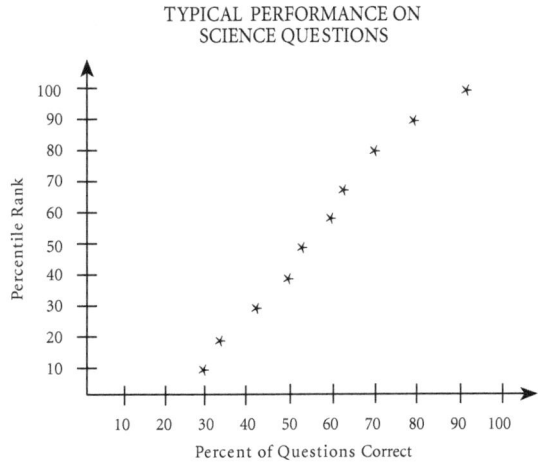

1. A test taker who scores in approximately the 40th percentile has correctly answered about what fraction of the questions?

    A. $\frac{9}{10}$

    B. $\frac{2}{3}$

    C. $\frac{1}{2}$

    D. $\frac{1}{5}$

The correct answer is (C). The point with 40th percentile as its *y*-coordinate has an *x*-coordinate approximately above the 50 percent point on the horizontal axis (percent correct). Fifty percent is the same as $\frac{1}{2}$. Note that this question involves a little simple arithmetic (translating a percent into a fraction)—not uncommon for Science questions.

Experiment Questions

Other Science questions require that you understand how experiments are designed and what they prove.

A scientist adds one drop of nitric acid to beakers A, B, and C. Each beaker contains water from a different stream. The water in beaker A came from Stream A, that in beaker B came from Stream B, and that in beaker C came from Stream C. In beakers B and C, small precipitates form, but not in beaker A.

12. Which of the following could properly be inferred on the basis of the experiment?

    F. Stream A is more polluted than Streams B or C.
    G. Streams B and C are more polluted than Stream A.
    H. Stream A contains material that neutralizes nitric acid.
    J. Streams B and C contain some substance that reacts in the presence of nitric acid.

The answer is (J). Since a precipitate forms when nitric acid is added to beakers B and C, which contain water from streams B and C, something in these streams must be involved. However, we don't know that it is pollution, so choices (F) and (G) are unwarranted. We also don't know exactly why no precipitate formed in beaker A, so (H) is also an unwarranted conclusion.

Principle Questions

The remaining Science questions require you either to apply a principle logically or to identify ways to defend or attack a principle. Some questions will involve two scientists stating opposing views on the same subject. Or a passage might describe a theory about how "V-shaped" valleys are typically formed on Earth—by water erosion through soft rock. Then the following question might be asked:

16. Which of the following is most likely to be a V-shaped valley?

    F. A valley formed by glaciers
    G. A river valley that is cut into very hard basalt
    H. A valley formed by wind erosion
    J. A river valley in a region of soft shale rocks

The answer is (J), because this is consistent with the passage as described.

WRITING

Time Tip

The Writing test is 40 minutes long and features one essay question. While it is optional, many colleges require it.

Format and Directions

The ACT Writing test is designed to gauge your ability to compose a clear and logical argument and effectively present that argument in written form.

The essay prompt will present a specific issue and three perspectives. You are asked to analyze multiple perspectives on a complex issue and to arrive at a point of view on that issue. Then you must state your point of view clearly and support it with clear and relevant examples. The directions will look like this:

> This is a test of your writing skills. You will have forty (40) minutes to write an essay in English. Before you begin planning and writing your essay, read the writing prompt carefully to understand exactly what you are being asked to do. Your essay will be evaluated on the evidence it provides of your ability to do the following:
>
> - Express judgments by evaluating the three perspectives given in the prompt, taking a position on an issue, and explaining the relationship among all four ideas
> - Develop a position by using logical reasoning and by supporting your ideas

- Maintain a focus on the topic throughout the essay
- Organize ideas in a logical way
- Use language clearly and effectively according to the conventions of standard written English

You may use the unlined pages in this test booklet to plan your essay. These pages will not be scored. **You must write your essay in pencil on the lined pages in the answer folder.** Your writing on those lined pages will be scored. You may not need all the lined pages, but to ensure you have enough room to finish, do NOT skip lines. You may write corrections or additions neatly between the lines of your essay, but do NOT write in the margins of the lined pages. **Illegible essays cannot be scored, so you must write (or print) clearly.**

If you finish before time is called you may review your work. Lay your pencil down immediately when time is called.

For more information on the Writing test, turn to Step Fifteen: Writing Skills and Strategies.

Step Three
General Test-Taking Strategies

Step 3 Preview

Introduction

Do Question Triage

Put the Material into a Form You Can Understand
- Mark Up Your Test Booklet
- Reword the Questions
- Draw Diagrams

Ignore Irrelevant Issues

Check Back

Answer the Right Question

Look for the Hidden Answer

Guess Intelligently

Be Careful with the Answer Grid

Use the Letters of the Answer Choices to Stay on Track

Keep Track of Time

Take Control of Your Test

INTRODUCTION

Now that you have some idea about the ACT, it's time to start developing strategies for dealing with it. Here are the top 10 general test strategies for success on the ACT.

DO QUESTION TRIAGE

In a hospital emergency room, the triage nurse is the person who evaluates each patient and decides which ones get attention first and which ones should be treated later. You should do the same thing on the ACT.

Performing question triage is one of the most important ways of controlling your test-taking experience. There are some questions on the ACT that most students could never answer correctly, no matter how much time or effort they spent on them. For example:

57. If $\sec^2 x = 4$, which of the following could be $\sin x$?

    A. 1.73205

    B. 3.14159

    C. $\sqrt{3}$

    D. $\dfrac{\sqrt{3}}{2}$

    E. Cannot be determined from the given information.

Clearly, even if you could manage to come up with an answer to this question, it would take some time. But would it be worth the time? We think not.

This question clearly illustrates our point: you should perform question triage on the ACT.

Test Tip

The first time you look at each question, make a quick decision about how hard and time-consuming it looks. Then decide whether to answer it now or skip it and do it later.

- If the question looks comprehensible and of reasonable difficulty, do it right away.
- If the question looks tough and time-consuming, but ultimately doable, skip it, circle the question number, and come back to it later.
- If the question looks impossible, forget about it. Guess and move on.

For the English, Reading, and Science tests, the best plan of attack is to do each passage as a block. Make a longish first pass through the questions (the "triage" pass), doing the easy ones, guessing on the impossible ones, and skipping any that look like they might cause trouble. Then make a second pass (the "cleanup" pass), and do those questions you think you can solve with some extra effort. This will be easier if you've marked these questions in your test booklet. For Math, you use the same two-pass plan, except that you move through the whole subject test twice.

• •

Kaplan's Two-Pass Plan
Make two passes through each group of questions—a triage pass and a cleanup pass.

• •

Make sure you take pains to grid your answers in the right place. It's easy to misgrid when you're skipping around, so be careful. And of course: be certain you have an answer gridded for every question by the time the test is over!

PUT THE MATERIAL INTO A FORM YOU CAN UNDERSTAND

ACT questions are rarely presented in the simplest, most helpful way. In fact, your main job for many questions is to figure out what the question means so you can solve it.

Because the material is presented in such an complex way, one of your best strategies is to recast (reword) the material into a form you can handle.

Mark Up Your Test Booklet
This strategy should be employed on all four subject tests. In Reading, for example, the passages can be overwhelming. The secret is to put the passages into a form you can understand and use. Circle or underline the main idea, for one thing. And make yourself a road map of the passage, making brief notes about each paragraph so you understand how it all fits together. That way, you'll also know *where* to find certain types of information you'll need.

Reword the Questions

You'll find that you also need to do some recasting of the questions. For instance, take the following question.

15. According to Figure 1, at approximately what latitude would calculations using an estimated value at sea level of $g = 9.80$ m/sec^2 produce the least error?

    A. 0°
    B. 20°
    C. 40°
    D. 80°

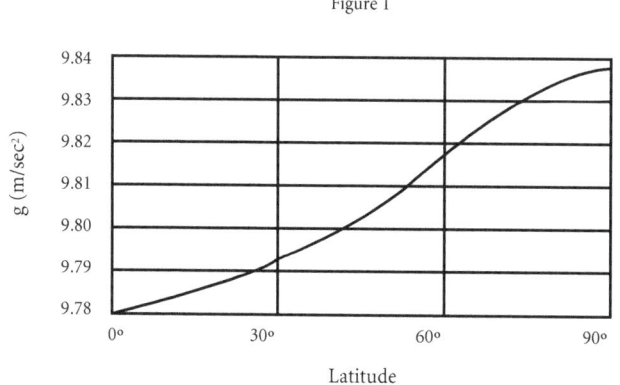

Figure 1

At what latitude would the calculations using a value of $g = 9.80$ m/sec^2 produce the least error? What does that mean?

Take a deep breath. Ask yourself: where would an estimate of 9.80 m/sec^2 produce the least error? In a latitude where 9.80 m/sec^2 is the real value of g. If you find the latitude at which the real value of g is 9.80 m/sec^2, then using 9.80 m/sec^2 as an estimate there would produce no error at all.

So, in other words, what this question is asking is: at what latitude does $g = 9.80$ m/sec^2? In that form, you can answer it easily. The answer is choice (C), which you can get by reading the chart.

Draw Diagrams

Sometimes, putting the material into usable form involves drawing with your pencil.

2. Jason bought a painting with a frame 1 inch wide. If the dimensions of the outside of the frame are 5 inches by 7 inches, which of the following could be the length of one side of the painting inside the frame?

    F. 3 inches

    G. 4 inches

    H. $5\frac{1}{2}$ inches

    J. $6\frac{1}{2}$ inches

    K. 7 inches

Just looking at the question the first time, you might be tempted simply to subtract 1 inch from the outside dimensions and think that the inside dimensions are 4 by 6 inches (and pick (G)). Why isn't this correct? Because the frame goes all the way around—both above and below the painting, both to the right and to the left. This would have been clear if you had put the problem in a form you could understand and use.

You might make the situation graphic by actually sketching out the painting frame:

When you draw the picture frame like this, you realize that if the outside dimensions are 5 by 7 inches, the inside dimensions must be 3 by 5 inches. Thus, the correct answer is (F).

What Does That Say?

Put everything into a form you can understand.

IGNORE IRRELEVANT ISSUES

It's easy to waste time on ACT questions by considering irrelevant issues. Just because an issue looks interesting, or just because you're worried about something, doesn't make it important. For example:

... China was certainly one of the cradles of civilization. <u>It's obvious that, China has a long history.</u> As is the case with other ancient cultures, the early history of China is lost in mythology. ...

14. F. NO CHANGE
    G. It's obvious that China has a long history.
    H. Obviously; China has a long history.
    J. OMIT the underlined portion.

In this question, the test makers are counting on you to waste time worrying about punctuation. Does that comma belong? Can you use a semicolon here? These issues might be worrisome, but there's a much bigger issue here—namely, does the sentence belong in the passage at all? No, it doesn't. If China has an ancient culture and was a cradle of civilization, it must have a long history, so the sentence really is "obvious." Redundancy is the relevant issue here, not punctuation. Choice (J) is correct.

CHECK BACK

Remember, all of the information you need is in the test itself. You shouldn't be afraid to refer to it.

In Reading and Science, always refer to the place in the passage where the answer to a question can be found (the question stem will often contain a line reference or a reference to a specific table, graph, or experiment to help you out). Your chosen answer should match the passage—not in exact vocabulary or units of measurement, perhaps, but in meaning.

Checking back is especially important in Reading and Science. Often, the wrong answers will be "misplaced details"—details taken from different parts of the passage. These misplaced details don't answer the question properly but might sound good to you if you aren't careful. By checking back with the passage, you can avoid making such wrong choices.

• •

Remember

Don't pick an answer just because it contains key words you remember from the passage. Many wrong answer choices are distortions; they use the right words but say the wrong things about them. Look for choices that contain the same ideas you find in the passage.

• •

ANSWER THE RIGHT QUESTION

This strategy is a natural extension of the last. As we said, the ACT test makers often include among the wrong answers to a question the *correct answer to a different question*. Under time pressure, it's easy for you to fall for one of these red herrings, thinking that you know what's being asked for when you really don't. For example:

7. What is the value of $3x$ if $9x = 5y + 2$ and $y + 4 = 2y - 10$?

   A. 5
   B. 8
   C. 14
   D. 24
   E. 72

To solve this problem, we need to find y first, even though the question asks about x (because x here is given only in terms of y). You could solve the second equation like this:

$y + 4 = 2y - 10$	given
$4 = y - 10$	by subtracting y from both sides
$14 = y$	by adding 10 to both sides

But (C), 14, isn't the right answer here, because the question doesn't ask for y—it asks about x. You can use the value of y to find x, however, by plugging the calculated value of y into the first equation:

$9x = 5y + 2$	given
$9x = 5(14) + 2$	because $y = 14$
$9x = 70 + 2$	$5 \times 14 = 70$
$9x = 72$	

But (E), 72, isn't the answer either, because the question doesn't ask for 9x. It doesn't ask for x either, so if you picked (B), 8, you'd be wrong as well. Remember to refer to the question. The question asks for 3x. So we need to divide 9x by 3:

$9x = 72$ from your calculation
$3x = 24$ dividing by 3

Thus, the answer is (D).

Doing all the right work but then getting the wrong answer can be seriously frustrating. So be sure to answer the right question.

What Was the Question?
Check the question stem again before choosing an answer.

LOOK FOR THE HIDDEN ANSWER

On many ACT questions, the right answer is hidden in one way or another. It might be hidden by being written in a way that you aren't likely to expect. For example, you might work out a problem and get 0.5 as your answer, but then find that 0.5 isn't among the answer choices. Then you notice that one choice reads $\frac{1}{2}$.

But there's another way the ACT can hide answers. Many ACT questions have more than one possible right solution, though only one correct answer choice is given. Often, the ACT will hide that answer by offering one of the less obvious possible answers to a question. For example:

2. If $3x^2 + 5 = 17$, which of the following could be the value of x ?

    A. -3
    B. -2
    C. 0
    D. 1
    E. 4

You quickly solve this very straightforward problem like so:

$3x^2 + 5 = 17$ given
$3x^2 = 12$ by subtracting 5
$x^2 = 4$ dividing by 3
$x = 2$ taking square root of both sides

Having arrived at an answer, you confidently look for it among the choices. But 2 isn't a choice. The explanation? This question has two possible solutions, not just one. The square root of 4 can be either 2 or −2, so (B) is the answer.

Keep in mind that though there is only one right answer choice for each question, that right answer may not be the one that occurs to you first. A common mistake is to pick an answer that seems "sort of" like the answer you're looking for even when you know it's wrong. Don't settle for second best.

GUESS INTELLIGENTLY

On the ACT, an unanswered question is always wrong, but even a wild guess may be right. In fact, smart guessing can make a big difference in your score.

A Shot in the Dark
Always guess on every ACT question you can't answer.

You'll be doing two different kinds of guessing during your two passes through any subject test:

- Blind guessing (which you do mostly on questions you deem too hard or time-consuming to try)
- Considered guessing (which you do mostly on questions that you do some work on, but can't make headway with)

When you guess blindly, you just choose any letter you feel like choosing. When you guess in a considered way, on the other hand, you've usually done enough work on a question to eliminate at least one or two choices. If you can eliminate any choices, you increase the odds that you'll guess correctly.

BE CAREFUL WITH THE ANSWER GRID

Your ACT score is based on the answers you select on your answer grid. Even if you work out every question correctly, you'll get a low score if you misgrid your answers. So be careful! Don't disdain the process of filling in those little "bubbles" on the grid. Sure, it's pretty mindless, but under time pressure it's easy to make mistakes.

It's important to develop a disciplined strategy for filling in the answer grid. We find that gridding the answers in groups rather than one question at a time works best.

Gridding Strategy

As you figure out each question in the test booklet, circle the answer choice you come up with. Then transfer those answers to the answer grid in groups of five or more.

The English, Reading, and Science tests are divided naturally into groups of questions—the passages. For most students, it makes sense to circle your answers in your test booklet as you work them out. Then when you're finished with each passage and its questions, fill in the answers as a group on your answer grid.

In Math, the strategy has to be different because the Math test isn't broken up into natural groups. The best strategy is to mark your answers in the test booklet and then grid them when you reach the end of each page or two. Since there are usually about five math questions per page, you'll probably be gridding five or ten math answers at a time.

No matter what subject you're working on, however, you should start gridding your answers one at a time near the end of the session. You don't want to be caught with ungridded answers when time is called.

Time Strategy

When there are five minutes left in a subject test, start gridding your answers one-by-one. With a minute or two left, fill in everything you've left blank. Remember, even one question left blank could affect your score.

USE THE LETTERS OF THE ANSWER CHOICES TO STAY ON TRACK

One oddity about the ACT is that even-numbered questions have F, G, H, J (and K in Math) as answer choices, rather than A, B, C, D (and E in Math). This might be confusing at first, but you can make it work for you. A common mistake with the answer grid is to enter an answer one row up or down accidentally. On the ACT, that won't happen if you pay attention to the letter in the answer. If you're looking for an A and you see only F, G, H, J, and K, you'll know you're in the wrong row on the answer grid.

KEEP TRACK OF TIME

It's important to keep track of time while you take the ACT. During your two passes through each subject test, you really have to pace yourself. On average, English, Reading, and Science questions should take about 30 seconds each. Math questions should average less than one minute each.

Set your watch to 12:00 at the beginning of each subject test, so it will be easy to check your time. Don't rely on proctors, even if they promise that they'll dutifully call out the time every five, ten, or fifteen minutes. Proctors get distracted once in a while.

For English, Reading, and Science questions, it's useful to check your timing as you grid the answers for each passage. English and Reading passages should take about nine minutes each. Science passages should average about five minutes.

Remember that more basic questions should take less time, and harder ones will probably take more. In Math, for instance, you need to go much faster than one per minute during your first pass. But at the end, you may spend two or three minutes on each of the hardest problems you work out.

TAKE CONTROL OF YOUR TEST

A common thread in all 10 strategies is: take control. You are the master of the test-taking experience. Do the questions in the order you want and in the way you want. Use your time for one purpose—to maximize your score. Don't get bogged down or agonize. Remember, you don't earn points for suffering, but you do earn points for moving on to the next question and getting it right.

• •
Get with the Program
In the remaining steps, we'll provide you with the arsenal of tools and techniques you'll need to take control of the ACT.
• •

Part 2

The ACT English Test

Step Four
English Question Types and Strategies

Step 4 Preview

Kaplan's Three-Step Method for ACT English
- Step 1. Read Until You Have Enough Information to Identify the Issue
- Step 2. Eliminate Choices That Do NOT Address the Issue
- Step 3. Plug in the Remaining Choices, and Choose the One That Is Most Correct, Concise, and Relevant

Economy Questions
- Redundancy, Verbosity, Irrelevance
- When in Doubt . . .

Sense Questions
- Make It Make Sense
- Good Grammar Makes Good Sense

Nonstandard Format Questions
- Judging the Passage
- Reading-Type Questions

KAPLAN'S THREE-STEP METHOD FOR ACT ENGLISH

Here's our Three-Step Method for ACT English.

Step 1. Read Until You Have Enough Information to Identify the Issue

Instead of reading the passage and looking for an error, think about what issue the question is testing. In other words, "the issue" is the reason that the test maker included the question, and you only need to read enough of each sentence or passage to identify the issue in that question.

Step 2. Eliminate Choices That Do NOT Address the Issue

Once you know what issue the question is testing, go through the answers to see which choices address the issue and which do not. In some cases, there will be no error and you can select "NO CHANGE." But most will have errors and you'll need to select the answer that corrects it. The best way to do this is to eliminate choices that do not fix it.

Step 3. Plug in the Remaining Choices, and Choose the One That Is Most Correct, Concise, and Relevant

This step gives you three criteria on which to judge the results of plugging in each answer choice: the best answer uses wording that is correct, concise, and relevant. "Plugging in" means simply reading the answer choice in the sentence in place of the underlined portion; this way you can "hear" which is best.

Many grammar errors will sound wrong to your ear. Even the ones that don't will be recognizable to you if you study our 12 Classic Grammar Errors (Step Five) and create a "flag list" of the ones you're shaky on. Choose the answer that corrects the error and makes the sentence sound right.

Most ACT English test takers are so worried about grammar and punctuation that they don't think about anything else. That's the wrong mind-set. Don't think too much about technical rules. As indicated in the previous step, the first thing is to get rid of unnecessary or irrelevant words. Only after you've decided that the underlined selection *is* concise and relevant do you go on to Steps 2 and 3. This means that you won't necessarily have to go through all three steps on every English question. The answer can come at any point in Kaplan's Three-Step Method.

ECONOMY QUESTIONS

Almost all of us have padded papers at one time or another in our academic careers. The recipe for padding, in fact, is practically universal: you repeat yourself a few times. You trade short phrases for long-winded verbiage. You add a few offbeat ideas that don't really belong. And presto! Your six-page paper is transformed into a 10 page paper.

Step Four: English Question Types and Strategies

The ACT test makers know that most students pad when they write. And on the English subject test, they know how to punish you for it. In fact, almost one-third of the English questions on the ACT—we call them Economy questions—are testing for long-windedness, repetition, and irrelevance.

But there's hope. Once you know what ACT English is testing for, you can easily avoid making these common English mistakes. More than any other part of the exam, ACT English is predictable.

Try the following English mini-passage—and pay attention to the message conveyed as well.

On recent ACTs, the shortest answer is correct and absolutely right, for about
<u>1</u>
half of all English questions. Because this

is true, a student who knew no English
<u>2</u>

at all could earn—and justly so—an
<u>3</u>
English subject score of about 15. Such

a student could compare the choices

carefully and choose the single
<u>4</u>
shortest one every time. Where the
<u>4</u>
answers were same length, the

student could pick at random. On

recent published ACTs, guessing in this

way would have yielded between 35 and

38 correct answers out of 75 questions

Of course, you're going to do much

1. **A.** NO CHANGE
   B. correct
   C. right, that is, correct,
   D. correct, absolutely, and

2. **F.** NO CHANGE
   G. truthfully factual
   H. factually correct
   J. factual—and true too—

3. **A.** NO CHANGE
   B. , and justly so,
   C. and justify
   D. OMIT the underlined portion.

4. **F.** NO CHANGE
   G. singularly shortest one
   H. uniquely short item
   J. shortest one

better than that. You actually <u>are capable of speaking the English Language.</u> You
                                    5
may not know every little rule of English usage, but you certainly know *something*. Obviously, getting the question right because you *know* the <u>right answer</u>
                                                6
is better than getting it right because you guessed well. But you should always remember that the ACT test makers <u>like</u> the shortest answers.
7

5. **A.** NO CHANGE
    B. possess the capability of speaking that wonderful language called the language of England
    C. possess the capability of speaking in the land called England
    D. speak English

6. **F.** NO CHANGE
    G. best choice to select
    H. most correct answer of the choices given
    J. answer considered as correct

7. **A.** NO CHANGE
    B. have a habit of liking
    C. habitually tend to like
    D. are in the habit of liking

Answers: 1. B, 2. F, 3. D, 4. J, 5. D, 6. F, 7. A

In case you didn't notice, the shortest answer happens to be correct in all eight of the questions above. OMIT, where it is an option, is the shortest answer, since taking the material out leaves a shorter text than leaving anything in.

Redundancy, Verbosity, Irrelevance

In the previous passage, the wrong (long) answers are either redundant, verbose, or irrelevant. This means that they either make the passage say the same thing twice, force the reader to read more words than necessary, or introduce topics that are off the topic being discussed.

The ACT is very strict about redundancy, verbosity, and irrelevance. Wherever these flaws appear, your first impulse should be to correct them.

• •

Remember the Three Rules of Economy

Redundancy	• Never let the text in a sentence repeat itself.
Verbosity	• Remember that the best way to write something is the shortest way, as long as it's grammatically correct.
Irrelevance	• Omit the ideas that are not directly and logically tied in with the purpose of the passage.

• •

When in Doubt . . .

On a real ACT, more than 20 questions—almost one-third of all the English items—test your awareness of redundancy, verbosity, relevance, and similar issues. For these Economy questions, the shortest answer is very often correct. So your best bet is: when in doubt, take it out.

Because these issues of writing economy are so important to English questions of all kinds, we've made them the keystone for our recommended approach to the English test. When approaching English questions, the first question you should ask yourself is: "Does this stuff belong here? Can the passage or sentence work *without* it?"

SENSE QUESTIONS

Okay, you just saw that the ACT expects you to use words efficiently and that, in fact, the shortest answer is right remarkably often. But, obviously, the shortest answer is sometimes wrong. What could make it wrong? It may not mean what it says.

Take this example: "Abraham Lincoln's father was a model of hardworking self-sufficiency. He was born in a log cabin he built with his own hands." Well, that's a cute trick, being born in a cabin you built yourself. Presumably the writer means that Abe was born in a cabin that his *father* built. But the literal meaning of the example is that the father somehow managed to be born in a cabin that he himself had built.

It's possible, of course, to analyze this example in terms of the rules of apostrophe use and pronoun reference. But that's not practical for the ACT, even for a student who's good at grammar. There isn't time to carefully analyze every question, consider all the rules involved, and decide on an answer. You have to do 75 English questions in only 40 minutes—that's almost 2 questions per minute.

But there is plenty of time to approach examples like this one in a more pragmatic way. After deciding whether or not the selection in a question is concise and relevant (Step 1 in the Kaplan Three-Step Method), the next step isn't to remember lots of rules. It's to make sure that the sentence says exactly what it's supposed to *mean*. If not, your job is to fix it.

Make It Make Sense

Sense questions test meaning errors. Once you get the hang of them, these questions can actually be fun. Errors of meaning are often funny once you see them.

The Real-Life Robinson Crusoe

Most people—even those who've never read Daniel Defoe's *Robinson Crusoe*—are familiar with the strange story of the sailor shipwrecked on a far-flung Pacific island. Relatively few of them, however, know that Crusoe's story. It was actually based on the real-life adventures of a Scottish seaman, Alexander Selkirk. Selkirk came to the Pacific as a member of a 1703 privateering expedition led by a captain named William Dampier. During the voyage, Selkirk became dissatisfied with conditions aboard ship. After a bitter quarrel with his captain, he put Selkirk ashore on tiny Mas a Tierra, one of the islands of Juan Fernandez, off the coast of Chile. Stranded, Selkirk lived there alone—in much the same manner as Defoe's Crusoe—until 1709, when

1. **A.** NO CHANGE
   B. story: was
   C. story, was
   D. story was

2. **F.** NO CHANGE
   G. Quarreling with his captain, the boat was put ashore
   H. Having quarreled with his captain, Selkirk was put ashore
   J. Having quarreled with his captain, they put Selkirk ashore

3. **A.** NO CHANGE
   B. same manner that
   C. identical manner that
   D. identical way as

he was finally rescued by another English privateer.

Upon his return to England, Selkirk found himself a <u>celebrity, his</u> strange tale had already become the talk of pubs and coffeehouses throughout the British Isles. The story even reached the ears of Richard Steele, who featured it in his periodical, *The Tatler*. Eventually, <u>he became</u> the subject of a best-selling book, *A Cruizing Voyage Round the World*, by Woodes Rogers. <u>And while</u> there is some evidence that Defoe, a journalist, may actually have interviewed Selkirk personally, most literary historians believe that it was the reprinting of the Rogers book in 1718 that served as the real stimulus for Defoe's novel.

In *Crusoe*, which <u>has been published</u> in 1719, Defoe took substantial liberties with the Selkirk story. For example, while Selkirk's presence on the island was of

4. **F.** NO CHANGE
   G. celebrity, but his
   H. celebrity. His
   J. celebrity his

5. **A.** NO CHANGE
   B. Selkirk became
   C. his became
   D. he becomes

6. **F.** NO CHANGE
   G. But since
   H. And therefore
   J. OMIT the underlined portion and start the sentence with "There."

7. **A.** NO CHANGE
   B. was published
   C. had been published
   D. will have been published

course known for many people (certainly
              8
everyone in the crew that stranded him

there), no one in the novel is aware of

Crusoe's survival of the wreck and

presence on the island. Moreover, while

Selkirk's exile lasted just six years,

Crusoe's goes on for a much more

dramatic, though less credible, twenty-eight

(over four times as long). But Defoe's
           9
most blatant embellishment of the tale

is the invention of the character of Friday,

for whom there was no counterpart

whatsoever in the real-life story.

 Because of its basis in fact, *Robinson*
  10
Crusoe is often regarded as the first

major novel in English literature. Still
                                    11
popular today, contemporary audiences
                11
enjoyed the book as well. In fact, two
         11
sequels, in which Crusoe returns to the

island after his rescue, were eventually

published. Though to little acclaim.
      12

8. F. NO CHANGE
  G. widely known among people
  H. known about many for people
  J. known to many people

9. A. NO CHANGE
  B. (much longer)
  C. (a much longer time, of course)
  D. OMIT the underlined portion.

10. F. NO CHANGE
  G. Despite
  H. Resulting from
  J. As a consequence of

11. A. NO CHANGE
  B. Still read today, Defoe's contemporaries also enjoyed it.
  C. Viewed by many even then as a classic, the book is still popular to this day.
  D. Read widely in its day, modern people still like the book.

12. F. NO CHANGE
  G. published, though
  H. published although
  J. published; although

Meanwhile, Selkirk himself never gave a hoot about returning to the island that had made him famous. Legend has it that he never gave up his eccentric living habits, spending his last years in a cave teaching alley cats to dance in his spare time. One wonders if even Defoe himself could have invented a more fitting end to the bizarre story of his shipwrecked sailor.

13.
- A. NO CHANGE
- B. evinced himself as desirous of returning
- C. could whip up a head of steam to return
- D. expressed any desire to return

Questions 14 and 15 ask about the passage as a whole.

14. Given the tone and subject matter of the text, is the last sentence an appropriate way to end the essay?
- F. Yes, because some doubt must be shed on Defoe's creativity.
- G. Yes, because the essay is about the relationship between the real Selkirk and Defoe's fictionalized version of him.
- H. No, because there's nothing "bizarre" about Selkirk's story as it is related here.
- J. No, because the essay focuses more on Selkirk than on Defoe's fictionalized version of him.

15. This essay would be most appropriate as part of a:
- A. scholarly study of 18th-century maritime history.
- B. study of the geography of the islands off Chile.
- C. history of privateering in the Pacific.
- D. popular history of English literature.

Answers:
1. D, 2. H, 3. A, 4. H, 5. B, 6. F, 7. B, 8. J, 9. D, 10. G, 11. C, 12. G, 13. D, 14. G, 15. D

You may have found these Sense questions harder than the Economy questions. The shortest answers here aren't right nearly as often. But, all other things being equal, the shortest answer is still your best bet. In this case, the correct answers for 6 out of 15 questions (numbers 1, 3, 7, 9, 10, and 13) were the shortest answers.

On some of the questions in the passage, you may have had no trouble completing Kaplan's Three-Step Method. Question 9, for example, presented material that was clearly redundant. We certainly know that 28 years is longer than 6 (and if we're really up on our math, we can even figure out that 28 is "more than four times" 6), so including any parenthetical aside like the one given would be unnecessary. Remember, when in doubt, take it out. As we saw earlier, if a question includes an OMIT option, or if some answers are much longer than others, it is usually testing writing economy.

In the rest of the questions in this passage, the answers differ in other ways. They may join or separate sentences, rearrange things, or add words that affect the meaning of the sentences. When the answers are all about the same length, as in most of the questions here, the question is more likely to test sense. Consider the shortest answer first, but don't be as quick to select it and move on. Think about the effect each choice has on the *meaning* of the sentence, and pick longer answers if the shortest one doesn't make sense.

Good Grammar Makes Good Sense

The ACT test makers include questions like those in the previous passage to test many different rules of writing mechanics. Though it's not *necessary* to think about rules to answer the questions, familiarity with the rules can give you an alternative approach. The more ways you have to think about a question, the more likely you are to find the right answer.

We'll discuss some of these examples in groups based on what they're designed to test. That way we can show you how the basic strategic approach of "make it make sense" can get you the answers without a lot of technical analysis. Let's start with question 1:

. . . Relatively few of them, however,

know that Crusoe's <u>story. It was actually</u>   1.   **A.** NO CHANGE
                     1   **B.** story: was
based on the real-life adventures of a   **C.** story, was
                                                          D. story was

Scottish seaman, Alexander Selkirk.

If the underlined section for question 1 were left as it is, the second sentence of the passage would be incomplete. It wouldn't make sense. "Relatively few people know that Crusoe's story" what? To make that make sense, you've got to continue the sentence so that it can tell us what it is that few people know about Crusoe's story. The three alternatives all do that, but (B) introduces a nonsensical colon, while (C) adds a comma when there's no pause in the sentence. (D), however, continues the sentence—adding nothing unnecessary, but making it complete.

Completeness

What question 1 is testing is something we call *completeness*—the requirement that every sentence should consist of an entire thought. Don't just blindly judge the completeness of a sentence by whether it contains a subject and a verb. The alleged sentence—"Relatively few of them, however, know that Crusoe's story."—actually *does* contain a subject and a verb, but it's still not complete. It leaves a thought hanging. Don't leave thoughts hanging on the ACT. The test makers don't like it one bit.

Question 12 also tests this concept of completeness.

Sentence Structure

Technically, of course, questions 1 and 12 test the broader topic of sentence structure, of which completeness is one part. The rules of good sentence structure require that every sentence contain a complete thought. A "sentence" without a complete thought is called a *fragment*. A "sentence" with *too many* complete thoughts (usually connected by commas) is called a *run-on*. That's what we find in question 4:

Upon his return to England, Selkirk found himself a <u>celebrity, his</u> strange tale had already become the talk of pubs and coffeehouses throughout the British Isles.

4. F. NO CHANGE
   G. celebrity, but his
   H. celebrity. His
   J. celebrity his

Here, we have two complete thoughts: (1) Selkirk found himself a celebrity upon his return, and (2) his tale was talked about at the pubs and coffeehouses. You can't just run these two complete thoughts together with a comma, as the underlined portion does. And you certainly can't just run them together without a comma or anything else, as choice (J) does. You can relate the two thoughts with a comma and a linking word (*and, for instance*), but choice (G)'s inclusion of the word *but* makes no sense. It implies a contrast, while the two complete thoughts are actually very similar. Thus, you should create two sentences, one for each thought. That's what the correct choice, (H), does.

Remember

Make sure every sentence contains at least one, but not more than one, complete thought.

Modifiers

Question 2 tests modifier problems:

After a bitter quarrel with his captain, he
put Selkirk ashore on tiny Mas a Tierra,
one of the islands of Juan Fernandez, . . .

2. F. NO CHANGE
   G. Quarreling with his captain, the boat was put ashore
   H. Having quarreled with his captain, Selkirk was put ashore
   J. Having quarreled with his captain, they put Selkirk ashore

In a well-written sentence, it must be clear exactly what words or phrases are modifying (or referring to) what other words or phrases in the sentence. In the underlined portion here, the clause "after a bitter quarrel with his captain" should modify the pronoun that follows it—*he*. But it doesn't. The *he* who put Selkirk ashore must be the captain, but it can't be the captain who had "a bitter quarrel with his captain." That doesn't make sense (unless the captain quarrels with himself). So put the thing modified next to the thing modifying it. The person who quarreled with his captain was Selkirk—not the boat and not *they*, whoever *they* are—so (H) is correct.

If you recognized the problem with question 2 as a misplaced modifier, that's great. Fantastic, even. But you didn't have to know the technicalities to get the right answer here. You just had to make the sentence make sense.

Question 11, which we won't discuss here, is another question testing modifier placement.

Mind Your Modifiers
Make sure that modifiers are as close as possible to the things they modify.

Idiom

Question 3 tests a rather hazy linguistic concept known as *idiom*. The word *idiomatic* refers to language that, well, uses words in the right way. Many words have special rules. If you're a native speaker of the language, you probably picked up many of these rules by ear before your eighth birthday; if you're not a native speaker, you had to learn them one by one.

Stranded, Selkirk lived there alone—in much the same manner as Defoe's Crusoe—until 1709, when he was finally rescued by another . . .

3. A. NO CHANGE
   B. same manner that
   C. identical manner that
   D. identical way as

The sentence as written actually makes perfect sense. Selkirk lived in "much the same manner as" Defoe's Crusoe. The phrase "much the same" calls for us to complete the comparison between Selkirk's and Crusoe's ways of life. Note how (B) and (C) would create completeness problems—in much the same (or identical) manner that Defoe's Crusoe what? Choice (D), meanwhile, is just plain unidiomatic. In English, we just don't say, "in much the identical way," because the word *identical* is an absolute. You can't be more or partially identical; either you are or aren't identical to something else. But even if you didn't analyze (D) carefully, it should have just sounded wrong to your ear. (Trusting your ear can be a great way to get correct answers on the English subject test.)

You'll notice that question 8 tests another idiom problem—the phrase *known to*.

Pronouns

Remember, the object of grammar rules is to make sure that the meaning of language is conveyed clearly. Sometimes, the test will throw you a sentence in which the meaning of a pronoun is unclear. You won't be sure to whom or what the pronoun is referring. That's the kind of problem you were given in question 5:

The story even reached the ears of

Richard Steele, who featured it in his

periodical, *The Tatler*. Eventually, he
                                    ―
                                    5
became the subject of a best-selling
―
5
book . . .

5. **A.** NO CHANGE
    B. Selkirk became
    C. his became
    D. he becomes

The intended meaning of the pronoun *he* here is as a substitute for Selkirk. But what's the closest male name to the pronoun? Richard Steele, the publisher of *The Tatler*. That creates an unclear situation. Make it clear. Choice (B) takes care of the problem by naming Selkirk explicitly. (C) would create a sense problem. His what became the subject of a book? Meanwhile, (D) shifts the verb tense into the present, which makes no sense since this book was written over 250 years ago.

Make It Clear
Make sure it's perfectly clear to what or to whom all pronouns refer.

Logic

Structural clues are signal words that an author uses to show where he or she is going in a piece of writing. They show how all of the pieces logically fit together. If the author uses the structural clue *on the other hand*, that means a contrast is coming up. If he or she uses the clue *moreover*, that means that a continuation is coming up—an addition that is more or less in the same vein as what came before.

Many ACT English questions mix up the logic of a piece of writing by giving you the wrong structural clue or other logic word. That's what happened in question 10:

<u>Because of</u> its basis in fact, *Robinson*
10
Crusoe is often regarded as the first

major novel in English literature.

10. **F.** NO CHANGE
    G. Despite
    H. Resulting from
    J. As a consequence of

As written, this sentence means that *Crusoe* was regarded as the first major novel because it was based on fact. But that makes no sense. If it was based on fact (which implies nonfiction), that would contradict its being regarded as a novel (which implies fiction). To show that contrast logically, you need a contrast word like *despite*. That's why (G) is correct here. (G) makes the sentence make sense.

Question 6 also tests logic. *And while* is the right answer, because it first conveys a sense of continuation with the preceding sentence, and then a sense of contrast with the second half of the sentence.

• •

Where Is It Going?

Make sure structural clues make logical sense.

• •

Verb Usage

Verbs change form depending on who's doing the action and when he or she is doing it. Verbs must match their subject and the tense of the surrounding context. Take a look at question 7.

In *Crusoe*, which <u>has been published</u> in
7
1719, Defoe took substantial liberties

with the Selkirk story.

7. **A.** NO CHANGE
   B. was published
   C. had been published
   D. will have been published

The publication of *Robinson Crusoe* is something that took place in 1719—the past, in other words. So the underlined portion, which puts the verb in the present perfect tense, is flawed. Choices (C) and (D), meanwhile, would put the verb into the wrong tenses. (C) makes it seem as if publication of the book happened before Defoe took his liberties with the story. But that's nonsensical. The liberties were taken in the writing of the book. (D), meanwhile, does strange things with the time sequence. But keep things simple. The book was published in the past; Defoe also took his substantial liberties in more or less the same past. So just use the simple past tense. The book *was published* in 1719, choice (B).

Actions: Who Did What When?
Make sure all verbs match their subject and the tense of the surrounding context.

Tone

The passages on the English subject test vary in tone. Some are formal; others are informal. Usually, you'll know which is which without having to think about it. If a passage contains slang, a few exclamation points, and a joke or two, the tone is informal. If it sounds like something a Latin instructor would say, it's probably formal.

Good style requires that the tone of a piece of writing be at the same level throughout. Sometimes the underlined portion might not fit the tone of the rest of the passage. If so, it's up to you to correct it.

Look at question 13:

... Meanwhile, Selkirk himself never gave a hoot about returning to the island that had made him famous.
             13

13. **A.** NO CHANGE
    B. evinced himself as desirous of returning
    C. could whip up a head of steam to return
    D. expressed any desire to return

Selkirk "never gave a hoot" about going back? That's slang (and pretty outdated slang, too). It certainly doesn't belong in this passage. This text isn't the most formally written piece of prose in the world, but it's certainly no place for a phrase like "gave a hoot" or (just as bad) "whip up a head of steam," (C). (B), meanwhile, goes too far in the opposite direction. "Evinced himself as desirous of returning" sounds like something no human being would say. But the rest of the passage sounds human. It makes no sense to shift tonal gears in the middle of a passage. Choose (D).

Take Care with Tone

Keep the tone consistent with the rest of the text.

NONSTANDARD FORMAT QUESTIONS

Some questions ask about the passage as a whole. They're looking for the main point—the gist of the passage—as well as the overall tone and style.

Judging the Passage

Question 14 asks you to judge the passage. Was the last sentence an appropriate ending or not? Most passages will have a well-defined theme, laid out in a logical way. Choose the answer that best continues the logical "flow" of the passage. Some questions on the test will ask you if a passage fits a specified requirement, and often the answer is no.

14. Given the tone and subject matter of the text, is the last sentence an appropriate way to end the essay?

   F. Yes, because it is necessary to shed some doubt on Defoe's creativity.
   G. Yes, because the essay is about the relationship between the real Selkirk and Defoe's fictionalized version of him.
   H. No, because there is nothing "bizarre" about Selkirk's story as it is related here.
   J. No, because the essay focuses more on Selkirk than on Defoe's fictionalized version of him.

Think of the passage as a whole. It's been comparing Selkirk's real life with the one that Defoe made up for Robinson Crusoe. Ending in this way, therefore, with an ironic reference to Defoe writing a more fitting end to Selkirk's life, is perfectly appropriate. The answer to the question, then, should be yes. (F) says yes, but gives a nonsensical reason for saying yes. Why is it necessary to shed doubt on Defoe's creativity? Does the author hold a grudge against Defoe? Not that we can tell. So (G) is the best answer here.

Look at the Big Picture

Make sure that your answer is in keeping with the logical "flow" of the passage.

Reading-Type Questions

If you thought question 15 looked like a Reading question hiding in the English part of the exam, you were right. As mentioned earlier, one reason that you should focus on what the passage means, rather than on picky rules of grammar or punctuation, is that the ACT often asks Reading-type questions.

15. This essay would be most appropriate as part of a:

   A. scholarly study of 18th-century maritime history.
   B. study of the geography of the islands off Chile.
   C. history of privateering in the Pacific.
   D. popular history of English literature.

What was this passage principally about? How Defoe's *Robinson Crusoe* was loosely based on the life of a real shipwrecked sailor, Alexander Selkirk. Would that kind of thing belong in a study of geography (B)? No; the focus is on the fictionalization of a historical life, not on the physical features of the islands off Chile. The passage isn't principally about privateering or maritime history either, so (C) and (A) are wrong, too. This passage is about the relationship of a true story and a famous fictionalized story. And its tone isn't overly scholarly, either. So it probably belongs in a popular history of English literature, (D).

In this step, we've introduced you to ACT English questions and talked about the first two question types—Economy and Sense questions. In the next step, we'll cover what we call Technicality questions, where it really does help to know a handful of grammar rules. But remember that common sense is your best guide on this subject test.

Keys to Success

"When in doubt, take it out," and "Make it make sense."

Step Five
Twelve Classic Grammar Errors

Step 5 Preview

Introduction

Trusting Your Ear
- Formal or Informal?

"Listening" Carefully: Practice Passage

Twelve Classic Grammar Errors
- Error 1: *It* and *They* (Singulars and Plurals)
- Error 2: Commas or Dashes (Parenthetical Phrases)
- Error 3: Run-Ons and Comma Splices
- Error 4: Fragments
- Error 5: Misunderstood Punctuation Marks
- Error 6: *-ly* Endings (Adverbs and Adjectives)
- Error 7: *Its* and *It's* (Apostrophe Use)
- Error 8: *There, Their, They're* and *Are, Our* (Proper Word Usage)
- Error 9: *Sang, Sung, Brang, Brung,* etc. (Verb Forms)
- Error 10: *-er* and *-est, More* and *Most* (Comparatives and Superlatives)
- Error 11: Confusing *Between* and *Among*
- Error 12: Confusing *Less* and *Fewer*

INTRODUCTION

In the first English step, we discussed English questions that hinged mostly on common sense. But there are also some English questions—we call them Technicality questions—that may seem harder because they test for the technical rules of grammar. These require you to correct errors that don't necessarily harm the economy or sense of the sentence. But don't worry; you don't have to be a grammar whiz to get these questions right. Luckily, you can often detect these errors because they "sound funny." Most of the time on the ACT, it's safe to trust your ear.

TRUSTING YOUR EAR

Which of the following "sounds right" and which "sounds funny"?

- Bob doesn't know the value of the house he lives in.
- Bob don't know the value of the house he lives in.

The first sounds a lot better, right? And for many of these questions, all you need to do is to "listen" carefully in this way. You may not know the formal rules of grammar, punctuation, and diction, but you communicate in English every day. You wouldn't be communicating unless you had a decent feel for the rules.

Formal or Informal?

You might have caught an apparent error in *both* of the previous examples—ending a sentence with a preposition such as *in*. This is undesirable in extremely formal writing. But ACT passages aren't usually that formal. The test makers expect you to have a feel for the level of formality in writing. If the passage is informal, pick informal answers. If the passage is slightly formal (as most ACT passages are), pick slightly formal answers. If the passage is extremely formal, pick extremely formal answers. For example, if the passage starts off with, "You'll just love Bermuda—great beaches, good living . . . ," it won't end like this: "and an infinitely fascinating array of flora and fauna which may conceivably exceed, in range and scope, that of any alternative. . . ." That ending is too formal. Pick something like this: "You'll just love Bermuda—great beaches, good living, and a lot of exotic plants and animals."

Make It Match
Choose answers that match the level of formality of the entire passage.

"LISTENING" CAREFULLY: PRACTICE PASSAGE

In the following short passage, you may well be able to determine an answer by "listening" carefully to each choice.

The History of Halloween

Halloween was first celebrated among various Celtic tribes in Ireland in the fifth century B.C. It traditionally took place on the official last day of summer—October 31, and was named "All Hallows Eve." It was believed that all persons who had died during the previous year returned on this day to select persons or animals to inhabit for the next twelve months, until they could pass peaceful into the afterlife.

1.
   A. NO CHANGE
   B. among varied
   C. between the various
   D. between various

2.
   F. NO CHANGE
   G. 31—and
   H. 31. And
   J. 31; and

3.
   A. NO CHANGE
   B. pass peacefully
   C. passed peacefully
   D. be passing peaceful

On All Hallows Eve, the Celts were dressing up as demons and monsters to frighten the spirits away, and tried to make their homes as coldest as possible to prevent any stray ghosts from crossing their thresholds. Late at night, the townspeople typically gathered outside the village, where a druidic priest would light a

4.
   F. NO CHANGE
   G. were dressed
   H. dressed
   J. are dressed

5.
   A. NO CHANGE
   B. colder
   C. coldest
   D. as cold

huge bonfire to frighten away ghosts and to honor the sun god for the past summer's harvest. Any villager whom was
           6
suspected of being possessed would be captured, after which they might be
                                   7
sacrificed in the bonfire as a warning to other spirits seeking to possess the living.

When the Romans invaded the British Isles, they adopted Celtic—not Saxon—Halloween rituals, but outlawed human sacrifice in A.D. 61. Instead, they used effigies for their sacrifices. In time, as belief in spirit possession waned,
      8
Halloween rituals lost their serious aspect and had been instead performed for
     9
amusement.

Irish immigrants, fleeing from the potato famine in the 1840s, brought there
                              10
Halloween customs to the United States. In New England, Halloween became a night of costumes and practical jokes. Some

6. F. NO CHANGE
   G. whom were
   H. who was
   J. who were

7. A. NO CHANGE
   B. it
   C. he or she
   D. those

8. F. NO CHANGE
   G. belief for
   H. believing about
   J. belief of

9. A. NO CHANGE
   B. having been
   C. have been
   D. were

10. F. NO CHANGE
    G. brought they're
    H. brought their
    J. their brought-in

Step Five: Twelve Classic Grammar Errors

favorite pranks <u>included unhinging</u> front
gates and overturning outhouses. The
Irish also introduced the custom of carving
jack-o'-lanterns. The ancient Celts
probably began the tradition by hollowing
out a large turnip, carving its face, and
lighting it from inside with a candle. Since
there were <u>far less</u> turnips in New
England than in Ireland, the Irish
immigrants were forced to settle for
pumpkins.

    Gradually, Halloween celebrations
spread to other regions of the United
States. Halloween has been a popular
holiday ever since, <u>although these days
it's principal celebrants are children</u>
rather than adults.

11. **A.** NO CHANGE
    B. include unhinging
    C. had included unhinged
    D. includes unhinged

12. **F.** NO CHANGE
    G. lots less
    H. not as much
    J. far fewer

13. **A.** NO CHANGE
    B. although these days its
    C. while now it's
    D. while not its

14. **F.** NO CHANGE
    G. rather then
    H. rather
    J. else then

ANSWER	PROBLEM
1. A	*among/between* distinction (see Classic Grammar Error 11)
2. G	commas and dashes mixed (see Classic Grammar Error 2)
3. B	use of adjectives and adverbs (see Classic Grammar Error 6)
4. H	unnecessary *-ing* ending
5. D	comparative/superlative (see Classic Grammar Error 10)
6. H	*who/whom* confusion
7. C	pronoun usage error (see Classic Grammar Error 1)
8. F	preposition usage
9. D	tense problem with *to be*
10. H	*they're/there/their* mixup (see Classic Grammar Error 8)
11. A	verb tense usage (see Classic Grammar Error 9)
12. J	*less/fewer* confusion (see Classic Grammar Error 12)
13. B	*it's/its* confusion (see Classic Grammar Error 7)
14. F	*then/than* usage

TWELVE CLASSIC GRAMMAR ERRORS

Many students could rely almost exclusively on their ear to correct many of the previous errors. But there are a few English questions on the ACT that contain errors your ear probably won't or can't catch. If you have a good ear for English, there may be only a handful of such questions on the test. If not, there may be many more. For these, you'll have to think about the rules more formally. But fortunately, only a small number of rules are typically involved, and we'll discuss the most common ones in this step. Even more fortunately, most of the technicalities tested on the ACT boil down to one general principle: make it all match.

The rest of this step is designed to help you build your own "flag list" of common errors on the ACT that your ear might not catch. Consider each classic error. If it seems like common sense to you (or, better, if the error just *sounds* like bad English to you, while the correction *sounds* like good English), you probably don't have to add it to your flag list. If, on the other hand, the error doesn't seem obvious, add it to your list.

As we'll see, making things match works in two ways. Some rules force you to match one part of the sentence with another. Other rules force you to match the right word or word form with the meaning intended.

Error 1: *It* and *They* (Singulars and Plurals)

The "matching" rule tested most on the ACT is this: singular nouns must match with singular verbs and pronouns, and plural nouns must match with plural verbs and pronouns. The most common error in this area involves the use of the word *they*. It's plural, but in everyday speech, we incorrectly use it as singular.

SENTENCE:	"If a student won't study, they won't do well."
PROBLEM:	A *student* (singular) and *they* (plural) don't match.
CORRECTION:	"If students won't study, they won't do well." "If a student won't study, he (or she) won't do well."

Make It All Match

Watch for subject-verb and noun-pronoun agreement.

Error 2: Commas or Dashes (Parenthetical Phrases)

Parenthetical phrases must *begin* and *end* with the same punctuation mark. Such phrases can be recognized because without them, the sentence would still be complete. For instance: "Bob, on his way to the store, saw a large lizard in the street." If you dropped the phrase "on his way to the store," the sentence would still be complete. Thus, this phrase is parenthetical. It could be marked off with commas, parentheses, or dashes. But the same mark is needed at both ends of the phrase.

SENTENCE:	"Bob—on his way to the store, saw a lizard."
PROBLEM:	The parenthetical phrase starts with a dash but finishes with a comma.
CORRECTION:	"Bob, on his way to the store, saw a lizard."

Finish What You Started

Make sure parenthetical phrases begin and end with the same punctuation mark.

Error 3: Run-Ons and Comma Splices

The ACT test makers expect you to understand what makes a sentence and what doesn't. You can't combine two sentences into one with a comma (though you can with a semicolon or conjunction).

SENTENCE:	"Ed's a slacker, Sara isn't."
PROBLEM:	Two sentences are spliced together with a comma.
CORRECTION:	"Ed's a slacker, but Sara isn't." "Ed's a slacker; Sara isn't." "Ed, unlike Sara, is a slacker."

Usually, only one thing should happen in each sentence. There should be one "major event." There are only a few ways to put more than one event in a sentence. One way is to connect the sentences with a comma and a conjunction (a word such as *and* or *but*), as in the first correction. Or, as in the second, a semicolon can stand in for such a word. The other way is to "subordinate" one event to the other in a clause, as in the third correction.

Error 4: Fragments

This rule goes hand-in-hand with the previous one. A "fragment" is writing that could be a subordinate part of a sentence, but not a whole sentence itself.

SENTENCE: "Emily listened to music. While she studied."
PROBLEM: "She studied" would be a sentence, but *while* makes this a fragment.
CORRECTION: "Emily listened to music while she studied."

Make Sure Sentences Are Complete
Look out for sentence fragments and run-on sentences.

Error 5: Misunderstood Punctuation Marks

The test makers don't test tricky rules of punctuation. But they do expect you to know what the punctuation marks mean and to match their use to their meanings. Here are some common ones:

- Comma (,)—Represents a pause. In many cases, a comma is optional. But never use a comma where a pause would be confusing, as in: "I want to go, to the, store."
- Semicolon (;)—Used to separate two complete but closely related thoughts.
- Colon (:)—Works like an "=" sign, connecting two equivalent things. Colons are usually used to begin a list.
- Dash (—)—Can be used for any kind of pause, usually a long one or one indicating a significant shift in thought.

Error 6: *-ly* Endings (Adverbs and Adjectives)

The test makers expect you to understand the difference between adverbs (the *-ly* words) and adjectives. The two are similar because they're both modifiers. They modify, refer to, or describe another word or phrase in the sentence. But nouns and pronouns must be modified by *adjectives*, while other words, especially verbs and adjectives themselves, must be modified by *adverbs*.

Step Five: Twelve Classic Grammar Errors

SENTENCE: "Anna is an extreme gifted child, and she speaks beautiful, too."

PROBLEM: *Extreme* and *beautiful* are adjectives, but they're supposed to modify an adjective (*gifted*) and a verb (*speaks*) here, so they should be adverbs.

CORRECTION: "Anna is an extremely gifted child, and she speaks beautifully, too."

Don't Mix Up Your Modifiers

Nouns and pronouns are modified by adjectives. Verbs and adjectives are modified by adverbs.

Error 7: *Its* and *It's* (Apostrophe Use)

Probably the trickiest rule is the proper use of apostrophes. Apostrophes are used primarily for two purposes: possessives and contractions. When you make a noun (not a pronoun) possessive by adding an -s, you use an apostrophe. For example: *Bob's, the water's, a noodle's*. But you *never* use an apostrophe to make a pronoun possessive—pronouns have special possessive forms. You would never write *her's*. (One exception is the pronoun *one*, as in, "One's hand is attached to one's wrist.") When you run two words together to form a contraction, you use an apostrophe to join them. For example: *I'm, he's, they're*.

Apostrophes also have a few unusual uses, but luckily they're almost never tested on the ACT. So master the basics and you'll be in good shape.

The most common apostrophe issue on the ACT is usage of *its* and *it's*. These two words follow the same rule as do *his* and *he's*. Both *its* and *his* are possessive pronouns—so they have no apostrophes. Both *it's* and *he's* are contractions—so they do have apostrophes.

SENTENCE: "The company claims its illegal to use it's name that way."

PROBLEM: *It's* is a contraction of *it is*; *its* is the possessive form of *it*.

CORRECTION: "The company claims it's illegal to use its name that way."

Remember

It's is a contraction for *it is*, while *its* shows possession.

Error 8: *There, Their, They're* and *Are, Our* (Proper Word Usage)

Some students confuse the words *there*, *their*, and *they're*. Contractions use apostrophes—so *they're* is the contraction for *they are*. You can tell when to use *there* because it's spelled like *here*, and the words *here* and *there* both indicate location. *Their* means "of or belonging to them." You'll just have to remember that one the old-fashioned way.

Students also frequently confuse the words *are* (a verb) and *our* (a possessive). You can remember that *our* is spelled like *your*, another (less confusing) possessive.

• •

Location, Possession, Contraction
Learn to distinguish the words there, their, and they're.
• •

Error 9: *Sang, Sung, Brang, Brung*, etc. (Verb Forms)

When you have to consider different forms of the same verb (for example, *live, lives, lived*), ask yourself who did it and when did they do it? We would say, "I now live" but "he now lives." In these sentences, the *who* is different—and so the verb changes. Similarly, we would say, "I now live" but "I lived in the past." In these sentences, the *when* is different—so the verb changes.

Most verbs are "regular" in this way. You add *-s* when the subject is *he, she,* or *it* and the time is now (present tense). You add *-d* for times in the past. For times in the future, or several steps back in the past, there are no special endings; you use the words *will, will have, have,* and *had*. I *will* live. I *will have* lived for 25 years by the time the next decade begins. I *had* lived in Nebraska, but we moved. I *have* lived in Indiana since then.

But a few verbs are irregular. They have special forms. For example, we say *sang* rather than *singed* and *have sung* rather than *have singed* or *have sang*. Each of these verbs must be learned separately.

One irregular verb commonly tested on the ACT is *bring*.

SENTENCE: "I've brung my umbrella to work."
PROBLEM: *Brang* and *brung* aren't used in standard English.
CORRECTION: "I've brought my umbrella to work."

Error 10: *-er* and *-est, More* and *Most* (Comparatives and Superlatives)

Whenever you see the endings *-er* or *-est,* or the words *more* or *most,* double-check to make sure they're used logically. Words with *-er* or with *more* should be used to compare only two things. If there are more than two things involved, use *-est* or *most*.

SENTENCE:	"Bob is the fastest of the two runners."
PROBLEM:	The comparison is between just two things, so the *-est* ending is inappropriate.
CORRECTION:	"Bob is the faster of the two runners."

Don't use the words *more* or *most* if you can use the *-er* and *-est* endings instead. Say, "I think vanilla is tastier than chocolate," not "I think vanilla is more tasty than chocolate." Never use both *more* or *most* and an *-est* or *-er* ending. Don't say, "Of the five flavors of frozen yogurt I've eaten, strawberry delight is the most tastiest." Just say it's "the tastiest."

Error 11: Confusing *Between* and *Among*

As a rule, use the word *between* only when there are two things involved, or when comparisons in a larger group are made between pairs of things. When there are more than two things, or an unknown number of things, use *among*.

SENTENCES:	"I will walk among the two halves of the class." "I will walk between the many students in class."
PROBLEM:	Use *between* for two things; *among* for more than two.
CORRECTION:	"I will walk between the two halves of the class." "I will walk among the many students in class."

Error 12: Confusing *Less* and *Fewer*

Make sure that you use the word *less* only for uncountable things. When things can be counted, use *fewer*.

SENTENCE:	"I have fewer water than I thought, so I can fill less buckets."
PROBLEM:	You can count buckets; you can't count water.
CORRECTION:	"I have less water than I thought, so I can fill fewer buckets."

• •
Hint
People are always countable, so you should always use *fewer* when writing about them.
• •

Part 3

The ACT Math Test

Step Six

Math Question Types and Strategies

Step 6 Preview

Introduction

Question Breakdown

Be a Thinker—Not a Number Cruncher

Kaplan's Four-Step Method for ACT Math
- Step 1. What Is the Question?
- Step 2. What Information Am I Given?
- Step 3. What Can I Do with the Information?
- Step 4. Am I Finished?

Important Math Concepts

Kaplan's Two-Pass Plan for ACT Math

Know When to Skip a Question

What to Do When You're Stuck
- Guesstimating
- Eyeballing

INTRODUCTION

All that matters on the ACT is correct answers. On the Math test, your goal is to get as many correct answers as you can in 60 minutes. It doesn't matter what you do (short of cheating, naturally) to get those correct answers. What matters is using quick methods that get you a solid number of correct answers.

The Answer Is What Counts

Worry about right answers, not "right" ways of solving problems.

QUESTION BREAKDOWN

The Math test includes the following:

- 24 pre-algebra and elementary algebra questions
- 9 intermediate algebra questions
- 9 coordinate geometry questions
- 14 plane geometry questions
- 4 trigonometry questions

You don't need to get all 60 questions right. The average ACT student gets fewer than half of the math questions right. You need only about 40 correct answers to get a math score over 25—just two right out of every three questions gets you a great score.

BE A THINKER—NOT A NUMBER CRUNCHER

One reason you're given limited time for the Math test is that the ACT is testing your ability to think, not your willingness to do a lot of mindless calculations. They're looking for creative thinkers, not human calculators. So one of your guiding principles for ACT Math should be: Work less, but work smarter.

If you want to get the best score you can, you need to be always on the lookout for quicker ways to solve problems. Here's an example that could take a lot more time than it needs to.

1. When $\frac{4}{11}$ is converted to a decimal, the 50th digit after the decimal point is:

   A. 2
   B. 3
   C. 4
   D. 5
   E. 6

It seems that when you convert $\frac{4}{11}$ to a decimal, there are at least 50 digits after the decimal point. The question asks for the 50th. One way to answer this question would be to divide 11 into 4, carrying the division out to 50 decimal places. That method would work, but it would take forever. It's not worth spending that much time on one question.

Look for Patterns

No ACT Math question should take more than a minute, if you know what you're doing. There has to be a faster way to solve this problem. There must be some kind of pattern you can take advantage of.

And what kind of pattern might there be with a decimal? How about a repeating decimal!

In fact, that's exactly what you have here. The decimal equivalent of $\frac{4}{11}$ is a repeating decimal:

$$\frac{4}{11} = .3636363636\ldots$$

The first, third, fifth, seventh, and ninth digits are each 3. The second, fourth, sixth, eighth, and tenth digits are each 6. To put it simply, odd-numbered digits are 3s and even-numbered digits are 6s. The 50th digit is an even-numbered digit, so it's a 6 and the answer is (E).

What looked at first glance like a "fractions-and-decimals" problem turned out to be something of an "odds-and-evens" problem.

If you don't use creative shortcuts on problems like this one, you'll get bogged down, you'll run out of time, and you won't get a lot of questions right.

Question 1 demonstrates how the ACT designs problems to reward clever thinking and to punish students who blindly "go through the motions."

But how do you get yourself into a creative mind-set on the Math test? For one thing, you have to take the time to understand thoroughly each problem you decide to work on. Most students are so nervous about time that they skim each math problem and almost immediately start computing with their pencils. But that's the wrong way of thinking. Sometimes on the ACT, you have to take time to save time. A few extra moments spent understanding a Math problem can save many extra moments of computation or other drudgery.

•••

Think About Each Question

Take the time to look for shortcuts that will save time in the long run.

•••

KAPLAN'S FOUR-STEP METHOD FOR ACT MATH

At Kaplan, we've developed this take-time-to-save-time philosophy into a Four-Step Method for solving ACT Math questions. The method is designed to help you find the fast, inventive solutions that the ACT rewards.

Step 1. What Is the Question?

Focus first on the question stem (the part before the answer choices) and make sure you understand it. Sometimes you'll want to read the stem twice or rephrase it in a way you can better understand. Think to yourself: "What kind of question is this? What am I looking for? What am I given?" Don't pay too much attention to the answer choices yet, though you may want to give them a quick glance just to see what form they're in.

Step 2. What Information Am I Given?

Now that you know what the question is asking, you need to figure out how to get from the problem to the answer. The best way to approach problems on the ACT is to ask yourself two things:

1. What information is provided in the question stem?
2. In what format do the answers appear?

For part 1, look at what information you're given along with what the question is asking. Do you have all of the information you need to answer the question like you would in a straightforward arithmetic or algebra problem? Are there additional computations you need to make in order to get to the answer? Note to yourself what information you have and what you may still need. Next, take a quick look at the answers—not to choose an answer yet, just to check out the format of your options. This will help you organize your thinking. For example, you may think that you need to solve for x in an equation, but then you see that all of the answers are given in terms of *x*, so you don't actually need to find *x*, just come up with a formula. If you are given information in fractions and see answers in decimals, you'll know that you need to convert from one to the other at some point.

For some questions, it will be clear to you what information you have and what you may need to find the answer. For others, you may not have all of the information you need and will need to do some computations before you can answer the question. That brings us to Step 3.

Step 3. What Can I Do with the Information?

Think for a moment and decide on a plan of attack. Don't start crunching numbers until you've given the question a little thought. "What's a quick and reliable way to find the correct answer?" Look for patterns and shortcuts, using common sense and your knowledge of the test to find the creative solutions that will get you more right answers in less time. If a question seems overwhelmingly complex, think about ways you can simplify the problem so that it's easier to understand. For example, you can write equivalent fractions so you can work with the information given more easily. Or draw a diagram to better understand a word problem. Try to answer the question without focusing on the answer choices. We'll go over even more strategies for finding answers in Step Eight.

Step 4. Am I Finished?

Before selecting an answer, reread the question to be sure that you have fully answered it. Some problems require several steps, and you may miss the last step if you don't check before you select. For example, a question may ask you to find three possible values of *x* and you've just found one, or it will ask for the area of a circle and you've only determined the radius—and the radius might be an answer choice! Since you will have identified the question in Step 1, double-checking that you're finished should take only a few seconds, and it can make a real difference on test day.

Once you get an answer—or once you get stuck—check the answer choices. If your answer is listed as one of the choices, chances are it's right; fill in the appropriate bubble and move on. But if you didn't get an answer, narrow down the choices as best you can, by a process of elimination, and then guess.

Each of these steps can happen in a matter of seconds. And it may not always be clear when you've finished with one step and moved on to the next. Sometimes you'll know how to attack a question the instant you read and understand it.

Let's look at the following:

2. If the sum of five consecutive even integers is equal to their product, what is the greatest of the five integers?

F. 4
G. 10
H. 14
J. 16
K. 20

Step 1. What Is the Question?

Before you can begin to answer this question, you have to figure out what it's asking, and to do that you need to know the meanings of *sum*, *product*, *consecutive*, *even*, and *integer*. Put the question stem into words you can understand. What it's really saying is that when you add up these five consecutive even integers, you get the same thing as when you multiply them.

Step 2. What Information Am I Given?

Start by examining the question. In this one, you're not given any specific integers in the question, but you know that you'll be dealing with integers—not variables—and that there are five of them and that they will be consecutive and even, so the difference between each integer in the sequence is 2. Now take a look at the answers. The lowest answer given is 4 and the highest is 20. You're looking for the greatest of the five integers in a sequence and the highest option you're given is 20, so you're not going to be working with huge numbers once you get down to finding the answer.

Step 3. What Can I Do With the Information?

How are we going to figure out what these five numbers are? We could set up an equation:

$$x + (x - 2) + (x - 4) + (x - 6) + (x - 8) = x(x - 2)(x - 4)(x - 6)(x - 8)$$

But there's a better way.

Let's stop and think logically about this. When we think about sums and products, it's natural to think mostly of positive integers. With positive integers, we would generally expect the product to be *greater* than the sum.

But what about negative integers? Hmm. Well, the sum of five negatives is negative, and the product of five negatives is also negative, and generally the product will be "more negative" than the sum. So with negative integers, the product will be *less* than the sum.

So when will the product and sum be the same? How about right at the boundary between positive and negative—that is, around 0? The five consecutive even integers with equal product and sum are −4, −2, 0, 2, and 4.

$$(-4) \times (-2) \times 0 \times 2 \times 4 = (-4) + (-2) + 0 + 2 + 4$$

The product and sum are both 0. You've done it!

Step 4. Am I Finished?

Double-check that you're answering the whole question. The question asks for the greatest of the five integers, which is 4, choice (F). Does it ask for anything else? Nope! You're done with this one, so move on to the next question.

Reword the Question

Make sure you know what a math question is asking.

Now let's look at a case in which the method of solution is not so obvious.

4. What is the greatest of the numbers 1^{50}, 50^1, 2^{25}, 25^2, 4^{10}?

   F. 1^{50}
   G. 50^1
   H. 2^{25}
   J. 25^2
   K. 4^{10}

Step 1. What Is the Question?

It's not hard to figure out what the question's asking: which of five numbers is the greatest?

Step 2. What Information Am I Given?

There are five numbers all written as powers, some of which you don't have time to calculate. How are you going to compare them?

Step 3. What Can I Do with the Information?

If all the powers had the same base or the same exponent, or if they could all be rewritten with a common base or exponent, you could compare all five at once. As it is, though, you should take two at a time.

Compare 1^{50} and 50^1 to start: $1^{50} = 1$, while $50^1 = 50$, so there's no way choice (F) could be the biggest.

Next compare 50^1 and 2^{25}. We don't have time to calculate 2^{25}, but we can see that it doesn't take anywhere near 25 factors of 2 to get over 50. In fact, 2^6 is 64, already more than 50, so 2^{25} is much, much more than 50. That eliminates (G).

Choice (J), 25^2, doesn't take too long to calculate: $25 \times 25 = 625$. How does that compare to 2^{25}? Once again, with a little thought, you'll realize that it doesn't take 25 factors of 2 to get over 625. That eliminates (J).

The last comparison is easy because choice (K), 4^{10}, can be rewritten as $(2^2)^{10} = 2^{20}$, which in that form is clearly less than 2^{25}. That eliminates (K).

Step 4. Am I Finished?

It looks like the answer is (H). Does that answer the question? Yes.

IMPORTANT MATH CONCEPTS

You've probably encountered every math term that appears on the ACT sometime in high school, but you may not remember what each one means. Here are a few small but important concepts that you may have forgotten:

- **"Integers" include 0 and negative whole numbers.**

    If a question says, "*x* and *y* are integers," it's not ruling out numbers such as 0 and −1.

- **"Evens and odds" include 0 and negative whole numbers.**

    Remember, 0 and −2 are even numbers, and −1 is an odd number.

- **"Prime numbers" do not include 1.**

    The technical definition of a prime number is "a positive integer with exactly two distinct positive integer factors." 2 is prime because it has exactly two positive factors: 1 and 2. Now, 4 is not prime because it has three positive factors (1, 2, and 4)—too many! And 1 is not prime because it has only one positive factor (1)—too few!

- **"Remainders" are integers.**

    If a question asks for the remainder when 15 is divided by 2, don't say, "15 divided by 2 is 7.5, so the remainder is 0.5." What you should say is: "15 divided by 2 is 7 with a remainder of 1."

- **The $\sqrt{}$ symbol represents the positive square root only.**

    The equation $x^2 = 9$ has two solutions: 3 and −3. But when you see $\sqrt{9}$, it means positive 3 only.

- **"Rectangles" include squares.**
  - A rectangle is a four-sided figure with four right angles, whether or not the length and width are the same. When a question refers to "rectangle *ABCD*," it's not ruling out a square.

Know Your Terminology
Learn the small but important concepts that can help you earn points.

KAPLAN'S TWO-PASS PLAN FOR ACT MATH

We recommend that you plan two "passes" through the Math test.

- **First Pass:** Examine each question in order. Do every question you understand. Don't skip too hastily—sometimes it takes a few seconds of thought to see how to do something—but don't get bogged down. Never spend more than a minute on any question in the first pass. This first pass should take about 45 minutes.
- **Second Pass:** Use the last 15 minutes to go back to the questions that stumped you the first time. Sometimes a fresh second look is all you need, and you might suddenly see what to do. In most cases, though, you'll still be stumped by the question stem, so it's time to give the answer choices a try. Work by process of elimination, and guess.

No Third Pass
Don't plan on visiting a question a third time; it's inefficient to go back and forth that much. Always grid in an answer choice on the second pass; every question should be answered.

Don't worry if you don't work on every question in the Math test. The average ACT test taker gets fewer than half of the problems right. You can score in the top quarter of all ACT test takers if you can do just half of the questions on the test, get every single one of them right, and guess blindly on the other half. If you did just *one-third* of the questions and got every one right, then guessed blindly on the other 40 questions, you would still earn an average score.

KNOW WHEN TO SKIP A QUESTION

At any time during the Kaplan Four-Step Method, you could choose to skip the question. Almost everyone should skip at least some questions the first time through. (But remember, don't leave these questions blank. Always go back and guess if you have to.)

It can be harder to decide when to skip a question if you understand it, but then get stuck in Step 2. Suppose you just don't see how to solve it. Don't give up too quickly. Sometimes it takes a half-minute or so before you see the light. But don't get bogged down, either.

• •
Time Tip
Never spend more than a minute on a question the first time through. Be prepared to leave a question and come back to it later. Often, on the second try, you'll see something you didn't see earlier.
• •

Eventually, you're going to grid in answer choices for all the questions, even the ones you don't understand. The first time through, though, concentrate on the questions you understand.

WHAT TO DO WHEN YOU'RE STUCK

Let's say you're on your second pass. You've done some good work on a particular question, but you just can't get an answer. What you *don't* want to do is stall and waste time. What you *do* want to do is take your best shot at the question and move on. Guesstimating and Eyeballing are two handy methods for doing just that.

Guesstimating

Sometimes when you understand a question but can't figure out how to solve it, you can at least get a general idea of how big the answer is—what is sometimes called a "ballpark estimate," or "guesstimate." You may not know whether you are looking at something the size of an African elephant or the size of an Indian elephant, but you may be pretty sure it isn't the size of a mouse and it isn't the size of a battleship.

Here's a question that's not hard to understand but is hard to solve if you don't remember the rules for simplifying and adding radicals:

5. $\dfrac{\sqrt{32} + \sqrt{24}}{\sqrt{8}} = ?$

   A. $\sqrt{7}$
   B. $\sqrt{2} + \sqrt{3}$
   C. $2 + \sqrt{3}$
   D. $\sqrt{2} + 3$
   E. 7

Step 1. What Is the Question?

The question wants you to simplify the given expression, which includes three radicals. In other words, turn the radicals into numbers you can use, then work out the fraction.

Step 2. What Information Am I Given?

In this case, you are given numbers under a radical in a fractional form. No variables, no words, just a straightforward problem…albeit one that might take some simplification to figure out.

Step 3. What Can I Do with the Information?

The best way to solve this question would be to apply the rules of radicals—but what if you don't remember them? Don't give up; you can still guesstimate. In the question stem, the numbers under the radicals are not too far away from perfect squares. You could round $\sqrt{32}$ off to $\sqrt{36}$, which is 6. You could round 24 to $\sqrt{25}$, which is 5. And you could round $\sqrt{8}$ off to $\sqrt{9}$, which is 3. So the expression is now $\frac{6+5}{3}$, which is $3\frac{2}{3}$. That's just a guesstimate, of course—the actual value might be something a bit less or a bit more than that.

Now look at the answer choices. Choice (A), $\sqrt{7}$, is less than 3, so it's too small. Choice (B), $\sqrt{2} + \sqrt{3}$, is about 1.4 + 1.7, or just barely more than 3, so it seems a little small, too. Choice (C), $2 + \sqrt{3}$, is about 2 + 1.7, or about 3.7—that's very close to our guesstimate. We still have to check the other choices. Choice (D), $\sqrt{2} + 3$, is about 1.4 + 3, or 4.4—too big. And choice (E), 7, is obviously way too big. Looks like our best bet is (C)—and (C), in fact, is the correct answer.

Step 4. Am I Finished?

Since this is a straightforward math problem, with no hidden traps or extra steps, you're finished and can move on.

Keep Moving

It pays to learn the approximate value of these three irrational numbers:

$\sqrt{2} \approx 1.4$
$\sqrt{3} \approx 1.7$
$\pi \approx 3.14$

Eyeballing

There is another simple but powerful strategy that should give you at least a 50-50 chance on almost every diagram question: when in doubt, use your eyes. Trust common sense and careful thinking; don't worry if you've forgotten most of the geometry you ever knew. For almost half of all diagram questions, you can get a reasonable answer without solving anything. Just eyeball it.

The math directions say, "Illustrative figures are NOT necessarily drawn to scale," but in fact they almost always are. You're never really supposed to just eyeball the figure, but it makes a lot more sense than random guessing. Occasionally, Eyeballing can narrow the choices down to one likely candidate.

Here's a difficult geometry question that you might just decide to eyeball:

6. In the figure below, points *A*, *B*, and *C* lie on a circle centered at *O*. Triangle *AOC* is equilateral, and the length of *OC* is 3 inches. What is the length, in inches, of arc *ABC* ?

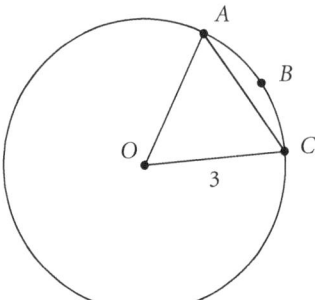

F. 3
G. π
H. 2π
J. 3π
K. 6π

Step 1. What Is the Question?

We're looking for the length in inches of the arc that goes from *A* to *C*.

Step 2. What Information Am I Given?

There's an "equilateral" triangle that connects the center and two points on the circumference of a circle. The length $\overline{OC}$ is 3 inches.

Step 3. What Can I do with the Information?

What you're "supposed" to do to answer this question is recall and apply the formula for the length of an arc. But suppose you don't remember that formula (most people don't). Should you give up and take a wild guess?

No. You can Eyeball it. If you understand the question well enough to realize that *equilateral* means that all sides are equal, then you know immediately that side $\overline{AC}$ is 3 inches long. Now look at arc *ABC* compared to side $\overline{AC}$. Suppose you were an ant, and you had to walk from *A* to *C*. If you walked along line segment $\overline{AC}$, it would be a 3-inch trip. About how long a walk would it be along arc *ABC*? Clearly more, but not much more, than 3 inches.

Now look at the answer choices. Choice (F), 3, is no good; we know the arc is more than 3 inches. All the other choices are in terms of π. Just think of π as "a bit more than 3," and you will quickly see that only one answer choice is in the right ballpark. Choice (G), π, would be "a bit more than 3," which sounds pretty good. Choice (H), 2π, would be "something more than 6"—way too big. Choices (J) and (K) are even bigger. It looks like the answer has to be (G)—and it is.

Step 4. Am I Finished?

You've found the correct answer by estimating and eliminating the incorrect answers. You're finished! This is a pretty hard question. Not many ACT students would be able to solve it the textbook way. If you did, great! That's the way to do it if you know how. Solving the question is always more reliable than Eyeballing.

But when you don't know how to solve a diagram question, or if you think it would take forever to get an answer, Eyeballing and eliminating answer choices sure beat wild guessing. Sometimes, as with question 6, you might even be able to narrow down the choices to the one that's probably correct.

• •

When to Eyeball

Eyeball a geometry question if you don't have the time or knowledge to solve it.

• •

This step has introduced you to the methods for success on ACT Math. In the next Math step, we'll give you some advice about calculator use, and in the final two Math steps, we'll talk about specific strategies for the two major areas of ACT Math—algebra and geometry.

Step Seven
Calculator Techniques

Step 7 Preview

Introduction
- Using Calculators

Think Before You Calculate

Using the Calculator to Save Time

Calculators: The Game Plan
- Know Your Calculator
- Backsolving and Picking Numbers

INTRODUCTION

Using Calculators

Students are permitted to use calculators on the Math test. The good news for non-calculator users is that you never absolutely need to use a calculator to answer the questions on the ACT. No Math question will require messy or tedious calculations. But while the calculator can't answer questions for you, it can keep you from making computational errors on questions you know how to solve.

Nevertheless, a calculator can actually cost you time if you overuse it. Take a look at this example:

1. The sum of all the integers from 1 to 44, inclusive, is subtracted from the sum of all the integers from 7 to 50, inclusive. What is the result?

   A. 6
   B. 44
   C. 50
   D. 264
   E. 300

You could add all the integers from 1 through 44, and then all the integers from 7 through 50, and then subtract the first sum from the second. And then punch all the numbers into the calculator. And then hope you didn't hit any wrong buttons.

• •

Remember

If a question seems to involve a lot of calculation, look for a quicker way.

• •

But that's the long way and the wrong way. That way involves hitting over 250 keys on your calculator. It'll take too long, and you're too likely to make a mistake. The amount of computation involved in solving this question tells you that there must be an easier way. Remember, no ACT question absolutely requires the use of a calculator.

THINK BEFORE YOU CALCULATE

Let's look at that question again:

1. The sum of all the integers from 1 to 44, inclusive, is subtracted from the sum of all the integers from 7 to 50, inclusive. What is the result?

   A. 6
   B. 44
   C. 50
   D. 264
   E. 300

A calculator can help you on this question, but you have to think first. Both sums contain the same number of consecutive integers, and each integer in the first sum has a corresponding integer six greater than it in the second sum. Here's the scratch work:

1	7
+2	+8
+3	+9
.	.
.	.
.	.
+42	+48
+43	+49
+44	+50

This means there are 44 pairs of integers that are each 6 apart. So the total difference between the two sums will be the difference between each pair of integers, times the number of pairs. Now you can pull out your calculator, punch "6 × 44 =" and get the correct answer of 264 with little or no time wasted. Mark (D) in your test booklet and move on.

Here's another way to solve it. Both sets of integers contain the integers 7 through 44, inclusive. Think of 7 + 8 + 9 + 10 + . . . + 50 as (7 + 8 + 9 + 10 + . . . + 44) + (45 + 46 + 47 + 48 + 49 + 50). Now think of 1 + 2 + 3 + 4 + . . . + 44 as (1 + 2 + 3 + 4 + 5 + 6) + (7 + 8 + 9 + 10 + . . . + 44).

So (7 + 8 + 9 + 10 + . . . + 50) − (1 + 2 + 3 + 4 + . . . + 44) =
(45 + 46 + 47 + 48 + 49 + 50) − (1 + 2 + 3 + 4 + 5 + 6) =
(45 − 1) + (46 − 2) + (47 − 3) + (48 − 4) + (49 − 5) + (50 − 6) =
44 + 44 + 44 + 44 + 44 + 44 = 6(44) = 264.

USING THE CALCULATOR TO SAVE TIME

Of course, there will be many questions for which using a calculator can save you time. Here's an ACT trig question that's much easier with a calculator:

2. sin 495° =

   F. $\dfrac{-\sqrt{2}}{2}$

   G. $\dfrac{-1}{2}$

   H. $\dfrac{1}{2}$

   J. $\dfrac{\sqrt{2}}{2}$

   K. $\dfrac{3\sqrt{2}}{2}$

Without a calculator, this is difficult. To find a trigonometric function of an angle greater than or equal to 90°, sketch a circle of radius 1 and centered at the origin of the coordinate grid. Start from the point (1, 0) and rotate the appropriate number of degrees counterclockwise. When you rotate counterclockwise 495°, you rotate 360° (which brings you back to where you started), and then an additional 135°. That puts you 45° into the second quadrant. Now you need to know whether sine is positive or negative in the second quadrant.

With a calculator, this problem becomes simple. Just punch in "sin 495°" and you get 0.7071067811865. (F) and (G) are negative, so they're out, and 0.7071067811865 is clearly not equal to $\dfrac{1}{2}$, so (H) is also wrong. That leaves only (J) or (K). Now, $\sqrt{2}$ is greater than 1, so if you multiply it by another number greater than 1 (namely $\dfrac{3}{2}$), the result is obviously greater than 1. So you can eliminate (K), leaving (J) as the correct answer. With a calculator, you can get this question right without really understanding it.

CALCULATORS: THE GAME PLAN

Keys to Choosing a Calculator

The key to effective calculator use is practice, so don't buy one the night before the test. If you don't already have a calculator (and intend to use one on the test), buy one now. Make sure you buy an extra set of fresh batteries that you can bring with you on test day. You don't want to be stuck with a dead calculator in the middle of a question!

Step Seven: Calculator Techniques

Unless you plan to study math or science in college, you won't need a calculator with anything more complex than trig functions. Bear in mind that you're better off bringing a simple model that you're familiar with than an esoteric model you don't know how to use.

The following calculators are **not** allowed on the test: pocket organizers, computers, models with writing pads, computers with QWERTY keyboards, calculators with built-in computer algebra systems, paper tapes, power cords, wireless transmitters, noisy calculators, Cray supercomputers. Some of these are permitted with specific modifications; see www.actstudent.org for details.

Know Your Calculator

Practicing with your calculator is the best way to get a sense of where it can help and save time.

3. $(7.3 + 0.8) - 3(1.98 + 0.69) =$

    A. −0.99
    B. −0.09
    C. 0
    D. 0.09
    E. 0.99

This question basically involves straightforward computation, so you'd be right if you reached for your calculator. However, if you just start punching the numbers in as they appear in the question, you might come up with the wrong answer. When you're performing a string of computations, you know that you need to follow the right order of operations. The problem is, your calculator might not know this. Some calculators have parentheses keys and do follow PEMDAS, so it's important to know your machine and what its capabilities are. PEMDAS stands for *parentheses* first, then *exponents*, then *multiplication and division* (left to right), and last, *addition and subtraction* (left to right).

If your calculator doesn't follow the order of operations, you'd need to perform the operations within parentheses separately. You'd get 8.1 − 3(2.67). Multiplication comes before subtraction, so you'd get 8.1 − 8.01, and then finally 0.09, choice (D).

4. A certain bank issues 3-letter identification codes to its customers. If each letter can be used only once per code, how many different codes are possible?

    F. 26
    G. 78
    H. 326
    J. 15,600
    K. 17,576

For the first letter in the code, you can choose any of the 26 letters in the alphabet. For the second letter, you can choose from all the letters except the one you used in the first spot, so there are 26 − 1 = 25 possibilities. For the third there are 26 − 2 = 24 possibilities. So the total number of different codes possible is equal to 26 × 25 × 24. Using your calculator, you find there are 15,600 codes—choice (J).

Backsolving and Picking Numbers

A calculator can help you in Backsolving (plugging the answer choices back into the question stem) and Picking Numbers (substituting numbers for the variables in the question).

5. Which of the following fractions is greater than 0.68 and less than 0.72?

   A. $\frac{5}{9}$

   B. $\frac{3}{5}$

   C. $\frac{7}{11}$

   D. $\frac{2}{3}$

   E. $\frac{5}{7}$

Here, you have to convert the fractions in the answer choices to decimals and see which one falls in the range of values given to you in the question. If you're familiar with common decimal and fraction conversions, you might know that choice (B), $\frac{3}{5} = 0.6$, is too small and choice (D), $\frac{2}{3}$, approximately 0.67, is also too small. But you'd still have to check out the other three choices. Your calculator can make short work of this, showing you that choice (A), $\frac{5}{9} = 0.5\overline{5}$, choice (C), $\frac{7}{11} = 0.\overline{63}$, and choice (E), $\frac{5}{7} \approx 0.71$. Only 0.71 falls between 0.68 and 0.72, so (E) is correct.

Step Eight
Algebra, Coordinate Geometry, Percents, and Averages

Step 8 Preview

Introduction

Textbook Algebra and Coordinate Geometry Questions

Complex Algebra and Coordinate Geometry Questions
- Restate the Problem
- Remove the Disguise
- Pick Numbers
- Backsolve

Story Problems
- Percent Problems
- Average Problems
- Probability Problems

INTRODUCTION

The main idea of the first Math step was: don't jump in headfirst and start crunching numbers until you've given the question some thought. Make sure you know what you're doing, and that what you're doing won't take too long.

As we saw, sometimes you'll know how to proceed as soon as you understand the question. A good number of ACT algebra and coordinate geometry questions are straightforward textbook questions you may already be prepared for.

TEXTBOOK ALGEBRA AND COORDINATE GEOMETRY QUESTIONS

When you take the ACT, you can be sure you'll see some of the following questions with only slight variations. We're assuming that you know how to do these basic kinds of questions. If not, take time now to learn these important math concepts. Turn to the Super Busy Resources and review the following concepts in 100 Essential Math Concepts.

By test day, then, you should know how to do the following:

1. **Evaluate an algebraic expression.**
   Example: If $x = -2$, then $x^2 + 5x - 6 = ?$

2. **Multiply binomials.**
   Example: $(x + 3)(x + 4) = ?$

3. **Factor a polynomial.**
   Example: What is the complete factorization of $x^2 - 5x + 6$?

4. **Solve a quadratic equation.**
   Example: If $x^2 + 12 = 7x$, what are the two possible values of x?

5. **Simplify an algebraic fraction.**
   Example: For all $x \neq \pm 3$, $\dfrac{x^2 - x - 12}{x^2 - 9} = ?$

6. **Solve a linear equation.**
   Example: If $5x - 12 = -2x + 9$, then $x = ?$

7. **Solve a system of equations.**
   Example: If $4x + 3y = 8$, and $x + y = 3$, what is the value of x?

8. **Solve an inequality.**
   Example: What are all the values of x for which $-5x + 7 < -3$?

9. **Find the distance between two points in the (x, y) coordinate plane.**
   Example: What is the distance between the points with (x, y) coordinates $(-2, 2)$ and $(1, -2)$?

10. **Find the slope of a line from its equation.**
    Example: What is the slope of the line with the equation $2x + 3y = 4$?

These questions are all so straightforward, they could have come out of a high school algebra textbook. These are the questions you should do the way you were taught.

COMPLEX ALGEBRA AND COORDINATE GEOMETRY QUESTIONS

The techniques you'd use on textbook questions are the techniques you've been taught in high school math classes. In this book, we're focused on algebra and coordinate geometry situations where the quick and reliable solution method is not so obvious and where often the best method is one your algebra teacher never taught you.

It's bound to happen at some point during the test. You look at a question and you don't see what to do. Don't freak out. Think about it for a few seconds before you give up. When you don't see the quick and reliable approach right away, shake up the problem a little. Try one of these "shake-it-up" techniques:

1. **Restate the question.**
2. **Remove the disguise.**
3. **Pick numbers.**
4. **Backsolve.**

Restate the Question

Often the way to get over that stymied feeling is to change your perspective. Have you ever watched people playing Scrabble™? In their search to form high-scoring words from their seven letters, they continually move the tiles around in their racks. Sometimes a good word becomes apparent only after rearranging the tiles. One might not see the seven-letter word in this arrangement:

R E B A G L A

But just reverse the tiles and a word almost reveals itself:

A L G A B E R

The same gimmick works on the ACT, too. When you get stuck, try looking at the question from a different angle. Rearrange the numbers or change fractions to decimals. Or factor, multiply out, or redraw the diagram. Do anything that might give you a fresh perspective.

Here's a question you might not know how to handle at first glance:

1. Which of the following is equivalent to $7^{77} - 7^{76}$?

   A. 7
   B. 7^{77-76}
   C. $7^{77} \div 76$
   D. $7(77 - 76)$
   E. $7^{76}(6)$

Here's a hint: Think of an easier question testing the same principles. The important thing to look for is the basic relationships involved—here, we have exponents and subtraction. That subtraction sign causes trouble, because none of the ordinary rules of exponents seem to apply when there is subtraction of "unlike" terms.

Another hint: How would you work with $x^2 - x$? Most test takers could come up with another expression for $x^2 - x$: they'd factor to $x(x - 1)$. So if the problem asked for $x^{77} - x^{76}$, they'd factor to $x^{76}(x - 1)$. The rule is no different for 7 than for x. Factoring out the 7^{76} gives you: $7^{76}(7 - 1)$, which is $7^{76}(6)$, or choice (E).

• •

Make Tough Questions Easier

On a complex question, think of how you would handle an easy problem that tests
the same principle.

• •

Sometimes an algebra question will include an expression that isn't of much use in its given form. Try restating the expression by either simplifying it or factoring it. For example:

2. If $\dfrac{x}{2} - \dfrac{x}{6}$ is an integer, which of the following statements must be true?

   F. x is positive.
   G. x is odd.
   H. x is even.
   J. x is a multiple of 3.
   K. x is a multiple of 6.

Reexpress it as: $\dfrac{x}{2} - \dfrac{x}{6} = \dfrac{3x}{6} - \dfrac{x}{6} = \dfrac{2x}{6} = \dfrac{x}{3}$

This form of the expression tells us a lot more. If $\frac{x}{3}$ is an integer, then x is equal to 3 times an integer:

$$\frac{x}{3} = \text{an integer}$$
$$x = 3 \times (\text{an integer})$$

So x is a multiple of 3, choice (J).

In Other Words
Restate expressions that don't make immediate sense.

Remove the Disguise

Sometimes it's hard to see the quick and reliable method right away because the true nature of the question is hidden behind a disguise. Look at this example:

3. What are the (x, y) coordinates of the point of intersection of the line representing the equation $5x + 2y = 4$ and the line representing the equation $x - 2y = 8$?

   A. (2, 3)
   B. (−2, 3)
   C. (2, −3)
   D. (−3, 2)
   E. (3, −2)

This may look like a coordinate geometry question, but do you really have to graph the lines to find the point of intersection? Remember, the ACT is looking for creative thinkers, not mindless calculators. Think about it—what's the significance of the point of intersection, the one point that the two lines have in common? That's the one point whose coordinates will satisfy both equations.

So what we realize now is that this is not a coordinate geometry question at all, but a "system of equations" question. All it's really asking you to do is solve the pair of equations for x and y. The question has nothing to do with slopes, intercepts, axes, or quadrants. It's a pure algebra question in disguise.

Now that we know we're looking at a system of equations, the method of solution presents itself more clearly. The first equation has $5x + 2y$, and the second equation has $x - 2y$. If we just add the equations, the *y* terms cancel:

$$5x + 2y = 4$$
$$x - 2y = 8$$
$$6x = 12$$

If $6x = 12$, then $x = 2$. Plug that back into either of the original equations and you'll find that $y = -3$. The point of intersection is (2, −3), and the answer is (C).

4. A geometer uses the following formula to estimate the area *A* of the shaded portion of a circle as shown in the figure below when only the height *h* and the length of the chord *c* are known:

$$A = \frac{2ch}{3} + \frac{h^3}{2c}$$

What is the geometer's estimate of the area, in square inches, of the shaded region if the height is 2 inches and the length of the chord is 6 inches?

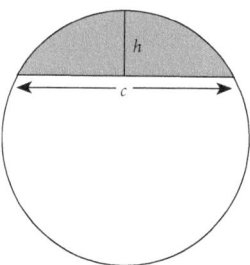

F. 6
G. $6\frac{2}{3}$
H. $7\frac{1}{2}$
J. $8\frac{2}{3}$
K. 12

At first glance, this looks like an esoteric geometry question.

Step Eight: Algebra, Coordinate Geometry, Percents, and Averages

But when you think about the question, you realize that you don't really have to understand the formula. In fact, this is not a geometry question at all; it's really just an "evaluate the algebraic expression" question in disguise. All you have to do is plug the given values $h = 2$ and $c = 6$ into the given formula:

$$A = \frac{2ch}{3} + \frac{h^3}{3}$$
$$= \frac{2(6)(2)}{3} + \frac{2^3}{2(6)}$$
$$= 8 + \frac{2}{3} = 8\frac{2}{3}$$

Choice (J) is correct.

Don't give up on a question too quickly just because it looks like it's testing something you never saw before. In many such cases, it's really a familiar problem in disguise.

Don't Be Intimidated
A complex question is often just an easier problem in disguise.

Pick Numbers

Sometimes you can get stuck on an algebra question just because it's too general or abstract. A good way to get a handle on such a question is to make it more explicit by temporarily substituting particular numbers for the variables. For example:

5. If a is an odd integer and b is an even integer, which of the following must be odd?

   A. $2a + b$
   B. $a + 2b$
   C. ab
   D. a^2b
   E. ab^2

Rather than try to think this one through abstractly, it's easier to pick numbers for a and b. There are rules that predict the evenness or oddness of sums, differences, and products, but there's no need to memorize those rules. When it comes to adding, subtracting, and multiplying evens and odds, what happens with one pair of numbers generally happens with all similar pairs.

Just say, for the time being, that $a = 1$ and $b = 2$. Plug those values into the answer choices, and there's a good chance only one choice will be odd:

A. $2a + b = 2(1) + 2 = 4$
B. $a + 2b = 1 + 2(2) = 5$
C. $ab = (1)(2) = 2$
D. $a^2b = (1)^2(2) = 2$
E. $ab^2 = (1)(2)^2 = 4$

Choice (B) was the only odd one for *a* = 1 and *b* = 2, so it *must* be the one that's odd no matter *what* odd number *a* is and even number *b* is.

Get Specific

Make abstract questions concrete by substituting numbers for variables.

Backsolve

With some Math questions, it may actually be easier to try out each answer choice until you find the one that works, rather than try to solve the question and then look among the choices for the answer. Since this approach involves working backward from the answer choices to the question stem, it's called Backsolving. Here's a good example:

6. All 200 tickets were sold for a particular concert. Some tickets cost $10 apiece, and the others cost $5 apiece. If total ticket sales were $1,750, how many of the more expensive tickets were sold?

   F. 20
   G. 75
   H. 100
   J. 150
   K. 175

There are ways to solve this question by setting up an equation or two, but if you're not comfortable with the algebraic approach to this one, why not just try out each answer choice?

The answer choices are generally listed in numerical order, and if the first number you try doesn't work, the process of plugging in that first number might tell you whether you'll need a smaller or a larger number. So when Backsolving, start off with the middle choice, choice (C) or (H), to be safe.

So start with choice (H). If 100 tickets went for $10, then the other 100 went for $5. The cost of 100 tickets at $10 is $1,000, and 100 tickets at $5 is $500, for a total of $1,500—too small. There must have been more than 100 $10 tickets.

Try choice (J) next. If 150 tickets went for $10, then the other 50 went for $5. The cost of 150 tickets at $10 is $1,500, and 50 tickets at $5 is $250, for a total of $1,750—that's it! The answer is (J).

Remember, all that matters is right answers—it doesn't matter how you get them.

Start in the Middle
When backsolving, start with the middle choice, (C) (or (H)).

STORY QUESTIONS

We find that about one-third of the questions on the Math subtest are Story questions. Although some Story questions present unique situations that must be analyzed on the spot, others are just variations on familiar themes.

Percent Questions
In Percent questions, you're usually given two numbers and asked to find a third. The key is to identify what you have and what you're looking for.

Dealing with Percent Questions
In Percent questions, identify the part, the percent, and the whole, and remember that
Part = Percent × Whole.

Put the numbers and the unknown into the general formula. Usually the part is associated with the word *is* and the whole is associated with the word *of*.

For example:

> 7. In a group of 250 students, 40 are seniors. What percentage of the group is seniors?
>
>   A. 1.6 percent
>   B. 6.25 percent
>   C. 10 percent
>   D. 16 percent
>   E. 40 percent

The percent is what we're looking for ("What percentage . . ."); the whole is 250 (". . . of the group . . ."); and the part is 40 (". . . is seniors"). Plug these into the general formula:

Part = Percent × Whole

40 = 250x

$x = \dfrac{40}{250} = 0.16 = 16$ percent, choice (D)

Percent Change Questions

Many ACT Percent questions concern percent change. To increase a number by a certain percent, calculate that percent of the original number and add it on. To decrease a number by a certain percent, calculate that percent of the original number and subtract. For example, to answer "What number is 30 percent greater than 80?" find 30 percent of 80—that's 24—and add that to 80: 80 + 24 = 104.

The ACT has ways of complicating Percent Change questions. Especially tricky are questions with multiple changes, such as a percent increase followed by another percent increase, or a percent increase followed by a percent decrease.

Here's a question, for example, that's not as simple as it seems:

8. If a positive number is increased by 70 percent, and then the result is decreased by 50 percent, which of the following accurately describes the net change?

   F. A 20 percent decrease
   G. A 15 percent decrease
   H. A 12 percent increase
   J. A 20 percent increase
   K. A 120 percent increase

The way to get a handle on this one is to Pick Numbers. Suppose the original number is 100. After a 70 percent increase, it rises to 170. That number, 170, is decreased by 50 percent, which means it's reduced by half to 85. The net change from 100 to 85 is a 15 percent decrease—choice (G).

Start with 100
Don't just add and subtract percents. Pick 100 as the original number and work from there.

Average Questions

Instead of giving you a list of values to plug into the average formula, ACT Average problems often have a slight spin. They tell you the average of a group of terms and ask you to find the value of the missing term. Here's a classic example:

9. To earn a B for the semester, Linda needs an average of at least 80 on the five tests. Her average for the first four test scores is 79. What is the minimum score she must get on the fifth test to earn a B for the semester?

   A. 80
   B. 81
   C. 82
   D. 83
   E. 84

The key to almost every Average question is to use the sum. Sums can be combined much more readily than averages. An average of 80 on five tests is more usefully thought of as a combined score of 400. To get a B for the semester, Linda's five test scores have to add up to 400 or more. The first four scores add up to 4 × 79 = 316. She needs 84 to get that 316 up to 400. The answer is (E).

Weighted Average Questions

Another spin ACT test makers use is to give you an average for part of a group and an average for the rest of the group and then ask for the combined average.

Be Careful

To get a combined average, it's usually wrong just to average the averages.

For example:

10. In a class of 10 boys and 15 girls, the boys' average score on the final exam was 80 and the girls' average score was 90. What was the average score for the whole class?

    F. 83
    G. 84
    H. 85
    J. 86
    K. 87

Don't just average 80 and 90 to get 85. That would work only if the class had exactly the same number of girls as boys. In this case, there are more girls, so they carry more "weight" in the overall class average. In other words, the class average should be somewhat closer to 90 (the girls' average) than to 80 (the boys' average).

As usual with averages, the key is to use the sum. The average score for the whole class is the total of the 25 individual scores divided by 25. We don't have 25 scores to add up, but we can use the boys' average and the girls' average to get two subtotals.

If 10 boys average 80, then their 10 scores add up to 10 × 80, or 800 total. If 15 girls average 90, then their 15 scores add up to 15 × 90, or 1,350 total. Add the boys' total to the girls' total: 800 + 1,350 = 2,150. That's the class total, which can be divided by 25 to get the class average: $\frac{2,150}{25}$ = 86. The answer is (J).

Probability Questions

Probabilities are part-to-whole ratios. The whole is the total number of possible outcomes. The part is the number of "favorable" outcomes. For example, if a drawer contains two black ties and five other ties, and you want a black tie, the total number of possible outcomes is 7 (the total number of ties), and the number of "favorable" outcomes is 2 (the number of black ties). The probability of choosing a black tie at random is $\frac{2}{7}$.

The Past Doesn't Matter

Remember, the probability of what will happen is not affected by what has happened already.

Because more than half the Math questions on the ACT involve algebra, it's a good idea to take some time before the day of the test to solidify your understanding of the basics. Keep things in perspective. Geometry's important, too, but algebra's more important.

Step Nine
Geometry

Step 9 Preview

Introduction

Textbook Geometry Questions

Complex Geometry Questions
- Find the Hidden Information
- Figureless Problems
- Multistep Problems

INTRODUCTION

The ACT Math test typically has 14 plane geometry questions and 4 trigonometry questions. Fortunately, a good number of the geometry questions are straightforward. Nothing is distorted or disguised. With these questions, you know what to do—if you know your geometry—the instant you understand them.

TEXTBOOK GEOMETRY QUESTIONS

When you take the ACT, there'll be a few questions requiring you to understand some of the following concepts. If you think you need additional review to improve these math skills, turn to the Super Busy Resources and review these in 100 Essential Math Concepts.

- **Finding the area of a square or other rectangle**
  The formula for the area of a rectangle is $A = l \times w$.
- **Finding the area of a circle**
  The formula for the area of a circle is $A = \pi r^2$, where r is the radius.
- **Finding the area of a trapezoid**
  The formula for the area of a trapezoid is $A = \left(\dfrac{b_1 + b_2}{2}\right)h$, where b_1 and b_2 are the lengths of the parallel sides.
- **Working with isosceles and equilateral triangles**
- **Working with special right triangles**
  45°-45°-90°; 30°-60°-90°; etcetera
- **Using the Pythagorean theorem**
  The Pythagorean theorem says:
  $(leg_1)^2 + (leg_2)^2 = (hypotenuse)^2$, or $a^2 + b^2 = c^2$
- **Working with similar triangles**
- **Working with parallel lines and transversals**
- **Finding the area of a triangle**
  The formula for the area of a triangle is $A = \dfrac{1}{2}bh$.
- **Figuring the length of an arc**

COMPLEX GEOMETRY QUESTIONS

Find the Hidden Information

Some ACT geometry questions are not all that they seem. It's not always obvious what the question's getting at. Sometimes you really have to think about the figure and the given information before that light bulb goes off in your head. Often, the inspiration that brings illumination is finding the hidden information.

Here's an example that doesn't come right out and say what it's all about:

1. In the figure below, △ABC is a right triangle and $\overline{AC}$ is perpendicular to $\overline{BD}$. If $\overline{AB}$ is 6 units long, and $\overline{AC}$ is 10 units long, how many units long is $\overline{AD}$?

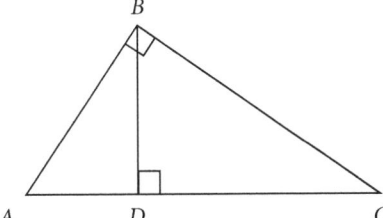

   A. 3
   B. $2\sqrt{3}$
   C. 3.6
   D. 4
   E. $3\sqrt{2}$

At first, this looks like a Pythagorean theorem question. In fact, the two given sides of △ABC identify it as the 6-8-10 version of the 3-4-5 special right triangle. So we know that BC = 8. So what? What good does that do us? How's that going to help us find AD?

The inspiration here is to realize that this is a "similar triangles" question. We don't see the word *similar* anywhere in the question stem, but the stem and the figure combined actually tell us that all three triangles in the figure—△ABC, △ADB, and △BDC—are similar. We know the triangles are similar because they all have the same three angle measures, therefore the same shape. Here are the three triangles separated and oriented to show the correspondences:

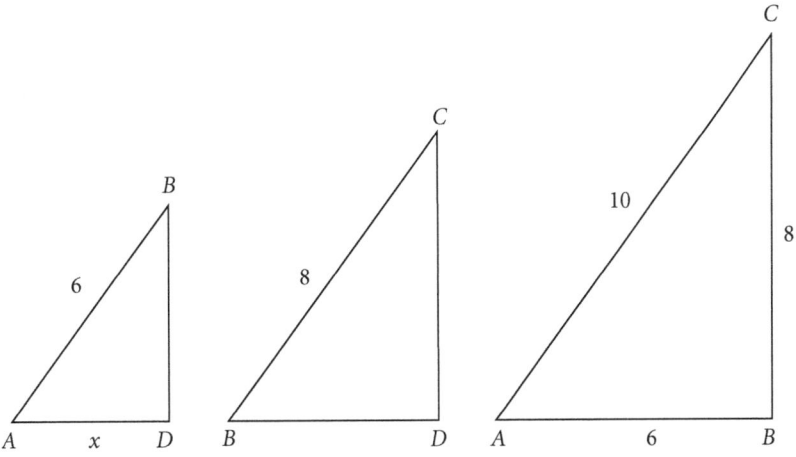

In this orientation, it's easy to see the proportion setup that will solve the questions:

$$\frac{10}{6} = \frac{6}{x}$$
$$10x = 36$$
$$x = 3.6, \text{ choice (C)}$$

More Than Meets the Eye

If you find yourself stuck on a question, look for hidden information.

Here's another example with hidden information:

2. In the figure below, the area of the circle centered at O is 25π, and $\overline{AC}$ is perpendicular to $\overline{OB}$. If $\overline{AC}$ is 8 units long, how many units long is $\overline{BD}$?

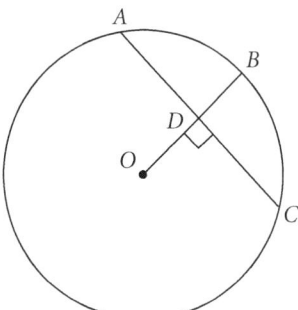

F. 2
G. 2.5
H. 3
J. 3.125
K. 4

It's not easy to see how to get $\overline{BD}$ from the given information. We can use the area—25π—to figure out the radius, and then we'd know the length of $\overline{OB}$:

$$\text{Area} = \pi r^2$$

$$25\pi = \pi r^2$$
$$25 = r^2$$
$$r = 5$$

So we know $\overline{OB}$ = 5, but what about $\overline{BD}$? If we knew $\overline{OD}$, we could subtract that from $\overline{OB}$ to get what we want. But do we know $\overline{OD}$?

The inspiration that will lead to a solution is that we can take advantage of the right angle at D. Look what happens when we take a pencil and physically add $\overline{OA}$ and $\overline{OC}$ to the figure:

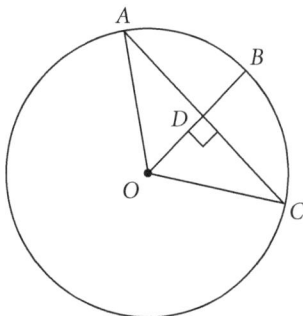

△OAD and △OCD are right triangles. A segment, $\overline{OB}$, perpendicular to a chord, $\overline{AC}$, divides the chord into two equal pieces. When we write in the lengths, we discover some special right triangles:

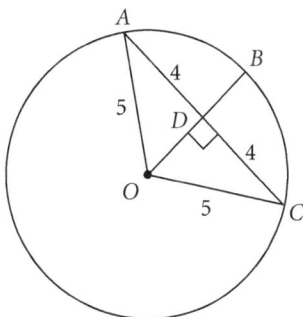

Now it's apparent that $\overline{OD}$ = 3. Since $\overline{OB}$ = 5, $\overline{BD}$ is 5 − 3 = 2. The answer is (F).

Draw on the Diagrams
Don't be afraid to pencil in additions to the given diagrams.

Figureless Questions

Some ACT geometry questions present an extra challenge because they don't provide a figure. You have to "figure it out" for yourself. Try this one:

> **3.** If one side of a right triangle is 3 units long, and a second side is 4 units long, which of the following could be the length, in units, of the third side?
>
> A. 1
> B. 2
> C. $\sqrt{7}$
> D. $3\sqrt{2}$
> E. $3\sqrt{3}$

The key to solving most Figureless questions is to sketch a diagram, but sometimes that's not so easy because you're given less information than you might like. Question 3 is the perfect example. It gives you two sides of a right triangle and asks for the third. Sounds familiar. And the two sides it gives you—3 and 4—really sound familiar. It's a 3-4-5, right?

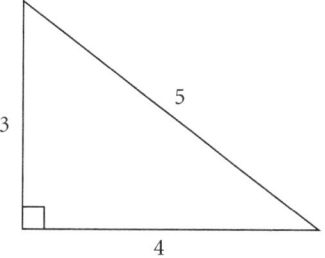

So the answer is 5 . . . whoops! There's no 5 among the answer choices! What's going on?

Better check back. Notice that the question asks, "which of the following could be the length . . . ?" That *could* is crucial. It suggests that there's more than one possibility. Our answer of 5 was too obvious. There's another one somewhere.

Can you think of another way of sketching the figure with the same given information? Who says that the 3 and 4 have to be the two legs? Look at what happens when you make one of them—the larger one, of course—the *hypotenuse*:

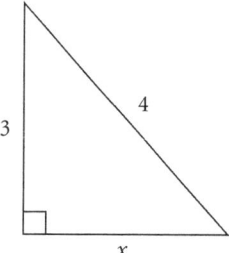

This is not a 3-4-5 triangle because in a 3-4-5, the 3 and the 4 are the legs. This is not a special right triangle. To figure out the length of the third side, we'll use the Pythagorean theorem:

$$(\text{leg}_1)^2 + (\text{leg}_2)^2 = (\text{hypotenuse})^2$$

$$3^2 + x^2 = 4^2$$
$$9 + x^2 = 16$$
$$x^2 = 7$$
$$x = \sqrt{7}$$

The answer is (C).

• •

Be an Artist
Sketch your own figures for figureless problems.

• •

Multistep Questions

Some of the toughest ACT geometry questions take many steps to solve and combine different geometry concepts. Here's an example:

4. In the figure below, $\overline{AB}$ is tangent to the circle at A. If the circumference of the circle is 12π units and $\overline{OB}$ is 12 units long, what is the area, in square units, of the shaded region?

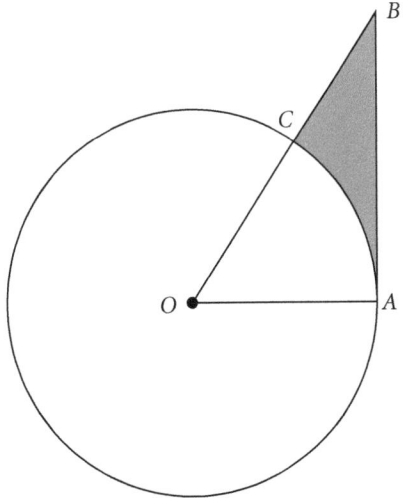

F. $18\sqrt{3} - 6\pi$
G. $24\sqrt{3} - 6\pi$
H. $18\sqrt{3} - 2\pi$
J. $12\pi - 12$
K. $24\sqrt{3} - 2\pi$

This is about as hard as they come on the ACT. It's by no means clear how the given information—the circumference of the circle and the length of $\overline{OB}$—will lead us to the area of the shaded region.

So what do you do? Give up? No.

Don't give up immediately unless you're really short on time or you know for sure you can't answer the question.

Rather than try to figure out every length and angle, take a more systematic approach. The shaded region is a shape that has no name, let alone an area formula. Like most shaded regions, this one is the difference between two familiar shapes with names and area formulas. Think of the shaded region in question 4 as:

(the area of ∆AOB) – (the area of sector AOC)

So we now know that we need to figure out the area of the triangle and the area of the sector.

First, the triangle. We are explicitly given $\overline{OB}$ = 12. We are also given that $\overline{AB}$ is tangent to the circle at A, which tells us that $\overline{OA}$ is a radius and that <OAB is a right angle. So if we can figure out the radius of the circle, we'll have two sides of a right triangle, which will enable us to figure out the third side, and then figure out the area.

We can get the radius from the given circumference. Plug what we know into the formula and solve for r:

$$\text{Circumference} = 2\pi r$$

$$12\pi = 2\pi r$$
$$r = \frac{12\pi}{2\pi} = 6$$

$\overline{OA}$ = 6. Aha! So it turns out that ∆AOB is no ordinary right triangle. Since one leg—6—is exactly half the hypotenuse—12—we're looking at a 30°-60°-90° triangle. By applying the well-known side ratios (1:√3:2) for a 30°-60°-90° triangle, we determine that $\overline{AB}$ = 6√3.

Now we can plug the lengths of the legs in for the base and altitude in the formula for the area of a triangle:

$$\text{Area} = \frac{1}{2}bh$$

$= \frac{1}{2}(6\sqrt{3})(6)$
$= 18\sqrt{3}$

Already it looks like the answer's going to be (F) or (H)—they're the choices that begin with $18\sqrt{3}$. We could just guess (F) or (H) and move on, but if we've come this far, we might as well go all the way.

Next, the area of the sector. Fortunately, while working on the triangle, we figured out the two things we need to get the area of the sector: the radius of the circle (6) and the measure of the central angle (60°). The radius tells us that the area of the whole circle (πr^2) is 36π. And the central angle tells us that the area of the sector is $\frac{60}{360}$, or $\frac{1}{6}$ of the area of the circle. $\frac{1}{6}$ of 36π is 6π. So the area of the shaded region is $18\sqrt{3} - 6\pi$, choice (F).

Break It Down
Break down complex problems into simpler steps.

A final bit of advice: Your goal on the ACT is to get as many points as possible, so focus your studies on the areas that are likely to generate the most points. Together, algebra and plane geometry make up the vast majority of ACT Math questions, so make sure you know how to do the basics in these areas.

Part 4

The ACT Reading Test

Step Ten
Skills Reading

Step 10 Preview

Introduction

Know Where You're Going
- Common Structural Clues

Kaplan's Three-Step Method for ACT Reading
- Step 1. Actively Read the Passage, Taking Notes as You Go
- Step 2. Examine the Question Stem, Looking for Clues
- Step 3. Predict the Answer and Select the Choice That Best Matches Your Prediction

Creating a Road Map
- Practice Making a Passage Map
- The General Outline

Special Passage Types
- The Prose Fiction Passage
- The Natural Science Passage
- Paired Passages

INTRODUCTION

The kind of reading rewarded by the ACT may not be what you expect. You may think that success on a test like this requires that you read very slowly and deliberately, making sure you remember everything. Well, we at Kaplan have found that this kind of reading won't work on the ACT. In fact, it's a sure way to run out of time halfway through the Reading test.

The real key to ACT Reading is to read very quickly but actively, getting a sense of the gist, or "main idea," of the passage and seeing how everything fits together to support that main idea. You should constantly try to think ahead. Look for the general outline of the passage—how it's structured. Don't worry about the details. You'll come back for those later.

Get a Sense of Direction
Read actively, with an eye toward where the author is going.

Fast, active reading, of course, requires a little more mental energy than slow, passive reading. But it pays off. Those who dwell on details—who passively let the passage reveal itself at its own pace—are sure to run out of time. Don't be that kind of reader! Again, the key is *take control*. Make the passage reveal itself to you on *your* schedule by skimming the passage, with an eye on structure rather than detail. Look for key words that tell you what the author is doing so that you can save yourself time. For example, read examples very, very quickly, just glancing over the words. When an author says "for example," you know that what follows is an example of a general point. Do you need to understand that specific example? Maybe, maybe not. If you *do*, you can come back and read the verbiage when you're attacking the questions. You'll know exactly where the author gave an example of general point *x* (or whatever). If you *don't* need to know the example for any of the questions, great! You haven't wasted much time on something that won't get you a point.

KNOW WHERE YOU'RE GOING

To help you know where an author is going, pay careful attention to "structural clues" (we discussed these briefly in Step Four). Words such as *but*, *nevertheless*, and *moreover* help you get a sense of where a piece of writing is going. You also should look for signal phrases such as *clearly*, *as a result*, or *no one can deny that* to determine the logic of the passage. Remember, you can come back for the details later, when you're doing the questions. What's important in reading the passage is to get a sense of how those details fit together to express the point or points of the passage.

For your reference, we've gathered together some important ways in which an author "tells" you where a Reading passage is going.

Common Structural Clues

Indicating a Contrast
but
however
on the other hand
nevertheless

Indicating a Continuation with a Similar or Complementary Thought
moreover
furthermore
; (a semicolon)

Indicating a Conclusion
therefore
thus

Indicating Reasons for a Conclusion
since
because of
due to

Indicating an Example or Illustration
for instance
for example

Now let's see how you can use this skill of active reading to develop a plan of attack for the ACT Reading test.

KAPLAN'S THREE-STEP METHOD FOR ACT READING

You must always remember that when reading for the ACT, you have a special purpose: to answer specific multiple-choice questions. And we've found that the best way to do this is initially to read a passage quickly and actively for general understanding, then refer to the passage to answer individual questions. Not everybody should use the exact same strategy, but we find that almost every ACT test taker can succeed by following these three basic steps:

Step 1. Actively read the passage, taking notes as you go.

Step 2. Examine the question stem, looking for clues.

Step 3. Predict the answer and select the choice that best matches your prediction.

For most students, these three tasks should together take up about nine minutes per passage. Less than three of those nine minutes should be spent prereading. The remaining time should be devoted to considering the questions and referring to the passage to check your answers.

As we mentioned earlier, you probably want to take two passes through the questions for each passage, getting the doable ones the first time around and coming back for the harder ones.

Step 1. Actively Read the Passage, Taking Notes as You Go

Unlike the English test, you should read the passage in the Reading test before looking at the questions and answers. As you read, use structural clues to anticipate how the parts of the passage fit together. In this reading, the main goals are:

- To understand the gist of the passage (the "main idea")
- To get an overall idea of how the passage is organized—a kind of road map—so that it will be easier to refer to later

Read a paragraph quickly; then pause to identify briefly the purpose of the paragraph and jot your notes for each paragraph in a nearby margin. Underlining or circling key phrases is OK, but labeling each paragraph is a more active approach and will help you understand the main ideas. Then, when you go through the questions, you'll have a clearer understanding of the passage and can easily find the information you need.

An important reminder: *don't read slowly, and don't get bogged down in individual details.* Most of the details in the passage aren't required for answering the questions, so why waste time worrying about them?

Get the Main Idea

Don't get bogged down in the details of the passage.

Step 2. Examine the Question Stem, Looking for Clues

The stem of an ACT Reading question can contain two kinds of clues. First, the test maker uses certain phrases repeatedly in question stems, such as *As stated in the passage* and *The author suggests*. A question stem can also include a line reference telling you where in the passage you should look for information. If there's no line reference, you have the notes you took in Step 1 to guide you.

It's All about the Question
Don't let the answer choices direct your thinking.

On the Reading test, you should think about the question stem *without looking at the choices*. In most cases, you won't be able to remember exactly what the passage said about the matter in question. That's all right. In fact, even if you do think you remember, don't trust your memory. Instead . . .

Step 3. Predict the Answer and Select the Choice That Best Matches Your Prediction

In Step 2, you figured out what the question was asking and where to find the answer; in Step 3, you predict an answer and then match your answer to the answer choices. It's important to make your prediction *before you read any of the multiple-choice answers*. This helps you focus your thinking and avoid wrong-answer traps.

Predict before You Peek
Answer the question in your own words, then look at the answer choices.

CREATING A ROAD MAP
Practice Making a Passage Map

Now practice taking notes on the full-length ACT passage that follows. We're not going to give you the questions until Step 11, when we'll talk about the different kinds of Reading questions and how to answer them. For now, just worry about the passage mapping part of the Kaplan Three-Step Method. Take three minutes or so, and read the passage. Remember to read quickly, with an eye to the structure of the passage. Make yourself a road map for the passage. And—most important of all—keep track of time and don't get bogged down in details!

Passage I

HUMANITIES: This passage comes from *Invitation to the Theatre*, copyright 1967 by George Kernodle; Harcourt, Brace, & World Inc., publisher.

Tragedy was the invention of the Greeks. In their Golden Age, the fifth century before Christ, they produced the world's greatest dramatists, new forms of tragedy and comedy
(5) that have been models ever since, and a theatre that every age goes back to for rediscovery of some basic principles. . . .

Since it derived from primitive religious rites, with masks and ceremonial costumes,
(10) and made use of music, dance, and poetry, the Greek drama was at the opposite pole from the modern realistic stage. In fact, probably no other theatre in history has made fuller use of the intensities of art. The
(15) masks, made of painted linen, wood, and plaster, brought down from primitive days the atmosphere of gods, heroes, and demons. Our nineteenth- and twentieth-century grandfathers thought masks must have been
(20) very artificial. Today, however, we appreciate their exciting intensity and can see that in a large theatre they were indispensable. If they allowed no fleeting change of expression during a single episode, they could give for
(25) each episode in turn more intense expression than any human face could. When Oedipus comes back with bleeding eyes, the new mask could be more terrible than any facial makeup the audience could endure, yet in
(30) its sculpted intensity more beautiful than a real face.

Most essential of all intensities, and hardest for us to understand, was the chorus. Yet many playwrights today are trying to find some
(35) equivalent to do for a modern play what the chorus did for the Greeks. During the episodes played by the actors, the chorus would only provide a background of group response, enlarging and reverberating the emotions
(40) of the actors, sometimes protesting and opposing but in general serving as ideal spectators to stir and lead the reactions of the audience. But between episodes, with the actors out of the way, the chorus took over.
(45) We have only the words, not the music or dance, and some translations of the odes are in such formal, old-fashioned language that it is hard to guess that they were accompanied by vigorous, sometimes even wild dances
(50) and symbolic actions that filled an orchestra that in some cities was sixty to ninety feet in diameter. Sometimes the chorus expressed simple horror or lament. Sometimes it chanted and acted out, in unison and in
(55) precise formations of rows and lines, the acts of violence the characters were enacting offstage. When Phaedra rushes offstage in *Hippolytus* to hang herself from the rafters, the members of the chorus, all fifteen of
(60) them, perform in mime and chant the act of tying the rope and swinging from the rafters. Sometimes the chorus tells or reenacts an incident of history or legend that throws light on the situation in the play. Sometimes
(65) the chorus puts into specific action what is a general intention in the mind of the main character. When Oedipus resolves to hunt out the guilty person and cleanse the city, he is speaking metaphorically, but the chorus
(70) invokes the gods of vengeance and dances a wild pursuit.

On the printed page, the choral odes seem static and formal, lyric and philosophical, emotional let-downs that punctuate the
(75) series of episodes, like intermissions between two acts of a play. The reader who skips the odes can get the main points of the play. A few are worth reading as independent poems, notably the famous one in *Antigone*
(80) beginning, "Many are the wonders of the world, but none is more wonderful than

man." Some modern acting versions omit the chorus or reduce it to a few background figures. Yet to the Greeks the odes were
(85) certainly more than mere poetic interludes: the wild Dionysian words and movements evoked primitive levels of the subconscious and at the same time served to transform primitive violence into charm and beauty
(90) and to add philosophical reflections on the meaning of human destiny.

For production today, we can only improvise some partial equivalent. In Athens the entire population was familiar with
(95) choral performances. Every year each of the tribes entered a dithyramb in a contest, rehearsing five hundred men and boys for weeks. Some modern composers have tried to write dramatic music for choruses: the most
(100) notable examples are the French composer Darius Milhaud, in the primitive rhythms, shouts, and chants of his operatic version of the *Oresteia*; George Gershwin, in the Negro funeral scenes of *Porgy and Bess*; and Kurt
(105) Weill, in the African choruses *for Lost in the Stars*, the musical dramatization of Alan Paton's novel, Cry, the Beloved Country. For revivals of Greek tragedies we have not dared use much music beyond a few phrases
(110) half shouted, half sung, and drumbeats and suggestive melodies in the background.

The General Outline

Your quick preread of the passage should have given you a sense of its general organization:

- **First paragraph**—introduces the topic of Greek tragedy
- **Second paragraph**—discusses use of masks (artificial but intense)
- **Third paragraph**—discusses use of chorus (also artificial but intense)
- **Fourth paragraph**—expands discussion to choral odes
- **Fifth paragraph**—concludes with discussion of how Greek tragedy is performed today and how it has influenced some modern art

And that's really all the road map you need going into the questions. Aside from that, you should take away a sense of the author's main point: Greek tragedy included many artificial devices, but these devices allowed it to rise to a high level of intensity.

You wouldn't need or even want to get more than this on your prereading of the passage. We know it's difficult for many students to accept, but it really is true: *Careful, detail-oriented reading does not pay on the ACT Reading section*. You just don't have the time.

• •

Don't Go without Your Road Map

Build a mental road map for all nonfiction passages—an outline of the major points covered.

• •

SPECIAL PASSAGES: PROSE FICTION, NATURAL SCIENCE, AND PAIRED PASSAGES

Now that you've learned the general approach, let's look more closely at the three kinds of ACT passage that give students the most trouble—the Prose Fiction passage, the Natural Science passage, and Paired Passages.

The passage breakdown for every ACT Reading section is as follows:

- **Prose Fiction**—one passage per test
- **Nonfiction**—three passages per test, one each in:
  — Social Science
  — Natural Science
  — Humanities

Your approach will be essentially the same for all three nonfiction passages, since they're all well-organized essays. We've just seen how to handle passages like this. Your approach to the Prose Fiction passage, however, will be somewhat different.

The Prose Fiction Passage

The Prose Fiction passage is usually a story in which characters, fully equipped with their own motivations and emotions, interact in revealing ways. For that reason, the passage won't break down into an orderly outline or road map, so don't even try to characterize the function of each paragraph. Pay attention instead to the *story*.

A Special Approach

Don't try to construct a mental road map for the Prose Fiction passage. Instead, pay attention to the story and the characters.

In the Prose Fiction passage, almost all the questions relate to the characters. Your job is to find the answers to the following general questions:

- *Who are these people?* What are they like? How are they related to each other?
- *What is their state of mind?* Are they angry, sad, reflective, excited?
- *What's really going on?* What's happening on the surface? What's happening beneath the surface?

Most of the fiction passages focus on one person or are written from the point of view of one of the characters. Figure out who this main character is, and pay special attention to what he or she is like. Read between the lines to determine unspoken emotions and attitudes. Little hints—a momentary pause, a pointed or sarcastic comment—are sometimes all you have to go on, so pay attention. In fact, you probably want to spend more time prereading the Prose Fiction passage than you do any of the other three passages. Get a good feel for the tone and style of the passage as a whole before going to the questions.

Fortunately, the questions for these passages tend to go more quickly than those for the other passages, so you'll be able to make up some of that lost time you spent reading the text.

Prose Fiction Passage Strategy

When prereading the Prose Fiction passage, ask yourself:
- Who are these people?
- What is their state of mind?
- What's really going on?

The Natural Science Passage

The Natural Science passage in the ACT Reading section is often similar in outward appearance to a passage on the Science Reasoning section. Illustrations, graphs, and tables of information may be included. Usually, though, the emphasis in Reading is more on understanding ideas rather than reading and analyzing experiments and data.

Approaching the Natural Science passage is not very different from approaching the other nonfiction passages, since many of those are well-organized essays laying out ideas in a straightforward, logical way. (However, some nonfiction passages—particularly the Humanities passage—are personal essays that require a focus on the author and tone.) But you may be more likely to find unfamiliar vocabulary in a Natural Science passage. Don't panic. Any unfamiliar terms will usually be defined explicitly in the passage or else will have definitions inferable from context.

In the Natural Science passage, it's extremely easy to lose yourself in complex details. Don't do it. *It's especially important not to get bogged down in the Natural Science passage!* Many students try to understand and remember everything as they read. But that's not the right ACT attitude. In your prereading of the passage, just get the gist and the outline; don't sweat the details. You'd be surprised how many questions you can answer on a passage you don't understand completely.

Get the Big Picture

When prereading the Natural Science passage, you must be even more careful than usual not to get bogged down in details.

Paired Passages

Also be on the lookout for Paired Passages on the ACT Reading test. Paired Passages provide two passages that deal with the same topic or related topics. Some questions ask about only one of the passages, while others ask you to consider both. The passage or passages each question addresses is clearly labeled. If you are tackling a set of paired passages, you want to follow the Kaplan Method for Paired Passages in which you divide and conquer.

The Kaplan Method for Paired Passages

Step 1: Read Passage A and answer the questions about it.

Step 2: Read Passage B and answer the questions about it.

Step 3: Answer questions asking about both passages.

The ACT will make clear which questions relate to Passage A, Passage B, and both Passages A and B, which is very helpful. By concentrating on one passage a time before you tackle questions that discuss both, you can avoid trap answer choices that refer to the wrong passage.

As you continue in your ACT training, don't forget the very first piece of Reading advice we offered: read actively. Always know where a passage is going, and keep an eye on the structure. Use this habit whenever you read on the ACT, not just in the Reading test. It helps in all of the subject areas.

Step Eleven
Reading Question Types and Strategies

Step 11 Preview

Introduction

Detail Questions

Inference Questions

Big Picture Questions

Proven Reading Strategies
- Find and Paraphrase
- Skipping Questions

INTRODUCTION

In the first Reading step, we discussed general strategies for approaching ACT Reading, with a special focus on prereading. Now let's look at the major question types you'll encounter. There are three main types of Reading questions on the test: Detail questions and Inference questions (which make up the bulk) and Big Picture questions (of which there are usually just a few).

The following passage is the same one you already preread. Now, however, you have the questions attached to it, so you can go through the entire process. Remember to use the Three-Step Method:

Step 1. Actively read the passage, taking notes as you go.

Step 2. Examine the question stem, looking for clues.

Step 3. Predict the answer, and select the choice that best matches your prediction.

We'll discuss selected questions from this set as examples of Detail, Inference, and Big Picture questions.

Passage I

HUMANITIES: This passage comes from *Invitation to the Theatre*, copyright 1967 by George Kernodle; Harcourt, Brace, & World Inc., publisher.

Tragedy was the invention of the Greeks. In their Golden Age, the fifth century before Christ, they produced the world's greatest dramatists, new forms of tragedy and comedy
(5) that have been models ever since, and a theatre that every age goes back to for rediscovery of some basic principles. . . .

Since it derived from primitive religious rites, with masks and ceremonial costumes,
(10) and made use of music, dance, and poetry, the Greek drama was at the opposite pole from the modern realistic stage. In fact, probably no other theatre in history has made fuller use of the intensities of art. The
(15) masks, made of painted linen, wood, and plaster, brought down from primitive days the atmosphere of gods, heroes, and demons. Our nineteenth- and twentieth-century grandfathers thought masks must have been
(20) very artificial. Today, however, we appreciate their exciting intensity and can see that in a large theatre they were indispensable. If they allowed no fleeting change of expression during a single episode, they could give for
(25) each episode in turn more intense expression than any human face could. When Oedipus comes back with bleeding eyes, the new mask could be more terrible than any facial makeup the audience could endure, yet in
(30) its sculpted intensity more beautiful than a real face.

Most essential of all intensities, and hardest for us to understand, was the chorus. Yet many playwrights today are trying to find some
(35) equivalent to do for a modern play what the chorus did for the Greeks. During the episodes played by the actors, the chorus would only provide a background of group response, enlarging and reverberating the emotions
(40) of the actors, sometimes protesting and opposing but in general serving as ideal spectators to stir and lead the reactions of the audience. But between episodes, with the actors out of the way, the chorus took over.

(45) We have only the words, not the music or dance, and some translations of the odes are in such formal, old-fashioned language that it is hard to guess that they were accompanied by vigorous, sometimes even wild dances
(50) and symbolic actions that filled an orchestra that in some cities was sixty to ninety feet in diameter. Sometimes the chorus expressed simple horror or lament. Sometimes it chanted and acted out, in unison and in
(55) precise formations of rows and lines, the acts of violence the characters were enacting offstage. When Phaedra rushes offstage in *Hippolytus* to hang herself from the rafters, the members of the chorus, all fifteen of
(60) them, perform in mime and chant the act of tying the rope and swinging from the rafters. Sometimes the chorus tells or reenacts an incident of history or legend that throws light on the situation in the play. Sometimes
(65) the chorus puts into specific action what is a general intention in the mind of the main character. When Oedipus resolves to hunt out the guilty person and cleanse the city, he is speaking metaphorically, but the chorus
(70) invokes the gods of vengeance and dances a wild pursuit.

On the printed page, the choral odes seem static and formal, lyric and philosophical, emotional let-downs that punctuate the
(75) series of episodes, like intermissions between two acts of a play. The reader who skips the odes can get the main points of the play. A few are worth reading as independent poems, notably the famous one in *Antigone*
(80) beginning, "Many are the wonders of the world, but none is more wonderful than man." Some modern acting versions omit the chorus or reduce it to a few background figures. Yet to the Greeks the odes were
(85) certainly more than mere poetic interludes: the wild Dionysian words and movements evoked primitive levels of the subconscious and at the same time served to transform primitive violence into charm and beauty

(90) and to add philosophical reflections on the meaning of human destiny.

For production today, we can only improvise some partial equivalent. In Athens the entire population was familiar with
(95) choral performances. Every year each of the tribes entered a dithyramb in a contest, rehearsing five hundred men and boys for weeks. Some modern composers have tried to write dramatic music for choruses: the most
(100) notable examples are the French composer Darius Milhaud, in the primitive rhythms, shouts, and chants of his operatic version of the *Oresteia*; George Gershwin, in the Negro funeral scenes of *Porgy and Bess*; and Kurt
(105) Weill, in the African choruses *for Lost in the Stars*, the musical dramatization of Alan Paton's novel, *Cry, the Beloved Country*. For revivals of Greek tragedies we have not dared use much music beyond a few phrases
(110) half shouted, half sung, and drumbeats and suggestive melodies in the background.

1. Combined with the passage's additional information, the fact that some Greek orchestras were sixty to ninety feet across suggests that:

   A. few spectators were able to see the stage.
   B. no one performer could dominate a performance.
   C. choruses and masks helped overcome the distance between actors and audience.
   D. Greek tragedies lacked the emotional force of modern theatrical productions.

2. Which of the following claims expresses the writer's opinion and not a fact?

   F. The Greek odes contained Dionysian words and movements.
   G. Greek theater has made greater use of the intensities of art than has any other theater in history.
   H. Many modern playwrights are trying to find an equivalent to the Greek chorus.
   J. The chorus was an essential part of Greek tragedy.

3. The description of the chorus's enactment of Phaedra's offstage suicide (lines 56–60) shows that, in contrast to modern theater, ancient Greek theater was:

   A. more violent.
   B. more concerned with satisfying an audience.
   C. more apt to be historically accurate.
   D. less concerned with a realistic portrayal of events.

4. It can be inferred that one consequence of the Greeks' use of masks was that:

   F. the actors often had to change masks between episodes.
   G. the characters in the play could not convey emotion.
   H. the actors wearing masks played nonspeaking roles.
   J. good acting ability was not important to the Greeks.

5. Which of the following is supported by the information in the second paragraph (lines 8–31)?

   A. Masks in Greek drama combined artistic beauty with emotional intensity.
   B. The use of masks in Greek drama was better appreciated in the nineteenth century than it is now.
   C. Masks in Greek drama were used to portray gods but never human beings.
   D. Contemporary scholars seriously doubt the importance of masks to Greek theater.

6. The author indicates in lines 67–68 that Oedipus's resolution "to hunt out the guilty person and cleanse the city" was:

   F. at odds with what he actually does later in the performance.
   G. misinterpreted by the chorus.
   H. dramatized by the actions of the chorus.
   J. angrily condemned by the chorus.

7. According to the passage, when actors were present on stage, the chorus would:

   A. look on as silently as spectators.
   B. inevitably agree with the actors' actions.
   C. communicate to the audience solely through mime.
   D. react to the performance as an audience might.

8. The main point of the fourth paragraph (lines 72–91) is that choral odes:

   F. should not be performed by modern choruses.
   G. have a meaning and beauty that are lost in modern adaptations.
   H. can be safely ignored by a modern-day reader.
   J. are worthwhile only in *Antigone*.

9. The passage suggests that modern revivals of Greek tragedies "have not dared use much music" (lines 108–109) because:

   A. modern instruments would appear out of place.
   B. to do so would require a greater understanding of how choral odes were performed.
   C. music would distract the audience from listening to the words of choral odes.
   D. such music is considered far too primitive for modern audiences.

10. *Porgy and Bess* and *Lost in the Stars* are modern plays that:

    F. are revivals of Greek tragedies.
    G. use music to evoke the subconscious.
    H. perform primitive Greek music.
    J. have made use of musical choruses.

Let's remind ourselves of the passage's general outline:

- **First paragraph**—introduces the topic of Greek tragedy
- **Second paragraph**—discusses use of masks (artificial but intense)
- **Third paragraph**—discusses use of chorus (also artificial but intense)
- **Fourth paragraph**—expands discussion to choral odes
- **Fifth paragraph**—concludes with discussion of how Greek tragedy is performed today and how it has influenced some modern art

Don't forget to phrase in your mind the author's main point: Greek tragedy included many artificial devices, but these devices allowed it to rise to a high level of intensity.

DETAIL QUESTIONS

Questions 6 and 7 are typical Detail questions. As you've seen, some Detail questions (such as 6) give you a line reference to help you out; others (such as 7) don't, forcing you to seek out the answer based on your own sense of how the passage is laid out (one of the two key reasons to preread the passage). With either type of Detail question, once you've found the part of the passage that a question refers to, the answer is often (though not always) pretty obvious.

• •

Look for the Answer in the Passage

Always refer to the passage before answering a question.

• •

Question 6 provides a line reference (lines 67–68), but to answer the question confidently, you should have also read a few lines before and a few lines after the cited lines. There you would have read: "Sometimes the chorus puts into action what is a general intention in the mind of the main character. When Oedipus resolves . . ." Clearly, the Oedipus example is meant to illustrate the point about the chorus acting out a character's intentions. So (H) is correct—it is dramatizing (or acting out) Oedipus's resolution. (By the way, choice (G) might have been tempting, but there's no real evidence that the chorus is misinterpreting, just that it's "putting a general intention into specific action.")

Question 7 is a Detail question *without* a line reference. Such questions are common on the ACT. This question's mention of the chorus should have sent you to the third paragraph, but that's a long paragraph, so you probably had to skim it to find the answer in lines 42–43, where the author claims that the chorus serves to "lead the reactions of the audience"—captured by correct choice (D).

Context Matters

When given a specific line reference, always read a few sentences before and after the cited lines to get a sense of the context.

INFERENCE QUESTIONS

For Inference questions, your job is to combine ideas logically to make an inference—something that's not stated explicitly in the passage but that is definitely said implicitly. Often, Inference questions have a word like *suggest*, *infer*, *inference*, or *imply* in the question stem to tip you off.

Read between the Lines

To succeed on these, you have to "read between the lines." Common sense is your best tool here. You use various bits of information in the passage as evidence for your own logical conclusion.

Like Detail questions, Inference questions only sometimes contain line references. Question 9 does, referring you to lines 108–109. But you really have to keep the context of the entire paragraph in mind when you make your inference. Why would modern revivals not have "dared" to use much music? Well, the paragraph opens by saying that modern productions "can only improvise some partial equivalent" to the choral odes. We can infer that since we can only improvise the odes, we don't understand very much about them. That's why the use of music would be considered daring and why choice (B) is correct.

Question 4 provides no line reference, but the mention of masks should have sent you to the second paragraph of the passage, where (according to your trusty road map) masks are discussed. Lines 23–24 explain that masks "allowed no fleeting change of expression during a single episode." Treat that as your first piece of evidence. Your second comes in lines 24–26: "[T]hey [the masks] could give for each episode in turn more intense expression than any human face could." Put those two pieces of evidence together—masks can't change expression during a *single* episode, but they can give expression for each episode *in turn*.

Clearly, the actors must have changed masks between episodes, so that they could express the different emotions that different episodes required. Choice (F) is correct.

Be a Detective

Making inferences requires that you combine bits of information from different parts of the passage.

One warning: be careful to keep your inferences as "close" to the passage as possible. Don't make wild leaps. An inference should seem to follow naturally and inevitably from the evidence provided in the passage.

No Flights of Fancy

Don't make your inferences too extreme.

BIG PICTURE QUESTIONS

There are a few questions in Reading that test your understanding of the theme, purpose, and organization of the passage. For these Big Picture questions, your main task is different from what it is for Detail or Inference questions, though you should still plan to find the answer in the passages.

Big Picture questions tend to focus on:

- The main point or purpose of a passage or part of a passage
- The author's attitude or tone
- The logic underlying the author's argument
- How ideas in different parts of the passage relate to each other
- The difference between fact and opinion

One way to see the Big Picture is to read actively. As you read, ask yourself, "What's the point of this? Why is the author saying this?"

Find Clues from Other Questions

If you're still stumped after reading the passage, try doing the Detail and Inference questions first—to help you fill in the Big Picture.

Question 8 asks for the main idea of a particular paragraph—namely, the fourth, which our general outline indicates as the paragraph about choral odes. Skimming that paragraph, you find reference to how the odes seem to us modern people—"static and formal" (line 73), "like intermissions between two acts of a play" (lines 75–76). Later, the author states, by way of contrast (note the use of the clue word *yet*): "Yet to the Greeks the odes were certainly more than mere poetic interludes" (lines 84–85). Clearly, the author in this paragraph wants to contrast our modern static view of the odes with the Greeks' view of them as something more. That idea is best captured by choice (G).

Question 2, meanwhile, is another common type of Big Picture question—one that requires that you distinguish between expressions of fact and opinion in the passage. A simple test for fact (versus opinion) is this: Can it be proven objectively? If so, it's a fact.

The content of Greek odes (F) is a matter of fact; you can go to a Greek ode and find out whether it does or doesn't contain Dionysian words. Similarly, the efforts of modern playwrights to find an equivalent to the Greek chorus (choice (H)) and the central importance of the chorus to Greek tragedy (J) can be factually verified.

But the "intensities of art" are a subjective matter. What one person thinks is intense might strike another as simply boring. So (G) is the expression of opinion the question is looking for.

PROVEN READING STRATEGIES

Find and Paraphrase

Don't Get Confused

Your task in Reading is to "find and paraphrase," not to "comprehend and remember."

The previous examples show that your real task in Reading is different from what you might expect. Your main job is to *find* the answers. In other words, "find and paraphrase." But students tend to think that their task in Reading is to "comprehend and remember." That's the wrong mind-set.

Here's a key to the Greek tragedy passage, so that you can check the answers to the questions not already discussed.

		(Nonfiction—Humanities)	
ANSWER	REFER TO	TYPE	COMMENTS
1. C	Lines 36–43 45–51	Inference	Q-stem emphasizes distance between audience and stage; masks and choruses help to "enlarge" the action so that it can be understood from a distance.
2. G	Throughout	Big Picture	Already discussed.
3. D	Lines 56–60	Inference	Combine info from lines 8–12, 52–67, 84–91.
4. F	Lines 22–26	Inference	Already discussed.
5. A	Lines 8–31	Inference	Combine info from lines 14–31.
6. H	Lines 68–71	Detail	Already discussed.
7. D	Lines 36–43	Detail	Already discussed.
8. G	Lines 72–91	Big Picture	Already discussed.
9. B	Lines 108–112	Inference	Already discussed.
10. J	Lines 97–111	Detail	"Some modern composers have tried to write dramatic music for choruses." (lines 98–99)

Skipping Questions

Now that you've done a full-length passage and questions, you've probably encountered at least a few questions that you found unanswerable. What do you *do* if you can't find the answer in the passage, or if you *can* find it but don't understand, or if you do understand but can't see an answer choice that makes sense? Skip the question. Skipping is probably more important in Reading than in any other ACT section. Many students find it useful to skip as many as half of the questions on the first pass through a set of Reading questions. That's fine.

Come Back to Difficult Questions

Answer the easy questions for each passage first. Skip the tough ones and come back to them later.

Second Time Around

On your second time through a Reading question, using the process of elimination is a good idea.

When you come back to a Reading question the second time, it usually makes sense to use the process of elimination. The first time around, you tried to find the *right* answer but you couldn't. So now try to identify the three *wrong* answers. Eliminating three choices is slower than finding one right choice, so don't make it your main strategy for Reading. But it's a good way to try a second attack on a question.

Another thing to consider when attacking a question for a second time is that the right answer may have been hidden. Maybe it's written in an unexpected way, with different vocabulary. Or maybe there is another good way to answer the question that you haven't thought of. But remember not to get bogged down when you come back to a question. Be willing to admit that there are some questions you just can't answer. Guess if you have to.

Part 5

The ACT Science Test

Step Twelve
Science Skills and Strategies

Step 12 Preview

Reading Skills for Science Reasoning

Kaplan's Three-Step Method for ACT Science
- Step 1. Map the Passage, Identifying and Marking the Purpose, Method, and Results of the Experiment
- Step 2. Scan Figures, Identifying Variables and Patterns
- Step 3. Find Support for the Answer in the Passage

Reading Tables and Graphs
- Look for Patterns and Trends

What to Do When You're Running Out of Time

> **Science Lowdown**
>
> Many ACT takers worry about "not knowing enough science" to do well on the Science test. But the fact of the matter is, you really don't need to be a science whiz to do well on the ACT. Knowing science is a plus, of course, and it certainly can help your work in the Science test. But you don't need to know a truckload of scientific facts to answer these science questions. The questions are answerable from the information in the passage.

READING SKILLS FOR SCIENCE REASONING

ACT Science requires many of the same skills that ACT Reading does. The difference between Reading and Science, however, is that the "details" you have to find in the Science passages almost all relate to numbers or scientific processes or both, and they are often contained in graphs and tables rather than in paragraph form. The secrets to finding most of these details are:

- **Learn to "read" graphs, tables, and research summaries.**
  Some questions involve only accurately retrieving data from a single graph or table, while others involve combining knowledge from two graphs or tables. Still others involve understanding experimental methods well enough to evaluate information.

- **Learn to look for patterns in the numbers that appear.**
  Do these numbers get bigger or smaller? Where are the highest numbers? Where are the lowest? At what point do the numbers change? A little calculation is sometimes required, but not much. In Science, you won't be computing with numbers so much as thinking about what they mean.

KAPLAN'S THREE-STEP METHOD FOR ACT SCIENCE

In the Science test, you have 35 minutes to complete six short passages and 40 questions. Each passage with questions should average five to six minutes. We recommend using just about one minute to preread, and then a total of about four minutes to consider the questions and refer to the passage (that's about 40 seconds per question). Here's a Three-Step Method that you can use as a guide for attacking passages in the Science test:

Step 1. Map the passage, identifying and marking the purpose, method, and results of the experiment.

Step 2. Scan figures, identifying variables and patterns.

Step 3. Find support for the answer in the passage.

These steps may seem familiar—they're pretty similar to the steps for the ACT Reading section. However, the way to attack the Science test is slightly different because you will have charts, graphs, and tables to interpret as well as text. Read through the explanations for each of these steps to see how the two tests differ.

Step 1. Map the Passage, Identifying and Marking the Purpose, Method, and Results of the Experiment

Almost all Science passages have the same general structure. They begin with an introduction, which you should always read first to orient yourself. As with the Reading section, your first step in the Science section is to read the passage actively and take notes. In this case, you are looking for three specific things: the purpose, method, and results of the experiment described.

Step 2. Scan Figures, Identifying Variables and Patterns

Next, take a look at the figures included with the passage. Try to get a general idea of what the figures are telling you about the experiment and how they relate to the information described in the passage. There will be some questions that ask you to interpret the figures only or the figures combined with the text so don't skip them!

• •
Don't Be Delayed by Details
Don't worry about details on your initial read-through.
• •

Step 3. Find Support for the Answer in the Passage

Most of your time in Science will be spent considering questions and referring to the passage to find the answers. Here's where you should do most of your really careful reading. It's essential that you understand exactly what the question is asking. Then go back to the passage and get a sense of what the answer should be before looking at the choices.

You have to be diligent about referring to the passage. Your preread should have given you an idea of where particular kinds of data can be found. Sometimes the questions themselves will direct you to the right place.

Be careful not to mix up units when taking information from graphs, tables, and summaries. Make sure you don't confuse opposites. The difference between a correct and an incorrect answer will often be a "decrease" where an "increase" should be. Always look for words like *not* and *except* in the questions.

Remember, a possible pitfall in answering the questions is relying too heavily on your own knowledge of science. In answering questions, use your knowledge of scientific *methods* and *procedures*; don't rely heavily on any knowledge of specific facts.

• •

Find the Answer in the Passage First

Always refer to the passage and the question stem before selecting an answer.

• •

READING TABLES AND GRAPHS

Most of the specific information in ACT Science passages is contained in tables or graphs, usually accompanied by explanatory material. *Knowing how to read data from tables and graphs is critical to success on the Science test.*

In order to read most graphs and tables, you have to do four things:

- Determine what is being represented.
- Determine what the axes (or columns and rows) represent.
- Take note of units of measurement.
- Look for trends in the data.

Let's say you saw the following graph in a Science passage:

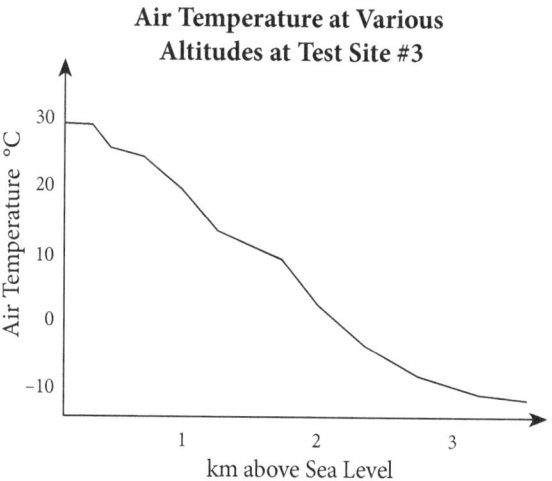

- **Determine what is being represented.** Most graphs and tables have titles that tell you what they represent. For some, though, you may have to get that information from the introduction. Here, the graph is representing how cold or hot the air is at various altitudes at Test Site #3.
- **Determine what the axes represent.** These, too, are usually labeled. In this graph, the *x*-axis represents kilometers above sea level, while the *y*-axis represents the air temperature in degrees Celsius.

- **Take note of units of measurement.** Note that distance here is measured in *kilometers*, not miles or feet. Temperature is measured in degrees *Celsius*, not Fahrenheit.
- **Look for trends in the data.** The pattern of the data in this graph is pretty clear. As you rise in altitude, the temperature drops—the higher the altitude, the lower the temperature.

The sloping line on the graph represents the various temperatures measured at the various altitudes. To find what the measured temperature was at, say, 2 km above sea level, find the 2 km point on the *x*-axis and trace your finger directly up from it until it hits the line. It does so at about the level of 3°C. In other words, at an altitude of 2 km above sea level at Test Site #3, the air temperature was about 3°C.

You should follow a similar procedure with tables of information. For instance, in the introduction to the passage in which the following table might have appeared, you would have learned that scientists were trying to determine the effects of two pollutants (Pb and Hg, lead and mercury) on the trout populations of a particular river. (Note: No introductory paragraph is included here, but there will be one on your exam.)

Location	Water Temperature (°C)	Presence of Pb (parts per million)	Presence of Hg (parts per million)	Population Density of Speckled Trout (# per 100 m^3)	Population Density of Brown Trout (# per 100 m^3)
1	15.4	0	3	5.5	7.9
2	16.1	0	1	12.2	3.5
3	16.3	1	67	0	0
4	15.8	54	3	15.3	5.7
5	16.0	2	4	24	9.5

- **Determine what is being represented.** There's no informative title for this table, but the introduction would have told you what the table represents.
- **Determine what the columns and rows represent.** In tables, you get columns and rows instead of *x*- and *y*-axes. But the principle is the same. Here, each row represents the data from a different numbered location on the river. Each column represents different data—water temperature, presence of the first pollutant, presence of the second pollutant, population of one kind of trout, population of another kind of trout.
- **Take note of units of measurement.** Temperature is measured in Celsius. The two pollutants are measured in parts-per-million (or ppm). The trout populations are measured in number per 100 cubic meters of river.
- **Look for trends in the data.** Glancing at the table, it looks like locations where the Hg concentration is high (as in Location 3), the trout population is virtually nonexistent. This

would seem to indicate that trout life and a high Hg concentration are incompatible. But notice the location where the other pollutant is abundant—in Location 4. Here, both trout populations seem to be more in line with other locations. That would seem to indicate that this other pollutant—Pb—is *not* as detrimental to trout populations as Hg is.

Look for Patterns and Trends

When you first examine a graph or table, don't focus on exact numbers. Look for patterns in the numbers. Don't assume that there is always a pattern or trend. Finding that there isn't a pattern is just as important as finding that there is one. Let's look at the three characteristic patterns in graphs and tables.

Extremes

Extremes—or maximums and minimums—are merely the highest and lowest points that things reach. In tables, the maximums and minimums will be represented by especially high and low numbers. In graphs, they will be represented by high and low x- and y-coordinates. In bar charts, they will be represented by the tallest and shortest bars.

In discussing the extremes in the trout populations table, we saw how isolating the locations at which trout populations and chemical concentrations were at their maximum and minimum values led us to a conclusion about the compatibility of trout and water containing high concentrations of Hg.

Critical Points

Critical points—or points of change—are values at which something dramatic happens. For example, at atmospheric pressure water freezes at 0°C and boils at about 100°C. If you examined water at various temperatures below the lower of these two critical points, it would be solid. If you examined water at various temperatures between the two points, it would be liquid. If you examined water above the higher critical point, it would be a gas.

When you scan the numbers in a chart or points on a graph, look for places where values bunch together, where an increasing trend switches to a decreasing trend, or where suddenly something special happens. At atmospheric pressure, 0°C is a critical point for water—as is 100°C—since something special happens: the substance changes form.

To find out how critical points can help you evaluate data, let's look at a graph representing the concentration of *E. coli* (a common type of bacterium) in relation to a location called Effluent Pipe 3.

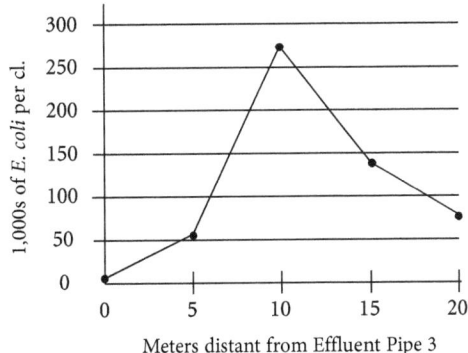
Meters distant from Effluent Pipe 3

Notice how the concentration is low very near Effluent Pipe 3. From there, it rises until about 10 meters away from the pipe, then it falls again, tapering off the farther you get from the pipe. There's a critical point, then, right around 10 meters from Effluent Pipe 3. Somehow, that vicinity is most conducive to the growth of *E. coli*. As you move closer to or farther away from that point, the concentration falls off. So in looking to explain the data, you'd want to focus on that location—10 meters from the pipe. What is it about that location that's so special? Why is it that more *E. coli* grows there?

Variation

Variation is a bit more complex than extremes or critical points. Variation refers to the way two different things change *in relation to each other*. Direct variation means that two things vary in the same way: when one gets bigger, the other does too; when one gets smaller, so does the other. Inverse variation means that two things vary in *opposite* ways: when one gets bigger, the other gets smaller, and vice versa. We saw an example of inverse variation in the air temperature graph, in which altitude and air temperature varied inversely—as altitude *increased*, air temperature *decreased*. Observing this inverse variation allowed us to draw conclusions about the relationship between altitude and air temperature.

When reading data, you should be on the lookout for the three characteristic patterns or trends:

- Extremes (maximums and minimums)
- Critical points (or points of change)
- Direct or inverse variation (or proportionality)

To do well on Science, you have to be able to read graphs and tables, paying special attention to trends and patterns in the data. And sometimes, that's all you need to do to get most of the points on a passage.

WHAT TO DO WHEN YOU'RE RUNNING OUT OF TIME

Let's conclude now with another quick point about getting quick points. If you're nearly out of time and you still have a whole Science passage left, you need to shift to last-minute strategies. Don't try to preread the passage, or you'll just run out of time before you answer any questions. Instead, scan the questions without reading the passage and look first for the ones that require only reading data off of a graph or table. You can often get a couple of quick points just by knowing how to find data quickly.

Last-Minute Strategy: Do the Data Representation Questions

When you're running out of time, go right to the questions without reading the passage, and do as many Data Interpretation questions as you can.

Again, the most important thing is to make sure you have gridded in at least a random guess on every question.

Step Thirteen
Experiment Questions

Step 13 Preview

Introduction

How Scientists Think
- General-to-Specific Thinking
- Specific-to-General Thinking

How Experiments Work
- A Controlled Situation
- Find What Varies

Handling Experiment Questions: Practice Passage
- Approaching the Passage

INTRODUCTION

To succeed on the ACT Science test, you must learn how to think like a scientist. You don't have to know very much science (although it certainly helps), but you should at least be familiar with how scientists go about getting and testing knowledge.

HOW SCIENTISTS THINK

Scientists use two very different kinds of logic, which (to keep things nontechnical) we'll call:

- General-to-specific thinking
- Specific-to-general thinking

General-to-Specific Thinking

In some cases, scientists have already discovered a law of nature and wish to apply their knowledge to a specific case. For example, a scientist may wish to know how fast a pebble (call it Pebble A) will be falling when it hits the ground 3 seconds after being dropped. There is a law of physics that says on Earth, falling objects accelerate at a rate of about 9.8 m/sec^2. The scientist could use this known general law to calculate the specific information she needs: After 3 seconds, the object would be falling at a rate of about 3 sec × 9.8 m/sec^2, or roughly 30 m/sec^2. You could think of this kind of logic as *general-to-specific*. The scientist uses a *general* rule (the acceleration of any object falling on Earth) to find a *specific* fact (the speed of Pebble A).

Specific-to-General Thinking

But scientists use a different kind of thinking in order to discover new laws of nature. In these cases, they examine many facts and then draw a general conclusion about what they've seen. For example, a scientist might watch hundreds of different kinds of frogs live and die and might notice that all of them developed from tadpoles. She might then announce a theory: all frogs develop from tadpoles. You could think of this kind of logic as specific-to-general. The scientist looks at many specific frogs to arrive at a general rule about all frogs.

This conclusion is called a hypothesis, not a fact or a truth, because the scientist has not checked every single frog in the universe. She knows that theoretically there *could* be a frog somewhere that grows, say, from pond scum or from a Dalmatian puppy. But until she finds such a frog, it is reasonable to think that her theory is correct. Many hypotheses, in fact, are so well documented that they become the equivalent of laws of nature.

Step Thirteen: Experiment Questions

Which Direction?
For Science questions, ask yourself whether you should be doing general-to-specific or specific-to-general thinking.

In your science classes in school, you mostly learn about general-to-specific thinking. Your teachers explain general rules of science to you and then expect you to apply these rules to solve problems. Some ACT Science questions are like that, too, but most are not. They test your ability to see the kinds of patterns in specific data that, as a scientist, you would use to formulate your own general hypotheses. We did something like this in Step Twelve, when we theorized—based on the trends we found in a table of data—that the pollutant Hg was in some way detrimental to trout populations.

Remember
Most questions on the ACT test specific-to-general thinking.

HOW EXPERIMENTS WORK

Many ACT Science passages describe experiments and expect you to understand how they're designed. Experiments help scientists do specific-to-general thinking in a reliable and efficient way. Consider the tadpole researcher we just mentioned. In a real-world situation, she would probably notice that some frogs develop from tadpoles and wonder if maybe they all did. Then she'd know what to look for and could check many frogs systematically. This process contains the two basic steps of any experiment:

- Form a hypothesis (guessing that all frogs come from tadpoles).
- Test a hypothesis (checking frogs to see if this guess was right).

Scientists are often interested in cause-and-effect relationships. Having formed her hypothesis about tadpoles, the scientist might wonder what causes a tadpole to become a frog, for instance. To test causal relationships, a special kind of experiment is needed. She must test one possible cause at a time in order to isolate which one actually produces the effect in question. For example, the scientist might inject tadpoles with several kinds of hormones. Some of these tadpoles might die. Others might grow into frogs normally. But a few—those injected with Hormone X, say—might remain tadpoles for an indefinite time. One reasonable explanation is that Hormone X in some way inhibited whatever causes normal frog development. In other words, the scientist would hypothesize a causal relationship between Hormone X and frog development.

A Controlled Situation

The relationship between Hormone X and frog development, however, would not be demonstrated very well if the scientist also fed different diets to different tadpoles, kept some in warmer water, or allowed some to have more room to swim than others—or if she didn't also watch tadpoles that were injected with no hormones at all but that were otherwise kept under the same conditions as the treated tadpoles. Why? Because if the "eternal tadpoles" had a diet that differed from that of the others, the scientist wouldn't know whether it was Hormone X or the special diet that kept the eternal tadpoles from becoming frogs. Moreover, if their water was warmer than that of the others, maybe it was the warmth that somehow kept the tadpoles from developing. And if she didn't watch untreated tadpoles (a control group), she couldn't be sure whether, under the same conditions, a normal, untreated tadpole would also remain undeveloped.

Thus, a scientist creating a well-designed experiment will do the following:

- Ensure that there's a single variable (like Hormone X) that varies from test to test, or group to group
- Ensure that all other factors (diet, temperatures, space, etcetera) remain the same
- Ensure that there is a control group (tadpoles who don't get any Hormone X at all) for comparison purposes

Find What Varies

One advantage to knowing how experiments work is that *you can tell what a researcher is trying to find out about by checking to see what she allows to vary.* That is what's being researched—in this case, Hormone X. Data about things other than hormones and tadpole-to-frog development would be outside the design of the experiment. Information about other factors might be interesting, but could not be part of a scientific proof.

For example, if some of the injected tadpoles that did grow into frogs later turned into princes, the data about the hormone they were given would not prove what causes frogs to become princes. However, the data could be used to design another experiment intended to explore what could make a frog into a prince.

Whenever you see an experiment in Science, therefore, ask yourself three things:

1. **What's the factor that's being varied?**—That is what's being tested.
2. **What's the control group?**—It's the group that has nothing special done to it.
3. **What do the results show?**—What differences exist between the results for the control group and those for the other group(s)? Or between the results for one treated group and those for another, differently treated group?

HANDLING EXPERIMENT QUESTIONS: PRACTICE PASSAGE

What follows is a complete Science passage organized around two experiments. Use the Three-Step Method (preread the passage, consider the question stem, refer to the passage before looking at the choices), but this time, since this is a passage that centers on experiments, remember to ask yourself the three questions you just read. Take five or six minutes to read the passage and do its questions.

Passage I

A mutualistic relationship between two species increases the chances of growth or survival for both of them. Several species of fungi form *mutualistic* relationships called mycorrhizae with the roots of plants. The benefits to each species are shown in the figure below.

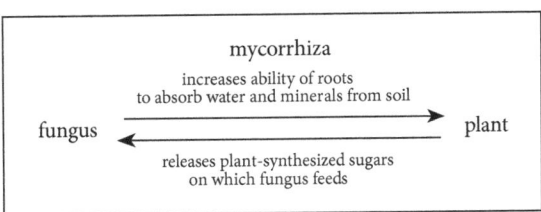

Some of the plant species that require or benefit from the presence of mycorrhizal fungi are noted below.

Cannot survive without mycorrhizae	Grow better with mycorrhizae

All conifers
Some deciduous trees
    (e.g. birch, beech)
Orchids
	Citrus trees
	Ericaceae (heath,
	    rhododendrons,
	    azaleas)
	Grapes
	Soy beans

Agronomists investigated the effects of mycorrhizae on plant growth and survival in the following studies.

Study 1

Three 4-acre plots were prepared with soil from a pine forest. The soil for Plot A was mixed with substantial quantities of cultured mycorrhizal fungi. The soil for Plot B contained only naturally occurring mycorrhizal fungi. The soil for Plot C was sterilized in order to kill any mycorrhizal fungi. Additionally, Plot C was lined with concrete. After planting, Plot C was covered with a fabric that filtered out microorganisms while permitting air and light to penetrate. Two hundred-fifty pine seedlings were planted in each of the three plots.

All plots were treated to the same environmental conditions. The six-month survival rates were recorded in the table below.

	# Seedlings alive after 6 months	Utilization of available K (average)	Utilization of available P (average)
Plot A	107	18%	62%
Plot B	34	10%	13%
Plot C	0	N/A	N/A

N/A = not applicable

Study 2

The roots of surviving seedlings from Plots A and B were analyzed to determine how efficiently they absorbed potassium (K) and phosphorus (P) from the soil. The results were added to the table.

1. The most likely purpose of the concrete liner was:

    A. to block the seedlings from sending out taproots to water below the plot.
    B. to prevent mycorrhizal fungi in the surrounding soil from colonizing the plot.
    C. to absorb potassium and phosphorus from the soil for later analysis.
    D. to provide a firm foundation for mycorrhizal fungi in the plot.

2. Mycorrhizae are highly susceptible to damage from acid rain. Given the information from the passage, acid rain is probably most harmful to:

    F. wheat fields.
    G. birch forests.
    H. orange groves.
    J. grape vines.

3. In a third study, pine seedlings were planted in soil from a different location. The soil was prepared as in Study 1. This time, the survival rates for seedlings planted in Plot A and Plot B were almost identical to each other. Which of the following theories would NOT help to explain these results?

    A. Sterilization killed all the naturally occurring mycorrhizal fungi in the new soil.
    B. The new soil was so mineral deficient that it could not sustain life.
    C. The new soil was naturally more fertile than that used in Study 1.
    D. Large quantities of mycorrhizal fungi occurred naturally in the new soil.

4. According to the passage, in which of the following ways do plants benefit from mycorrhizal associations?

   I. More efficient sugar production
   II. Enhanced ability to survive drought
   III. Increased mineral absorption

   F. I only
   G. III only
   H. II and III only
   J. I, II, and III

5. Which of the following generalizations is supported by the results of Study 2?

   A. Mycorrhizal fungi are essential for the survival of pine seedlings.
   B. Growth rates for pine seedlings may be improved by adding mycorrhizal fungi to the soil.
   C. Mycorrhizal fungi contain minerals that are not normally found in pine forest soil.
   D. Pine seedlings cannot absorb all the potassium that is present in the soil.

Answers: 1. B, 2. G, 3. A, 4. H, 5. D

Approaching the Passage

What's the Topic?

Notice how many diagrams and tables were used here. That's common in experiment passages, where information is given to you in a wide variety of forms. Typically, however, the experiments themselves are clearly labeled, as Study 1 and Study 2 were here.

A quick prereading of the introduction would have revealed the topic of the experiments here—the "mutualistic relationship" between some fungi and some plant roots, the relationship called *mycorrhiza* ("myco" for short). The first diagram just shows you who gets what out of this relationship. The benefit accruing to the plant (the arrow pointing to the word *plant*) is an increased ability to absorb water and minerals. The benefit accruing to the fungus (the other arrow) is the plant-synthesized sugars on which the fungus feeds. That's the mutual benefit the myco association creates.

Notice, by the way, that reading this first diagram alone is enough to answer question 4, which we'll do right now. The question is asking, essentially, what do the plants get out of the association? And we just answered that: increased ability to absorb water and minerals. Statement III is obviously correct, but so is Statement II, since increased water absorption would indeed enhance the plant's ability to survive drought (a drought is a shortage of water, after all). Statement I, though, is a distortion. We know that the fungi benefit from sugars produced by the plants, but we don't have any evidence that the association actually causes plants to produce sugar more efficiently. So I is out; II and III are in, making (H) the answer to question 4.

Data Analysis

But let's get back to the passage. We've just learned who gets what out of the myco association. Now we get a chart that shows what *kind* of plants enter into such associations. Some (those in the first column) are so dependent on myco associations that they can't live without them. Others (those in the second column) merely grow better with them; presumably they could live without them.

Again, there's a question we can answer based solely on information in this one table. Question 2 tells us that mycos are highly susceptible to acid rain, and then asks what kind of plant communities would be most harmed by acid rain. Well, if acid rain hurts mycos, then the plants that are most dependent on myco fungi (that is, the ones listed in the first column) would be the most harmed by acid rain. Of the four choices, only birch forests, choice (G), corresponds to something in column 1 of the table. Birch trees can't even survive without myco fungi, so anything that hurts myco fungi would inferrably hurt birch forests. (Grape vines and orange groves—which are citrus trees—would also be hurt by acid rain, but not as much, since they can survive without myco fungi. We're told nothing about wheat in the passage.)

• •

Don't Forget Data Analysis

Even in passages that center around experiments, there are plenty of Data Analysis questions.

• •

Analyzing Study 1

Now look at the first experiment. Three plots, each with differently treated soil, are planted with pine seedlings. Plot A gets soil with cultivated myco fungi; Plot B gets untreated soil with only naturally occurring myco fungi; and Plot C gets no myco fungi at all, since the soil has been sterilized and isolated (via the concrete lining and the fabric covering). Now ask yourself the three important experiment questions:

- **What factor is being varied?**

    The factor being varied is the amount of myco fungi in the soil. Plot A gets a lot; Plot B gets just the normal amount; Plot C gets none at all. It's clear, then, that the scientists are testing the effects of myco fungi on the growth of pine seedlings.

- **What's the control group?**

    The plants in Plot B are the control group, since they get untreated soil. To learn the effects of the fungi, then, the scientists will compare the results from fungi-rich Plot A with the control, and the results from fungi-poor Plot C with the same control.

Step Thirteen: Experiment Questions

- **What do the results show?**

The results are listed in the first column of the table in Study 1. And they are decisive: no seedlings at all survived in Plot C; 34 did in Plot B; and 107 did in Plot A. The minimums and maximums coincide. Minimum fungi = minimum number of surviving seedlings; maximum fungi = maximum number of surviving seedlings. Clearly there's a cause-and-effect relationship here. Myco fungi probably help pine seedlings survive.

Questions 1 and 3 can be answered solely on the basis of Study 1. Question 1 is merely a procedural question: Why the concrete liner in Plot C? Well, in the analysis of the experiment, we saw that the factor being varied was amount of myco fungi. Plot C was designed to have none at all. It follows, then, that the concrete liner was probably there to prevent any stray myco fungi from entering the sterilized soil—choice (B).

Question 3 actually sets up an extra experiment based on Study 1. The soils were prepared in the same way, except that the soil came from a different location. The results? The number of surviving seedlings from Plots A and B were almost identical. What can that mean? Well, Plot A was supposed to be the fungi-rich plot, whereas Plot B (the control) was supposed to be the fungi-normal plot. But here they have the same results (but notice that we're not told what those results are; it could be that no seedlings survived in any plots this time around).

The question is phrased so that the three wrong choices are things that could explain the results; the correct choice will be the one that can't. Choices B, C, and D all can explain the results, since they all show how similar results could have been derived from Plots A and B. If the new soil just couldn't support life—fungi or no fungi—Plots A and B would have produced similar results, namely, no seedlings surviving. On the other end of the spectrum, choices (C) and (D) show how the two plots might have produced similar high survival rates. If there were many myco fungi naturally in this soil (that's choice (D)), then there wouldn't be all that much difference between the soils in Plots A and B. And if the soil were naturally extremely fertile (that's choice (C)), there might be perfect survival rates no matter what the fungi situation. So all three of these answers would help to explain similar results in Plots A and B.

Choice (A), however, wouldn't help, since it talks about the sterilized soil that's in Plot C. The soil in Plot C won't affect the results in Plots A and B, so choice (A) is the answer here—the factor that doesn't help to explain the results.

Question 4 is in a slightly different format than the others, and you will probably encounter one or two questions in this format on the ACT. Don't let it phase you. The question asks you to interpret Passage 1, specifically the first figure; it doesn't relate to either of the studies at all. To answer the question correctly, you will need to refer to the first figure in the passage, and you will need to have understood that it is showing the benefits of mycorrhiza to each species. Before you look at the answer choices, go through the roman numerals and decide which are true. (This is similar to answering the questions in your own words as you're doing for the other questions.) Statement

I is misleading—the chart states that the plant-synthesized sugars are beneficial to fungi, but it does not indicate that the presence of fungi leads to more efficient sugar production by plants. Because this is not in the passage, it's not an answer to the question. Statements I and III are true, according to the chart. Scanning the answers, you'll see two choices, (F) and (J), which include Statement I, so they're out. Next, you need to decide between (G) and (H). While they're both true, (H) is the best answer because it includes Statements I and II.

Analyzing Study 2

This study takes the surviving seedlings from Plots A and B in Study 1 and just tests how much potassium (K) and phosphorus (P) the roots have absorbed. The results are listed in the second and third columns of the table. (Notice the N/A—not applicable—for Plot C in these columns, since there were no surviving seedlings to test in Plot C.) The data shows much better utilization of both substances in the Plot A seedlings, the seedlings that grew in a fungi-rich soil. This data would tend to support a theory that the myco fungi aid in the utilization of K and P, and that this in turn aids survival in pine seedlings.

The only question that hinges on Study 2 is question 5. It asks what generalization would be supported by the specific results of Study 2. Well, notice that Study 2 involved only measuring K and P. It did not involve survival rates (that was Study 1), so choice A can't be right. And neither study measured growth rates, so B is out. As for C, the minerals K and P were in the control group's soil, which was natural, untreated pine forest soil, so the results in choice (C) are clearly unsupported. But the data *did* show that not all of the potassium (K) could be absorbed by pine seedlings. Only 18 percent was absorbed in Plot A, while only 10 percent was absorbed in Plot B. That's a long way from 100 percent, so choice (D) seems a safe generalization to make.

Of course, not all experiments on the ACT Science test are specific-to-general experiments; some are general-to-specific procedures, with scientists making specific predictions based on accepted general premises. But the same kind of strict thinking—manipulating factors to narrow down possibilities—can get you points, no matter the direction of your thinking.

Step Fourteen
The Conflicting Viewpoints Passage

Step 14 Preview

Introduction

Prereading the Conflicting Viewpoints Passage

The Real Thing: Practice Passage and Key Strategies
- Identifying the Conflict
- Attacking the Questions

INTRODUCTION

On every Science test, you'll find one Conflicting Viewpoints passage, in which two or more scientists propose different theories about a particular scientific phenomenon. Often, the two theories are just differing interpretations of the same data. Other times, each scientist offers his own data to support his own opinion. In either case, it's essential that you know more or less what theory each scientist is proposing and that you pay careful attention to how and where their theories differ.

In the second Science step, we talked about how scientists think, and you should bring all of that learning to bear on the Conflicting Viewpoints passage. Since the scientists are disagreeing on interpretation, it's usually the case that they're engaging in specific-to-general thinking. They're each using specific data, sometimes the same specific data, but they're coming to very different general conclusions.

It's important to remember that your job is not to figure out which scientist is right and which is wrong. Instead, you'll be tested on whether you understand each scientist's position and the thinking behind it. That's what the questions will hinge on.

Don't Judge the Viewpoints

Don't waste time trying to figure out which scientist is "right." Just understand their different viewpoints.

PREREADING THE CONFLICTING VIEWPOINTS PASSAGE

When tackling the Conflicting Viewpoints passage, you'll probably want to spend a little more time than usual on the prereading step of the Kaplan Three-Step Method. On other Science passages, as we saw, your goal in prereading is to get a general idea of what's going on so that you can focus when you do the questions. But we find that it pays to spend a little extra time with the Conflicting Viewpoints passage in order to get a clearer idea of the opposing theories and the data behind them.

Remember the Three-Step Method

Step 1. Map the passage, identifying and marking the purpose, method, and results of the experiment.

Step 2. Scan figures, identifying variables and patterns.

Step 3. Find support for the answer in the passage.

The passage will usually consist of a short introduction laying out the scientific issue in question, followed by two different viewpoints on that issue. Sometimes these viewpoints are presented under the headings Scientist 1 and Scientist 2, or the headings might be Theory 1 and Theory 2, Hypothesis 1 and Hypothesis 2, or something similar.

A scientific viewpoint on the ACT usually consists of two parts:

- A statement of the general theory
- A summary of the data behind the theory

Usually, the very first line of each viewpoint expresses the general theory. So, for instance, Scientist 1's first sentence might be something like, "The universe will continue to expand indefinitely." That's Scientist 1's viewpoint boiled down to a single statement. Scientist 2's first sentence might then be, "The forces of gravity will eventually force the universe to stop expanding and to begin contracting." That's Scientist 2's viewpoint, and it is clearly in direct contradiction to Scientist 1's.

• •
If You're Confused
Don't panic if you don't understand both scientists' positions. Many questions will hinge on just one of the scientist's arguments.
• •

It's very important that you understand these basic statements of theory, and just as importantly, that you see how they're opposed to each other. In fact, you might want to circle the theory statement for each viewpoint, right there in the test booklet, to fix the two positions in your mind.

After each statement of theory will come the data that's behind it. As we said, sometimes the scientists are just drawing different interpretations from the same data. But usually, each will have different supporting data. There are two different kinds of data:

- Data that supports the scientist's own theory
- Data that weakens the opposing scientist's theory

It's normally a good idea to identify the major points of data for each theory. You might underline a phrase or sentence that crystallizes each, or even take note of whether it primarily supports the scientist's own theory or shoots holes in the opposing theory.

Once you understand each scientist's theory and the data behind it, you'll be ready to move on to the questions. Remember that some of the questions will refer to only one of the viewpoints. Whatever you do, *don't mix up the two viewpoints*! A question asking about, for example, the data supporting Theory 2 may have wrong answers that perfectly describe the data for Theory 1. If you're careless, you can easily fall for one of these wrong answers.

• •

Don't Mix Up the Viewpoints

Always double-check to make sure you haven't assigned Scientist 1's ideas to Scientist 2, and vice versa.

• •

THE REAL THING: PRACTICE PASSAGE AND KEY STRATEGIES

What follows is a complete Conflicting Viewpoints passage. Take six minutes or so to read the passage and do all seven questions.

Passage II

Tektites are natural, glassy objects that range in size from the diameter of a grain of sand to that of a human fist. They are found in only a few well-defined areas, called strewn fields. Two theories about the origin of tektites are presented below.

Scientist 1

Tektites almost certainly are extraterrestrial, probably lunar, in origin. Their forms show the characteristics of air-friction melting. In one study, flanged "flying saucer" shapes similar to those of australites (a common tektite form) were produced by ablating lenses of tektite glass in a heated airstream that simulated atmospheric entry.

Atmospheric forces also make terrestrial origin extremely improbable. Aerodynamic studies have shown that because of atmospheric density, tektite-like material ejected from Earth's surface would never attain a velocity much higher than that of the surrounding air, and therefore would not be shaped by atmospheric friction. Most likely, tektites were formed either from meteorites or from lunar material ejected in volcanic eruptions.

Analysis of specimen #14425 from the *Apollo 12* lunar mission shows that the sample strongly resembles some of the tektites from the Australasian strewn field. Also tektites contain only a small fraction of the water that is locked into the structure of terrestrial volcanic glass. And tektites never contain unmelted crystalline material; the otherwise similar terrestrial glass produced by some meteorite impacts always does.

Scientist 2

Nonlocal origin is extremely unlikely, given the narrow distribution of tektite strewn fields. Even if a tightly focused jet of lunar matter were to strike Earth, whatever was deflected by the atmosphere would remain in a solar orbit. The next time its orbit coincided with that of Earth, some of the matter would be captured by Earth's gravity and fall over a wide area.

Step Fourteen: The Conflicting Viewpoints Passage

There are striking similarities, not only between the composition of Earth's crust and that of most tektites, but between the proportions of various gases found in Earth's atmosphere and in the vesicles of certain tektites.

Tektites were probably formed by meteorite impacts. The shock wave produced by a major collision could temporarily displace the atmosphere above. Terrestrial material might then splatter to suborbital heights and undergo air-friction melting upon reentry. And tektite fields in the Ivory Coast and Ghana can be correlated with known impact craters.

1. The discovery that many tektites contain unmelted, crystalline material would:
    A. tend to weaken Scientist 1's argument.
    B. tend to weaken Scientist 2's argument.
    C. be incompatible with both scientists' views.
    D. be irrelevant to the controversy.

2. Which of the following is a reason given by Scientist 2 for believing that tektites originate on Earth?
    F. The density of Earth's atmosphere would prevent any similar lunar or extraterrestrial material from reaching Earth's surface.
    G. Tektites have a composition totally unlike that of any material ever brought back from the moon.
    H. Extraterrestrial material could not have been as widely dispersed as tektites are.
    J. Material ejected from the moon or beyond would eventually have been much more widely distributed on Earth.

3. Scientist 1 could best answer the point that some tektites have vesicles filled with gases in the same proportion as Earth's atmosphere by:
    A. countering that not all tektites have such gas-filled vesicles.
    B. demonstrating that molten material would be likely to trap some gases while falling through the terrestrial atmosphere.
    C. suggesting that those gases might occur in the same proportions in the moon's atmosphere.
    D. showing that similar vesicles, filled with these gases in the same proportions, are also found in some terrestrial volcanic glass.

4. How did Scientist 2 answer the argument that tektite-like material ejected from Earth could not reach a high enough velocity relative to the atmosphere to undergo air-friction melting?

   F. By asserting that a shock wave might cause a momentary change in atmosphere density, permitting subsequent aerodynamic heating
   G. By pointing out that periodic meteorite impacts have caused gradual changes in atmospheric density over the eons
   H. By attacking the validity of the aerodynamic studies cited by Scientist 1
   J. By referring to the correlation between tektite fields and known impact craters in the Ivory Coast and Ghana

5. The point of subjecting lenses of tektite glass to a heated airstream was to:

   A. determine their water content.
   B. see if gases became trapped in their vesicles.
   C. reproduce the effects of atmospheric entry.
   D. simulate the mechanism of meteorite formation.

6. Researchers could best counter the objections of Scientist 2 to Scientist 1's argument by:

   F. discovering some phenomenon that would quickly remove tektite-sized objects from orbit.
   G. proving that most common tektite shapes can be produced by aerodynamic heating.
   H. confirming that active volcanoes once existed on the moon.
   J. mapping the locations of all known tektite fields and impact craters.

7. Which of the following characteristics of tektites is LEAST consistent with the theory that tektites are of extraterrestrial origin?

   A. Low water content
   B. "Flying saucer" shapes
   C. Narrow distribution
   D. Absence of unmelted material

Answers: 1. A, 2. J, 3. B, 4. F, 5. C, 6. F, 7. C

Identifying the Conflict

Your prereading of the introduction should have revealed the topic at hand—namely, tektites, which are small glassy objects found in certain areas known as *strewn fields*. The conflict is about the *origin* of these objects; in other words, where did they come from?

Scientist 1's theory is expressed in his first sentence: "Tektites almost certainly are extraterrestrial, probably lunar, in origin." Put that into a form you can understand. Scientist 1 believes that tektites come from space, probably the moon. Scientist 2, on the other hand, has an opposing theory, also expressed in her first sentence: "Nonlocal origin is extremely unlikely." In other words, it's unlikely that tektites came from a nonlocal source. Instead, they probably came from a *local* source—right here on Earth. The conflict is clear. One says that tektites come from space; the other says they come from Earth itself. You might have even labeled the two positions "space origin" and "Earth origin."

But how do these scientists support their theories? Scientist 1 presents three points of data:

- Tektite shapes show characteristics of air-friction melting (supporting the theory of space origin).
- Atmospheric forces wouldn't be great enough to shape tektite-like material ejected from Earth's surface (weakening the theory of Earth origin).
- Tektites resemble moon rocks gathered by *Apollo 12* but not Earth rocks (strengthening the theory of space origin).

Scientist 2 also presents three points of data:

- Any matter coming from space would fall over a wide area instead of being concentrated in strewn fields (weakening the theory of space origin).
- There are striking similarities between tektites and the composition of Earth's crust (strengthening the theory of Earth origin).
- Meteorite impacts could create shock waves, explaining how terrestrial material could undergo air-friction melting (strengthening the theory of Earth origin by counteracting Scientist 1's first point).

Obviously, you wouldn't want to write out the supporting data for each theory the way we've done. But it probably would be a good idea to underline the key phrases in the data descriptions ("air-friction melting," "*Apollo 12*," etc.) and number them. What's important is that you have an idea of what data supports which theory. The questions will then force you to focus, once you get to them.

Attacking the Questions

Now let's quickly attack the questions:

Question 1 asks how it would affect the scientists' arguments if it were discovered that many tektites contain unmelted crystalline material. Well, Scientist 1 says that tektites *never* contain unmelted crystalline material and that the terrestrial glass produced by some meteorite impacts *always* does. Therefore, by showing a resemblance between tektites and Earth materials, this discovery would weaken Scientist 1's argument for extraterrestrial origin. Choice (A) is correct.

For question 2, you had to identify which answer choice was used by Scientist 2 to support the argument that tektites are terrestrial in origin. You should have been immediately drawn to choice (J), which expresses what we've identified as Scientist 2's first data point. Notice how choice (F) is a piece of evidence that Scientist 1 cites—remember not to confuse the viewpoints. As for (G), Scientist 2 says that tektites do resemble Earth materials, but never says that they *don't* resemble lunar materials. And choice (H) gets it backward; Scientist 2 says that extraterrestrial material *would* be widely dispersed and that the tektites are *not* widely dispersed.

For question 3, you need to find the best way for Scientist 1 to counter the point that some tektites have vesicles filled with gases in the same proportion as Earth's atmosphere. First, make sure you understand the meaning of that point. The idea that these gases must have been trapped in the vesicles—little holes—while the rock was actually being formed is being used by Scientist 2 to suggest that tektites are of terrestrial origin. Scientist 1 *could* say that not all tektites have such gas-filled vesicles (A) but that's not a great argument. If any reasonable number of them *do*, Scientist 1 would have to come up with an alternative explanation (Scientist 2 never claimed that *all* tektites contained these vesicles).

But if, as (B) suggests, Scientist 1 could demonstrate that molten material would be likely to trap some terrestrial gases while falling through Earth's atmosphere, that would explain how tektites might have come from beyond the Earth and still contain vesicles filled with Earth-like gases. Choice (C) is easy to eliminate if you know that the moon's atmosphere is extremely thin—almost nonexistent—and totally different in composition from Earth's atmosphere, so it doesn't make much sense to suggest that those gases might occur in the same proportions in the moon's atmosphere. Finally, since it's Scientist 2 who claims that tektites are terrestrial in origin, showing that similar gas-filled vesicles occur in some terrestrial volcanic glass (D) wouldn't help Scientist 1 at all.

In question 4, you're asked how Scientist 2 answered the argument that tektite-like material ejected from Earth could not reach a high enough velocity to undergo air-friction melting. Well, that was Scientist 2's third data point. The shock wave produced by a major meteorite collision could momentarily displace the atmosphere right above the impact site—just move the air out of the way for a very brief time—so when the splattered material reentered the atmosphere, it would undergo air-friction melting. That's basically what choice (F) says, so (F) is correct.

For question 5, subjecting lenses of tektite glass to a heated airstream was mentioned toward the beginning of Scientist 1's argument. The point was to simulate the entry of extraterrestrial tektite material through Earth's atmosphere, and that's closest to choice (C).

Question 6 shows again why it pays to keep straight whose viewpoint is whose. You can't counter the objections of Scientist 2 to Scientist 1's argument unless you know what Scientist 2 was objecting to. Scientist 2's first data point is the only one designed to weaken the opposing viewpoint. There, Scientist 2 takes issue with the idea that lunar material could strike Earth without being dispersed over a far wider area than the known strewn fields. But if, as correct choice (F) says, researchers found some force capable of removing tektite-sized objects from orbit *quickly*, it would demolish the objection that Scientist 2 raises in her first paragraph. The tektite material would strike Earth or be pulled away quickly instead of remaining in a solar orbit long enough to get captured by Earth's gravity and subsequently get distributed over a wide area of Earth.

Question 7 wasn't too tough if you read the question stem carefully. You want to find the tektite characteristic that is *least* consistent with the theory that tektites came from the moon or beyond. That's Scientist 1's theory, so you want to pick the answer choice that doesn't go with his argument. Scientist 1's evidence *does* include tektites' low water content, "flying saucer" shapes, and absence of unmelted material. The only answer choice that he didn't mention was the narrow distribution of the strewn fields. And with good reason. That's part of Scientist 2's argument *against* an extraterrestrial origin. So the correct answer is choice (C).

Identify the Evidence
Always be careful to take note of the evidence (data) each scientist uses.

Part 6

The ACT Writing Test

Step Fifteen
Writing Skills and Strategies

Step 15 Preview

Introduction

Just the Facts
- How Will Schools Use the Writing Test?
- Who Should Take the Writing Test?

How the ACT Essay Is Scored
- What Skills Are Tested?
- Do You Need to Prepare for the Essay?

Kaplan's Four-Step Method for the ACT Essay
- Step 1. Prompt
- Step 2. Plan
- Step 3. Produce
- Step 4. Proofread

Know the Score: Sample Essays
- Turning a 4 into a 6

Strategy Recap
- Information Banks
- Outside Reading
- Establish and Adhere to a Practice Schedule
- Self-Evaluation
- Get a Second Opinion
- If You're Not a "Writer"
- If English Is Your Second Language

INTRODUCTION

A growing number of colleges want an assessment of your written communication skills. If you consider yourself a good writer and are accustomed to scoring well on essays, there may be a temptation to skip this chapter. Don't. Top scores are not given out easily, and writing a scored first draft in under a half hour is unlike most of your past writing experiences.

Let's start with the facts.

JUST THE FACTS

Writing has always been an essential skill for college success. An optional Writing test will be available when you take the ACT. Some colleges require it; others do not. Before registering for the ACT, find out if the schools to which you're applying want applicants to take the Writing test.

The ACT English test already measures knowledge of effective writing skills, including grammar, punctuation, organization, and style. The Writing test will complement that evaluation of technical skill with an example of your simple, direct writing.

How Will Schools Use the Writing Test?

The ACT Writing test may be used for either admissions or course placement purposes, or both. About one-third of the schools using the ACT require the Writing test, and another 20 percent recommend but don't require it.

Students who take the Writing test will receive an English score, a Reading score, a Writing score, and a combined ELA score on a 1–36 scale. Copies of the essay (with the graders' comments) will also be available online for downloading. Schools that do not require the Writing test will also receive the Writing score for students who have taken the Writing test, unless the school specifically asks *not* to receive those results.

Who Should Take the Writing Test?

You should decide whether to take the ACT Writing test based on the admissions policies of the schools you will apply to and on the advice of your high school guidance counselors. A list of colleges requiring the test is maintained on the ACT website, www.act.org/aap/writing. If you are unsure about what schools you will apply to, you should plan to take the Writing test. However, testing will be available later if you decide not to take the Writing test and discover later that you need it.

HOW THE ACT ESSAY IS SCORED

Your essay will be graded on a scale of 1–36. Graders will be looking for an overall sense of your essay, not assigning separate scores for specific elements like grammar or organization. Two readers read and assign four subscores from 1 to 6 to each essay along four domains (Ideas and Analysis, Development and Support, Organization, Language Use and Conventions); then those scores are added together so that you receive four Writing subscores from 2 to 12. The subscores determine your overall Writing score of 1–36.

Statistically speaking, there will be few 36 Writing scores. If each grader gives your essay a 4 or 5, along with each of the subscore domains, that will place you at the upper range of those taking the exam.

What Skills Are Tested?

The readers realize you're writing under time pressure and expect you to make some mistakes. The content of your essay is not relevant; readers are not checking your facts (so go ahead and make them up if you have to). Nor will they judge you on your opinions. What they want is to see how well you can communicate a relevant, coherent point of view.

The test makers identify the following as the skills tested in the Writing test:

- Express judgments by evaluating the three perspectives given in the prompt, taking a position on an issue and explaining the relationship among all four ideas
- Develop a position by using logical reasoning and by supporting your ideas
- Maintain a focus on the topic throughout the essay
- Organize ideas in a logical way
- Use language clearly and effectively according to the conventions of standard written English

The Writing test is not principally a test of your grammar and punctuation (which are tested in the English test)—colleges want a chance to see your reasoning and communication skills.

The skill they didn't mention is speed. The skills they list would be relevant if you were writing an essay over the course of several weeks. On the ACT, you have to do all this in 40 minutes. This *cannot* be done using the process you learned for essay writing in the past. There is no time to write and rewrite, no choice of topic, no opportunity to do research.

Do You Need to Prepare for the Essay?

So the ACT essay is not like other writing experiences. It's a first draft that will be graded. Not only must it be complete and well organized, but it must also be easy for a grader to see that it is complete and well organized (and the grader may spend as little as a minute reading your essay). That's a lot to do in 40 minutes, so preparation and practice are a good idea.

KAPLAN'S FOUR-STEP METHOD FOR THE ACT ESSAY

Step 1. Prompt
Step 2. Plan
Step 3. Produce
Step 4. Proofread

If you plan your essay and adhere to your plan when you write, the result will be solidly organized. Between now and test day, you can't drastically change your overall writing skills—and you probably don't need to. If your plan is good, all you need to do in the writing and proofreading steps is draw on your strengths and avoid your weaknesses. Get to know what those are as you practice.

Write what counts: To maximize your score, use the Kaplan Method to help you focus on writing what the scorers will look for—*and nothing else*.

Step	An Upper-Level Essay	A Lower-Level Essay
Prompt	clearly develops a position on the issue	does not clearly state a position on the issue
Plan	supports with concrete, detailed examples	is general or repetitious
Produce	maintains clear focus and organization	digresses or has weak organization
Proofread	shows competent use of language	contains errors that reduce clarity

Kaplan has found this approach useful in its many years of experience with hundreds of sample essay statements on a wide range of tests. Let's look at what the test makers tell you about how the essays are scored.

To earn a 4 along the four domains, you must:
- Answer the question and engage with multiple perspectives on the given issue
- Develop ideas and support for claims
- Show logical thought and organization
- Avoid major or frequent errors that make your writing unclear

Remember

Organization and clarity are key to an above-average essay.

If the reader can't follow your train of thought—if ideas aren't clearly organized or if grammatical errors, misspellings, and incorrect word choices make your writing unclear—you can't do well.

Remember the Requirements

You can't earn a 5 or 6 if you haven't met the basic requirements for a 4, so think of the requirements as building blocks and be sure you have the foundation in place.

To earn a 5 along the four domains, all you have to add to a 4 is:

- Address the topic in depth.

That is, offer more examples and details. The graders love specific examples, and the more concrete your examples are, the more they clarify your thinking and keep you focused.

To earn a 6 along the four domains, all you have to add to a 5 is:

- Make transitions smoother and show variety in syntax and vocabulary.

Essay Tip

Use words from the prompt to tie paragraphs together, rather than relying exclusively on connectors like *however* and *therefore*. Vary your sentence structure, sometimes using simple sentences and other times using compound and complex ones. Adding a few college-level vocabulary words will also boost your score.

Now let's apply the Kaplan Method to a practice prompt.

Step 1. Prompt

The ACT Writing prompt usually relates to a topic that is broad enough for high school students to be able to relate to it. In most cases, the subject will be something fairly innocuous, like the possible advantages of including mandatory career-readiness programs in high schools. If by chance the prompt describes a situation you feel strongly about, be sure to still present your argument in a careful, thoughtful manner. Do NOT write an overly emotional response. You are being gauged on the strength of your argument, not the strength of your feelings.

Here's an example of a typical ACT Writing prompt:

BILINGUAL ACCREDITATION

While the United States has just one official national language, English is certainly not the only language in which Americans communicate. In fact, bilingual fluency is highly desirable in many professions, including business, education, and medicine. In an effort to ready students for success in their future careers, some high schools may consider instituting programs that would offer bilingual accreditation to students who successfully complete a significant portion of their schooling in a language other than English. Since bilingual certification is not a necessary component of traditional education, should schools be expected to explore this option for interested students? As American high schools aim to remain competitive as measured by increasingly rigorous international education standards, innovative programs such as bilingual certification may prove to be essential.

Read and carefully consider these perspectives. Each discusses relevant aspects of offering bilingual accreditation.

Perspective One	Perspective Two	Perspective Three
Schools should encourage bilingual fluency but should not be expected to offer special classes or programs. School administrators need to work on strengthening the existing curriculum rather than overcomplicating instruction by attempting to incorporate additional programs that do not reinforce traditional education.	Offering bilingual accreditation weakens the core of high school curriculum. A large enough portion of the student population already struggles to maintain passing grades when taught in English, and adding other languages would likely add to that number.	Bilingual accreditation should be offered, but it needs to be thoughtfully implemented. Courses taught in languages other than English need to be carefully selected to ensure that this program does not affect the integrity of the high school diploma.

Essay Task

Write a unified, coherent essay in which you evaluate multiple perspectives regarding bilingual accreditation. In your essay, be sure to:

- analyze and evaluate the perspectives given
- state and develop your own perspective on the issue
- explain the relationship between your perspective and those given

Your perspective may be in full agreement with any of the others, in partial agreement, or wholly different. Whatever the case, support your ideas with logical reasoning and detailed, persuasive examples.

Planning Your Essay

You may wish to consider the following as you think critically about the task:

Strengths and weaknesses of the three given perspectives

- What insights do they offer, and what do they fail to consider?
- Why might they be persuasive to others, or why might they fail to persuade?

Your own knowledge, experience, and values

- What is your perspective on this issue, and what are its strengths and weaknesses?
- How will you support your perspective in your essay?

As you read, be sure you understand the argument clearly. In this case, the argument is "Should schools be expected to explore bilingual accreditation for interested students, even though it is not a necessary component of traditional education?" You know you have the right question in this case because it is stated clearly in the prompt, but it may not always be. If the question is not stated this clearly, make sure you think through the issue thoroughly enough that you can take one clear position, being careful to not overcomplicate your thesis. Based on the structure of the prompt, you can use the three perspectives to help you determine your position. In this case, you can say, "High schools should promote bilingualism but shouldn't be required to offer bilingual classes," "High schools should avoid bilingual options," or "High schools should offer bilingual accreditation if it is carefully implemented." For this prompt, you do not want to try to argue all three positions since these perspectives feature diverse arguments.

Step 2: Plan

Take up to 8 minutes to analyze the prompt (Step 1) and build a plan before you write. This step is critical—a successful plan leads directly to a high-scoring essay. Focus on what kinds of reasoning and examples you can use to support your position.

Note: If you find you have better supporting evidence for a position different from the one you originally thought you would take, **change your position**.

Kaplan's Essay Template is an excellent way to organize your essay before you begin to write. This can easily be done in the 4 to 6 minutes you will invest in planning, and doing so will make the actual production **much** faster and smoother. Take a few minutes to write down notes about the prompt in Step 1. Then organize your notes using Kaplan's Essay Template. Your outline may look similar to the following:

¶1:   **Introductory paragraph**

- Introductory statement
- Thesis—*Schools should offer bilingual accreditation as long as courses offered in languages other than English are carefully selected.*

¶2:   **1st body paragraph**

- Describe Perspective One—*Students should be encouraged to become bilingual, but schools do not have the time or resources to add a bilingual certification program.*
    - Strengths/Weaknesses—*focuses on real-life concerns about curriculum*
    - Insights it offers/Insights it fails to consider—*fails to consider that bilingual accreditation could enhance curriculum*
    - Persuasive/Fails to persuade—*fails to persuade by ignoring possible benefits*
- Specifically state whether you agree, disagree, or partially agree/disagree with this perspective—*disagree*

¶3:   **2nd body paragraph**

- Describe Perspective Two—*Bilingual accreditation should not be included in any capacity because it will make school even harder than it is now.*
    - Strengths/Weaknesses—*considers how students may feel about the program*
    - Insights it offers/Insights it fails to consider—*does not consider the fact that some students struggle in school because English is not their primary language*
    - Persuasive/Fails to persuade—*fails to persuade because it dismisses the program without considering how it could help students*
- Specifically state whether you agree, disagree, or partially agree/disagree with this perspective—disagree

¶4:   **3rd body paragraph**

- Describe Perspective Three—***Bilingual accreditation should be offered, but it needs to be carefully organized so that all students receive education of the same quality.***
    - Strengths/Weaknesses—***considers the benefits to students***
    - Insights it offers/Insights it fails to consider—***does not consider that all courses taught in high schools are carefully selected***
    - Persuasive/Fails to persuade—***persuades because it recognizes that offering additional opportunity without sacrificing overall integrity benefits students***
- Specifically state whether you agree, disagree, or partially agree/disagree with this perspective—***agree***

¶5:   **4th body paragraph**

- Describe your thesis—***All students should have the opportunity to pursue bilingual accreditation as long as this opportunity is in addition to traditional course offerings; schools should accommodate students who wish to take classes in multiple languages as well as students who want to study only in English.***
    - Provide specific, relevant support—***traditional foreign language courses provide a foundation for this program***
    - Discuss the strengths/weaknesses of your thesis—***program is available to all students, which is good in terms of opportunity, but could be difficult to implement***
    - Explain how your thesis fits in among Perspectives One, Two, and Three—***agrees with Perspective Three***
- Include a single concluding sentence at the end of your 4th body paragraph to wrap up your essay.

Information banks: Don't wait until Test Day to think of examples you can use to support your ideas. Regardless of what question is raised in the prompt, you will draw your support from the things you know best and are most comfortable writing about—things you know a fair amount of concrete detail about.

Refresh your memory about your favorite or most memorable books, school subjects, historical events, personal experiences, activities—anything. By doing so, you strengthen mental connections to those ideas and details, making it easier to connect to the right examples on Test Day.

With that in mind:

- Use an effective *hook* to bring the reader in.
- Use *transitions* regularly—these are the "glue" that holds your ideas together.
- End with a *bang* to make your essay memorable.

Using a "hook" means avoiding an essay that opens (as thousands of other essays will): "In my opinion, ... because ..." Your opinion is not compelling to a reader who has graded hundreds of essays on the same subject. Make it something more exciting than that!

In today's global economy, students are looking for ways to ready themselves for an increasingly international future.

A "bang" means a closing that ties the essay together. A good choice can be a clear, succinct statement of your thesis in the essay or a vivid example that's right on point.

Enhancing instruction is always better than restricting learning, especially when the result is effective communication, desirable skills, and valuable experiences.

In summary, a good plan:

- Responds to the prompt
- Has an introduction
- Has strong examples, usually one per paragraph
- Has a strong conclusion

Step 3: Produce

You are not graded directly on word count, but graders know that filling out a thorough argument takes time and space—it will be hard to present all the elements of a strong argument in few words or only a couple of paragraphs. Nonetheless, don't think about your *number of words*; instead, think about the *strength of your arguments*.

Organization counts. Graders are far more able to follow—and be compelled by—your argument if they can see its distinct ingredients.

Write neatly. Graders may give you a zero if your essay is impossible to read. If your handwriting is a problem, print.

Stick with the plan. Resist any urge to introduce new ideas—no matter how good you think they are—or to digress from the central focus or organization of each paragraph.

Use topic sentences. Each paragraph should be organized around a topic sentence that you should finish in your mind before you start to write. These may begin as follows:

- *One example ...*
- *Another example ...*
- *Therefore, we can conclude ...*

You don't have to write it this way in the essay, but completing these sentences in your mind ensures that you focus on the idea that organizes each paragraph.

Choose words carefully. Use vocabulary you know well. New or fancy words that you have learned recently often stick out in a negative way. Using unfamiliar words in an essay often produces awkward, confusing thoughts—the opposite of what you want. Instead of impressing the graders, you would obscure your ideas. Two more points to keep in mind:

1. **Avoid using *I* excessively.** You are absolutely allowed to use personal examples ("At my school, we had this issue just last year, and I was very involved in the discussion …"), but avoid using your opinions or beliefs as evidence ("I really think …" "I believe …" "In my opinion …"). You base your argument on weak ground when it is founded on your thoughts, not what you can prove.

2. **Avoid slang.** Your tone should be personal and natural but academic. This is a school paper. Abbreviations such as those you might use in text messaging, online, or in personal emails are not appropriate here; at best, they're unprofessional, and at worst, the grader won't know what you're talking about.

Use transitions. Think about the relationship between ideas as you write and spell out your concepts clearly. Doing so allows the readers to follow your reasoning easily, and they'll appreciate it. **Use key words from the prompt as well as the kinds of words you've learned about in Reading that indicate contrast, opinion, relative importance, and support.**

Don't sweat the small stuff. Do not obsess over every little thing. If you cannot remember how to spell a word, do your best and just **keep going.** Even the top-scoring essays can have minor errors. The essay readers understand that you are writing first drafts and have no time for research or revision.

Step 4: Proofread

Always leave yourself 2 or 3 minutes to review your work—the time spent will definitely pay off. Very few of us can avoid the occasional confused sentence or omitted word when we write under pressure. Quickly review your essay to be sure your ideas are clearly stated.

Don't hesitate to make corrections to your essay—this is a timed first draft, not a term paper. But keep your writing clearly readable: use a single line through deletions and an asterisk to mark where text should be inserted.

During proofreading, remind yourself that **you don't have time to revise substantially.** This isn't the time for inserting new paragraphs, radically changing your tone, or (worst yet) changing your mind. Use your practice essays to learn the types of mistakes you tend to make and look for them.

Don't hesitate to make corrections on your essay—these are timed first drafts, not term papers. But keep it clear: Use a single line through deletions and an asterisk to mark where text should be inserted.

You don't have time to look for every minor error or to revise substantially. Learn the types of mistakes you tend to make and look for them. Some of the most common mistakes in students' essays are those found in the English test. Refer to Part Two of this book to review these common errors.

KNOW THE SCORE: SAMPLE ESSAYS

The best way to be sure you've learned what the readers will look for is to try scoring some essays yourself.

You Make the Call

Don't cheat yourself by reading our explanation without first deciding what holistic grade you would give the essay.

The graders will be scoring holistically, not checking off "points." To learn what makes a good essay, it may help to consider these questions, based on the test makers' scoring criteria:

- **Does the author answer the question?**
- **Is the author's position clearly stated?**
- **Does the body of the essay support and develop the position taken?**
- **Are there at least three supporting paragraphs?**
- **Is the relevance of each supporting paragraph clear?**
- **Is the essay a reasonable length?**
- **Is the essay organized, with a clear introduction, middle, and end?**
- **Did the author use one paragraph for each new idea?**
- **Is each sentence in a paragraph relevant to the point made in that paragraph?**
- **Are transitions clear?**
- **Is the essay easy to read? Is it engaging?**
- **Are sentences varied?**
- **Is vocabulary used effectively? Is college-level vocabulary used?**

Essay Tip

Don't just answer "yes" or "no"—locate specific text in the essay that answers the question.

Let's look at a sample essay based on the prompt and plan we've been looking at.

Sample Essay 1

> Some people think schools should encourage bilingualism but should not be expected to offer special classes or programs. Other people think offering bilingual accreditation weakens high school classes. Others say bilingual accreditation should be offered but it needs to be thoughtfully implemented. In my opinion, schools should definitely give the option of bilingualism.
>
> Firstly, schools should always encourage bilingualism. Students better in life with more than one language. Second, weakening high school doesn't make sense. More languages mean more learning.
>
> Finally and most importantly, there should be bilingual accreditation. Students won't be able to cognizant and value diverse languages if not given the opportunity. Extra certification on diplomas is good for getting kids into college. So high schools should have bilingual accreditation.

Score:_____ /6

It should have been fairly easy to see that this isn't a strong essay. This essay would get a score of 2 or 3 out of 6. The author does state a clear opinion, but half of the essay is a direct copy of the prompt—the graders will notice this and those sentences won't help the score. The time and space spent just quoting the prompt was completely wasted—it earned the writer zero points.

The rest of the essay is organized and uses transition words (*firstly* and *finally*). The author states her thesis, acknowledges the three perspectives provided in the prompt, and then offers a conclusion. However, none of this is discussed fully enough—no concrete details or examples are given. In the second paragraph, for instance, the author should have added examples that demonstrate how encouraging bilingual education is both beneficial to students and not a threat to the quality of high school curriculum.

The language is understandable, but there are significant errors affecting clarity. For instance, the second sentence of paragraph 2 is a fragment—there is no verb. Some vocabulary words are used without a clear understanding of their meaning: In paragraph 3, "won't be able to cognizant" is incorrect; perhaps the student meant "won't be able to understand."

It is possible that the writer couldn't think of good ideas to support each point, waited too long to start writing, and had to write in a hurry.

Let's look at another essay. Read it quickly and decide how you would score it.

Sample Essay 2

Some people think that schools should provide enough education in a different language for students to be certified as bilingual. Others think this will weaken the curriculum. Still others think the accreditation should be offered but carefully administered so that graduation from that school would indicate the completed high school curriculum, and this is the option I agree with.

The first option is to encourage bilingual fluency but not add any bilingual classes. Instead, the school administrators should make the existing curriculum better so that traditional education is really good. Certainly a high school curriculum should be as good as it can be and we should always be looking for ways to make it better. That often means adding new courses.

The second alternative is to not provide any bilingual education because there are enough students struggling with the curriculum in English. But this is a very weak argument because no one is suggesting that all students need to take bilingual classes, so just having those classes would not necessarily affect struggling students' grades.

Finally, people argue that students should be given the opportunity to learn in other languages and be accredited as bilingual, but that the courses given need to be carefully selected. In reality, all classes need to be carefully selected so this not a problem for bilingual classes. And if the classes selected were all optional, not required, it would not affect students who still want to learn everything in English. Since core classes might be given in two languages, and students select which one they want, all students still study the core curriculum and preserve the integrity of the diploma.

Being bilingual in a world with international interaction can't help but be useful. Expanding courses offered in a curriculum is always better than restricting them, especially when they serve such an important need as the ability to communicate with others in their own language. I fully support option three.

Score:_____ /6

This essay is pretty good—it would earn a 4. The position is clearly stated, and some supporting reasoning is given.

However, the reasoning is too general and the writing is too ordinary to earn the top score. Let's see how it could be improved.

Turning a 4 into a 6

The essay plunges right into the first point of view offered in the prompt. It could be improved by introducing the issue with a general statement, like:

> In today's world where international education standards are very high and the U.S. needs to remain competitive, educators are looking for ways to enhance high school curriculum. One way is offering classes in languages other than English.

In the last sentence of the first paragraph, the writer indicates that she agrees with Perspective Three. It is good to include your thesis in the introductory paragraph, but it would be better to make it clear where the position from the prompt ends and the author's position begins, perhaps like this:

> Still others think the accreditation should be offered but carefully administered so that graduation from that school would indicate the completed high school curriculum, and this is the option I agree with. <u>I would further argue that carefully implemented bilingual programs suit students who want to become fluent in two languages, but do not prevent others from pursuing their entire education in English.</u>

The second paragraph is relevant and organized—it covers one of the three positions offered in the prompt. But it would be better if the writer discussed this perspective using real-life information, such as:

> For instance, computer courses didn't exist a few years ago, but they are in the schools now because it's important for people to be able to use computers. It's the same thing with bilingual courses. Most of the world uses English as a second language and many people speak at least two languages. So it's only right that to stay competitive, U.S. students should be fluent in two languages too; this is particularly important in careers that require international work. Also, the argument simply says that these classes would only be for interested students, so it doesn't affect everyone. And finally, how can the schools encourage bilingual fluency if they don't provide a place for students to practice another language?

The third paragraph addresses Perspective Two. Discussing concrete ideas would bolster the essay. Plus, graders look to see if writers are able to provide analysis regarding how the perspectives related to each other. For example:

Students who struggle with the existing curriculum may find classes in another language, which may even be their home language. It may be more interesting, and they will do better overall. As I wrote before, adding important classes, such as computers, does not diminish the curriculum but strengthens it because it makes it more relevant to people today. Since bilingual classes are not required and therefore would not affect a student struggling to learn in English (and may even help if the student can take a class in his native language), this is an imprudent option and should not be implemented.

Paragraph four is pretty good, but expanding the discussion helps to increase your score. For instance:

Schools have always taught languages in high school, so a French or Spanish course taught as a bilingual class makes perfect sense. Bilingual classes are also appropriate for students who do well and want to challenge themselves. So a French literature class can be taught in French while students read in French also.

The fifth paragraph reiterates the writer's thesis, but it could benefit from reorganization and additional development, like:

Being bilingual in a world with international interaction can't help but be useful. I fully support option three because it opens up possibilities for all students without denying anyone a full high school curriculum leading to a meaningful diploma. Recognizing the benefits of being bilingual, and making bilingual courses available but optional, is the best of both worlds. Expanding courses offered in a curriculum is always better than impeding them, especially when they serve such an important need as the ability to communicate with others in their own language.

Here's how this essay would look with the improvements we've suggested:

In today's world where international education standards are very high and the U.S. needs to remain competitive, educators are looking for ways to enhance high school curriculum. One way is offering classes in languages other than English. Some people think that schools should provide enough education in a different language for students to be certified as bilingual. Others think this will weaken the curriculum. Still others think the accreditation should be offered but carefully administered so that graduation from that school would indicate the completed high school curriculum, and this is the option I agree with. I would further argue that carefully implemented bilingual programs suit students who want to become fluent in two languages, but do not prevent others from pursuing their entire education in English.

The first option is to encourage bilingual fluency but not add any bilingual classes. Instead, the school administrators should make the existing curriculum better so that traditional education is really good. Certainly a high school curriculum should be as good as it can be and we should always be looking for ways to make it better. That often means adding new courses. For instance, computer courses didn't exist a few years ago, but they are in the schools now because it's important for people to be able to use computers. It's the same thing with bilingual courses. Most of the world uses English as a second language, and many people speak at least two languages. So it's only right that to stay competitive, U.S. students should be fluent in two languages too; this is particularly important in careers that require international work. Also, the argument simply says that these classes would only be for interested students, so it doesn't affect everyone. And finally, how can the schools encourage bilingual fluency if they don't provide a place for students to practice another language?

The second alternative is to not provide any bilingual education because there are enough students struggling with the curriculum in English. But this is a very weak argument because no one is suggesting that all students need to take bilingual classes, so just having those classes would not necessarily affect struggling students' grades. Students who struggle with the existing curriculum may find classes in another language, which may even be their home language. It may be more interesting, and they will do better overall. As I wrote before, adding important classes, such as computers, does not diminish the curriculum but strengthens it because it makes it more relevant to people today. Since bilingual classes are not required and therefore would not affect a student struggling to learn in English (and may even help if the student can take a class in his native language), this is an imprudent option and should not be implemented.

Finally, people argue that students should be given the opportunity to learn in other languages and be accredited as bilingual, but that the courses given need to be carefully selected. In reality, all classes need to be carefully selected so this not a problem for bilingual classes. And if the classes selected were all optional, not required, it would not affect students who still want to learn everything in English. Since core classes might be given in two languages, and students select which one they want, all students still study the core curriculum and preserve the integrity of the diploma. Schools have always taught languages in high school so a French or Spanish course taught as a bilingual class makes perfect sense. Bilingual classes are also advantageous for students who do well and want to challenge themselves. So a French literature class can be taught in French while students read in French also.

Being bilingual in a world with international interaction can't help but be useful. I fully support option three because it opens up possibilities for all students without denying anyone a full

> high school curriculum leading to a meaningful diploma. Recognizing the benefits of being bilingual, and making bilingual courses available but optional, is the best of both worlds. Expanding courses offered in a curriculum is always better than restricting them, especially when they serve such an important need as the ability to communicate with others in their own language.

This is now a 6 essay. It addresses the task both fully and concretely. It addresses all three perspectives, refutes two opposing arguments, and then moves to the bulk of the author's own reasoning. The first paragraph introduces all the lines of reasoning that will be used, demonstrating to the reader that the writer knew right from the start where this essay was headed. The development of ideas is clear and logical, and the paragraphs reflect this organization.

The author shows a high level of skill with language. The transitions between paragraphs are clear and guide the reader through the reasoning. The sentence structure varies throughout the passage and is at times complex.

So what did we do to our 4 to make it a 6?

- We added examples and detail.
- We varied sentence structure and added stronger vocabulary (diminish, imprudent, advantageous).
- While length alone doesn't make a 6, we've added detail to our original essay.
- The conclusion, rather than being lost in the fifth paragraph, is now a strong, independent statement that concisely sums up the writer's point of view.

PART 7
Practice Test and Explanations

Practice Test

HOW TO TAKE THIS PRACTICE TEST

This practice test is a Kaplan-created tests, similar to the actual ACT. Before taking a Practice Test, find a quiet room where you can work uninterrupted for three and a half hours. Make sure you have a comfortable desk, your calculator, and several No. 2 pencils. Use the answer sheet to record your answers. Once you start a Practice Test, don't stop until you've finished. Remember: You can review any questions within a subject test, but you may not jump from one subject test to another.

You'll find the answers and explanations to the test questions immediately following the test.

ACT Practice Test
ANSWER SHEET

ENGLISH TEST

1. Ⓐ Ⓑ Ⓒ Ⓓ
2. Ⓕ Ⓖ Ⓗ Ⓙ
3. Ⓐ Ⓑ Ⓒ Ⓓ
4. Ⓕ Ⓖ Ⓗ Ⓙ
5. Ⓐ Ⓑ Ⓒ Ⓓ
6. Ⓕ Ⓖ Ⓗ Ⓙ
7. Ⓐ Ⓑ Ⓒ Ⓓ
8. Ⓕ Ⓖ Ⓗ Ⓙ
9. Ⓐ Ⓑ Ⓒ Ⓓ
10. Ⓕ Ⓖ Ⓗ Ⓙ
11. Ⓐ Ⓑ Ⓒ Ⓓ
12. Ⓕ Ⓖ Ⓗ Ⓙ
13. Ⓐ Ⓑ Ⓒ Ⓓ
14. Ⓕ Ⓖ Ⓗ Ⓙ
15. Ⓐ Ⓑ Ⓒ Ⓓ
16. Ⓕ Ⓖ Ⓗ Ⓙ
17. Ⓐ Ⓑ Ⓒ Ⓓ
18. Ⓕ Ⓖ Ⓗ Ⓙ
19. Ⓐ Ⓑ Ⓒ Ⓓ
20. Ⓕ Ⓖ Ⓗ Ⓙ
21. Ⓐ Ⓑ Ⓒ Ⓓ
22. Ⓕ Ⓖ Ⓗ Ⓙ
23. Ⓐ Ⓑ Ⓒ Ⓓ
24. Ⓕ Ⓖ Ⓗ Ⓙ
25. Ⓐ Ⓑ Ⓒ Ⓓ
26. Ⓕ Ⓖ Ⓗ Ⓙ
27. Ⓐ Ⓑ Ⓒ Ⓓ
28. Ⓕ Ⓖ Ⓗ Ⓙ
29. Ⓐ Ⓑ Ⓒ Ⓓ
30. Ⓕ Ⓖ Ⓗ Ⓙ
31. Ⓐ Ⓑ Ⓒ Ⓓ
32. Ⓕ Ⓖ Ⓗ Ⓙ
33. Ⓐ Ⓑ Ⓒ Ⓓ
34. Ⓕ Ⓖ Ⓗ Ⓙ
35. Ⓐ Ⓑ Ⓒ Ⓓ
36. Ⓕ Ⓖ Ⓗ Ⓙ
37. Ⓐ Ⓑ Ⓒ Ⓓ
38. Ⓕ Ⓖ Ⓗ Ⓙ
39. Ⓐ Ⓑ Ⓒ Ⓓ
40. Ⓕ Ⓖ Ⓗ Ⓙ
41. Ⓐ Ⓑ Ⓒ Ⓓ
42. Ⓕ Ⓖ Ⓗ Ⓙ
43. Ⓐ Ⓑ Ⓒ Ⓓ
44. Ⓕ Ⓖ Ⓗ Ⓙ
45. Ⓐ Ⓑ Ⓒ Ⓓ
46. Ⓕ Ⓖ Ⓗ Ⓙ
47. Ⓐ Ⓑ Ⓒ Ⓓ
48. Ⓕ Ⓖ Ⓗ Ⓙ
49. Ⓐ Ⓑ Ⓒ Ⓓ
50. Ⓕ Ⓖ Ⓗ Ⓙ
51. Ⓐ Ⓑ Ⓒ Ⓓ
52. Ⓕ Ⓖ Ⓗ Ⓙ
53. Ⓐ Ⓑ Ⓒ Ⓓ
54. Ⓕ Ⓖ Ⓗ Ⓙ
55. Ⓐ Ⓑ Ⓒ Ⓓ
56. Ⓕ Ⓖ Ⓗ Ⓙ
57. Ⓐ Ⓑ Ⓒ Ⓓ
58. Ⓕ Ⓖ Ⓗ Ⓙ
59. Ⓐ Ⓑ Ⓒ Ⓓ
60. Ⓕ Ⓖ Ⓗ Ⓙ
61. Ⓐ Ⓑ Ⓒ Ⓓ
62. Ⓕ Ⓖ Ⓗ Ⓙ
63. Ⓐ Ⓑ Ⓒ Ⓓ
64. Ⓕ Ⓖ Ⓗ Ⓙ
65. Ⓐ Ⓑ Ⓒ Ⓓ
66. Ⓕ Ⓖ Ⓗ Ⓙ
67. Ⓐ Ⓑ Ⓒ Ⓓ
68. Ⓕ Ⓖ Ⓗ Ⓙ
69. Ⓐ Ⓑ Ⓒ Ⓓ
70. Ⓕ Ⓖ Ⓗ Ⓙ
71. Ⓐ Ⓑ Ⓒ Ⓓ
72. Ⓕ Ⓖ Ⓗ Ⓙ
73. Ⓐ Ⓑ Ⓒ Ⓓ
74. Ⓕ Ⓖ Ⓗ Ⓙ
75. Ⓐ Ⓑ Ⓒ Ⓓ

MATHEMATICS TEST

1. Ⓐ Ⓑ Ⓒ Ⓓ Ⓔ
2. Ⓕ Ⓖ Ⓗ Ⓙ Ⓚ
3. Ⓐ Ⓑ Ⓒ Ⓓ Ⓔ
4. Ⓕ Ⓖ Ⓗ Ⓙ Ⓚ
5. Ⓐ Ⓑ Ⓒ Ⓓ Ⓔ
6. Ⓕ Ⓖ Ⓗ Ⓙ Ⓚ
7. Ⓐ Ⓑ Ⓒ Ⓓ Ⓔ
8. Ⓕ Ⓖ Ⓗ Ⓙ Ⓚ
9. Ⓐ Ⓑ Ⓒ Ⓓ Ⓔ
10. Ⓕ Ⓖ Ⓗ Ⓙ Ⓚ
11. Ⓐ Ⓑ Ⓒ Ⓓ Ⓔ
12. Ⓕ Ⓖ Ⓗ Ⓙ Ⓚ
13. Ⓐ Ⓑ Ⓒ Ⓓ Ⓔ
14. Ⓕ Ⓖ Ⓗ Ⓙ Ⓚ
15. Ⓐ Ⓑ Ⓒ Ⓓ Ⓔ
16. Ⓕ Ⓖ Ⓗ Ⓙ Ⓚ
17. Ⓐ Ⓑ Ⓒ Ⓓ Ⓔ
18. Ⓕ Ⓖ Ⓗ Ⓙ Ⓚ
19. Ⓐ Ⓑ Ⓒ Ⓓ Ⓔ
20. Ⓕ Ⓖ Ⓗ Ⓙ Ⓚ
21. Ⓐ Ⓑ Ⓒ Ⓓ Ⓔ
22. Ⓕ Ⓖ Ⓗ Ⓙ Ⓚ
23. Ⓐ Ⓑ Ⓒ Ⓓ Ⓔ
24. Ⓕ Ⓖ Ⓗ Ⓙ Ⓚ
25. Ⓐ Ⓑ Ⓒ Ⓓ Ⓔ
26. Ⓕ Ⓖ Ⓗ Ⓙ Ⓚ
27. Ⓐ Ⓑ Ⓒ Ⓓ Ⓔ
28. Ⓕ Ⓖ Ⓗ Ⓙ Ⓚ
29. Ⓐ Ⓑ Ⓒ Ⓓ Ⓔ
30. Ⓕ Ⓖ Ⓗ Ⓙ Ⓚ
31. Ⓐ Ⓑ Ⓒ Ⓓ Ⓔ
32. Ⓕ Ⓖ Ⓗ Ⓙ Ⓚ
33. Ⓐ Ⓑ Ⓒ Ⓓ Ⓔ
34. Ⓕ Ⓖ Ⓗ Ⓙ Ⓚ
35. Ⓐ Ⓑ Ⓒ Ⓓ Ⓔ
36. Ⓕ Ⓖ Ⓗ Ⓙ Ⓚ
37. Ⓐ Ⓑ Ⓒ Ⓓ Ⓔ
38. Ⓕ Ⓖ Ⓗ Ⓙ Ⓚ
39. Ⓐ Ⓑ Ⓒ Ⓓ Ⓔ
40. Ⓕ Ⓖ Ⓗ Ⓙ Ⓚ
41. Ⓐ Ⓑ Ⓒ Ⓓ Ⓔ
42. Ⓕ Ⓖ Ⓗ Ⓙ Ⓚ
43. Ⓐ Ⓑ Ⓒ Ⓓ Ⓔ
44. Ⓕ Ⓖ Ⓗ Ⓙ Ⓚ
45. Ⓐ Ⓑ Ⓒ Ⓓ Ⓔ
46. Ⓕ Ⓖ Ⓗ Ⓙ Ⓚ
47. Ⓐ Ⓑ Ⓒ Ⓓ Ⓔ
48. Ⓕ Ⓖ Ⓗ Ⓙ Ⓚ
49. Ⓐ Ⓑ Ⓒ Ⓓ Ⓔ
50. Ⓕ Ⓖ Ⓗ Ⓙ Ⓚ
51. Ⓐ Ⓑ Ⓒ Ⓓ Ⓔ
52. Ⓕ Ⓖ Ⓗ Ⓙ Ⓚ
53. Ⓐ Ⓑ Ⓒ Ⓓ Ⓔ
54. Ⓕ Ⓖ Ⓗ Ⓙ Ⓚ
55. Ⓐ Ⓑ Ⓒ Ⓓ Ⓔ
56. Ⓕ Ⓖ Ⓗ Ⓙ Ⓚ
57. Ⓐ Ⓑ Ⓒ Ⓓ Ⓔ
58. Ⓕ Ⓖ Ⓗ Ⓙ Ⓚ
59. Ⓐ Ⓑ Ⓒ Ⓓ Ⓔ
60. Ⓕ Ⓖ Ⓗ Ⓙ Ⓚ

READING TEST

1. Ⓐ Ⓑ Ⓒ Ⓓ
2. Ⓕ Ⓖ Ⓗ Ⓙ
3. Ⓐ Ⓑ Ⓒ Ⓓ
4. Ⓕ Ⓖ Ⓗ Ⓙ
5. Ⓐ Ⓑ Ⓒ Ⓓ
6. Ⓕ Ⓖ Ⓗ Ⓙ
7. Ⓐ Ⓑ Ⓒ Ⓓ
8. Ⓕ Ⓖ Ⓗ Ⓙ
9. Ⓐ Ⓑ Ⓒ Ⓓ
10. Ⓕ Ⓖ Ⓗ Ⓙ
11. Ⓐ Ⓑ Ⓒ Ⓓ
12. Ⓕ Ⓖ Ⓗ Ⓙ
13. Ⓐ Ⓑ Ⓒ Ⓓ
14. Ⓕ Ⓖ Ⓗ Ⓙ
15. Ⓐ Ⓑ Ⓒ Ⓓ
16. Ⓕ Ⓖ Ⓗ Ⓙ
17. Ⓐ Ⓑ Ⓒ Ⓓ
18. Ⓕ Ⓖ Ⓗ Ⓙ
19. Ⓐ Ⓑ Ⓒ Ⓓ
20. Ⓕ Ⓖ Ⓗ Ⓙ
21. Ⓐ Ⓑ Ⓒ Ⓓ
22. Ⓕ Ⓖ Ⓗ Ⓙ
23. Ⓐ Ⓑ Ⓒ Ⓓ
24. Ⓕ Ⓖ Ⓗ Ⓙ
25. Ⓐ Ⓑ Ⓒ Ⓓ
26. Ⓕ Ⓖ Ⓗ Ⓙ
27. Ⓐ Ⓑ Ⓒ Ⓓ
28. Ⓕ Ⓖ Ⓗ Ⓙ
29. Ⓐ Ⓑ Ⓒ Ⓓ
30. Ⓕ Ⓖ Ⓗ Ⓙ
31. Ⓐ Ⓑ Ⓒ Ⓓ
32. Ⓕ Ⓖ Ⓗ Ⓙ
33. Ⓐ Ⓑ Ⓒ Ⓓ
34. Ⓕ Ⓖ Ⓗ Ⓙ
35. Ⓐ Ⓑ Ⓒ Ⓓ
36. Ⓕ Ⓖ Ⓗ Ⓙ
37. Ⓐ Ⓑ Ⓒ Ⓓ
38. Ⓕ Ⓖ Ⓗ Ⓙ
39. Ⓐ Ⓑ Ⓒ Ⓓ
40. Ⓕ Ⓖ Ⓗ Ⓙ

SCIENCE TEST

1. Ⓐ Ⓑ Ⓒ Ⓓ
2. Ⓕ Ⓖ Ⓗ Ⓙ
3. Ⓐ Ⓑ Ⓒ Ⓓ
4. Ⓕ Ⓖ Ⓗ Ⓙ
5. Ⓐ Ⓑ Ⓒ Ⓓ
6. Ⓕ Ⓖ Ⓗ Ⓙ
7. Ⓐ Ⓑ Ⓒ Ⓓ
8. Ⓕ Ⓖ Ⓗ Ⓙ
9. Ⓐ Ⓑ Ⓒ Ⓓ
10. Ⓕ Ⓖ Ⓗ Ⓙ
11. Ⓐ Ⓑ Ⓒ Ⓓ
12. Ⓕ Ⓖ Ⓗ Ⓙ
13. Ⓐ Ⓑ Ⓒ Ⓓ
14. Ⓕ Ⓖ Ⓗ Ⓙ
15. Ⓐ Ⓑ Ⓒ Ⓓ
16. Ⓕ Ⓖ Ⓗ Ⓙ
17. Ⓐ Ⓑ Ⓒ Ⓓ
18. Ⓕ Ⓖ Ⓗ Ⓙ
19. Ⓐ Ⓑ Ⓒ Ⓓ
20. Ⓕ Ⓖ Ⓗ Ⓙ
21. Ⓐ Ⓑ Ⓒ Ⓓ
22. Ⓕ Ⓖ Ⓗ Ⓙ
23. Ⓐ Ⓑ Ⓒ Ⓓ
24. Ⓕ Ⓖ Ⓗ Ⓙ
25. Ⓐ Ⓑ Ⓒ Ⓓ
26. Ⓕ Ⓖ Ⓗ Ⓙ
27. Ⓐ Ⓑ Ⓒ Ⓓ
28. Ⓕ Ⓖ Ⓗ Ⓙ
29. Ⓐ Ⓑ Ⓒ Ⓓ
30. Ⓕ Ⓖ Ⓗ Ⓙ
31. Ⓐ Ⓑ Ⓒ Ⓓ
32. Ⓕ Ⓖ Ⓗ Ⓙ
33. Ⓐ Ⓑ Ⓒ Ⓓ
34. Ⓕ Ⓖ Ⓗ Ⓙ
35. Ⓐ Ⓑ Ⓒ Ⓓ
36. Ⓕ Ⓖ Ⓗ Ⓙ
37. Ⓐ Ⓑ Ⓒ Ⓓ
38. Ⓕ Ⓖ Ⓗ Ⓙ
39. Ⓐ Ⓑ Ⓒ Ⓓ
40. Ⓕ Ⓖ Ⓗ Ⓙ

ENGLISH TEST

45 Minutes—75 Questions

Directions: In the following five passages, certain words and phrases are underlined and numbered. In the right-hand column are alternatives for each underlined portion. Select the one that best conveys the idea, creates the most grammatically correct sentence, or is the most consistent with the style and tone of the passage. If you decide that the original version is best, select NO CHANGE. You may also find questions that ask about the entire passage or a section of the passage. These questions will correspond to small numbered boxes in the text. For these questions, decide which choice best accomplishes the purpose set out in the question stem. After you've selected the best choice, fill in the corresponding oval in your Answer Grid. For some questions, you'll need to read the context in order to answer correctly. Be sure to read until you have enough information to determine the correct answer choice.

PASSAGE I

ORIGINS OF URBAN LEGENDS

[1]

Since primitive times, societies have <u>created, and told</u> legends. Even before the development of written language, cultures would orally pass down these popular stories.

[2]

[2] These stories served the dual purpose of entertaining audiences and of transmitting values and beliefs from generation to generation.

1. **A.** NO CHANGE
   B. created then subsequently told
   C. created and told
   D. created, and told original

2. Suppose that the author wants to insert a sentence here to describe the different kinds of oral stories told by these societies. Which of the following sentences would best serve that purpose?
   F. These myths and tales varied in substance, from the humorous to the heroic.
   G. These myths and tales were often recited by paid storytellers.
   H. Unfortunately, no recording of the original myths and tales exists.
   J. Sometimes it took several evenings for the full story to be recited.

Indeed today we have many more permanent ways
      3
of handing down our beliefs to future generations, we
continue to create and tell legends. In our technological
society, a new form of folktale has emerged:
the urban legend.
 4

[3]

Urban legends are stories we all have heard; they
are supposed to have really happened, but are never
verifiable however. It seems that the people involved can
       5
never be found. Researchers of the urban legend call the
elusive participant in such supposed "real-life" events a
FOAF—a Friend of a Friend.

[4]

Urban legends have some characteristic features.
They are often humorous in nature with a surprise
ending and a conclusion. One such legend is the tale of
         6
the hunter who was returning home from an unsuccessful hunting trip. On his way home, he accidentally hit
and killed a deer on a deserted highway. Even though he
knew it was illegal, he decided to keep the deer, and he
loads it in the back of his station wagon. As the hunter
    7
continued driving, the deer,

he was only temporarily knocked unconscious by the
  8
car, woke up and began thrashing around. The hunter
panicked, stopped the car, ran to hide in the roadside
ditch, and watched the enraged deer destroy his car.

3. A. NO CHANGE
    B. However,
    C. Indeed,
    D. Although

4. F. NO CHANGE
    G. it is called the
    H. it being the
    J. known as the

5. A. NO CHANGE
    B. verifiable, however.
    C. verifiable, furthermore.
    D. verifiable.

6. F. NO CHANGE
    G. ending.
    H. ending, which is a conclusion.
    J. ending or conclusion.

7. A. NO CHANGE
    B. loaded it in
    C. is loading it in
    D. had loaded it in

8. F. NO CHANGE
    G. which being
    H. that is
    J. which was

[5]

One legend involves alligators in the sewer systems of major metropolitan areas. According to the story, before alligators were a protected species, people vacationing in Florida purchased baby alligators to take home as souvenirs.

Between 1930 and 1940, nearly a million alligators in Florida were killed for the value of their skin, used to make expensive leather products such as boots and wallets. After the novelty of having a pet alligator wore off, many people flushed their baby souvenirs down toilets. Legend has it that the baby alligators found a perfect growing and breeding environment in city sewer systems, where they thrive to this day on the ample supply of rats.

[6]

In addition to urban legends that are told from friend to friend, a growing number of urban legends are passed along through the Internet and email. One of the more popular stories are about a woman who was unwittingly charged $100 for a cookie recipe she requested at an upscale restaurant. To get her money's worth, this woman supposed copied the recipe for the delicious cookies and forwarded it via email to everyone she knew.

9. A. NO CHANGE
   B. species; people
   C. species. People
   D. species people

10. F. NO CHANGE
    G. Because their skin is used to make expensive leather products such as boots and wallets, nearly a million alligators in Florida were killed between 1930 and 1940.
    H. Killed between 1930 and 1940, the skin of nearly a million alligators from Florida was used to make expensive leather products such as boots and wallets.
    J. OMIT the underlined portion.

11. A. NO CHANGE
    B. would be about
    C. is about
    D. is dealing with

12. F. NO CHANGE
    G. woman supposedly
    H. women supposedly
    J. women supposed to

[7]

Although today's technology enhances our ability to tell and retell urban legends, the Internet can also serve as a monitor of urban legends. <u>Dedicated to commonly told urban legends, research is done by many websites.</u>

According to those websites, most legends, including the ones told here, have no basis in reality.

13.
- A. NO CHANGE
- B. Many websites are dedicated to researching the validity of commonly told urban legends.
- C. Researching the validity of commonly told urban legends, many websites are dedicated.
- D. OMIT the underlined portion.

Questions 14–15 ask about the preceding passage as a whole.

14. The author wants to insert the following sentence:

    Other urban legends seem to be designed to instill fear.

    What would be the most logical placement for this sentence?

    F. After the last sentence of paragraph 3
    G. After the second sentence of paragraph 4
    H. Before the first sentence of paragraph 5
    J. After the last sentence of paragraph 6

15. Suppose that the author had been assigned to write an essay comparing the purposes and topics of myths and legends in primitive societies and in our modern society. Would this essay fulfill that assignment?

    A. Yes, because the essay describes myths and legends from primitive societies and modern society.
    B. Yes, because the essay provides explanations of possible purposes and topics of myths and legends from primitive societies and modern society.
    C. No, because the essay does not provide enough information about the topics of the myths and legends of primitive societies to make a valid comparison.
    D. No, because the essay does not provide any information on the myths and legends of primitive societies.

PASSAGE II

HENRY DAVID THOREAU: A SUCCESSFUL LIFE

What does it mean to be successful? <u>Do one</u> meas-
                                      16
ure success by money? If I told you about a

man: working as a teacher, a land surveyor, and a
     17
factory worker (never holding any of these jobs for more than a few years), would that man sound like a success to you? If I told you that he spent

16. F. NO CHANGE
    G. Does we
    H. Does one
    J. Did you

17. A. NO CHANGE
    B. man who worked
    C. man and worked
    D. man, which working

two solitary years living alone in a small cabin that he
built for himself and that he spent those years looking at
plants and writing in a diary—would you think of him
as a celebrity or an important figure? What if I told you
that

he rarely ventured far from the town where he was
born, that he was thrown in jail for refusing to pay his
taxes, and that he died at the age of forty-five? Do any of
these facts seem to point to a man whose life should be
studied and emulated?

You may already know about this man. You may
even have read some of his writings. His name was:
Henry David Thoreau, and he was, in addition to the
jobs listed above, a poet, an essayist, a naturalist, and
a social critic. Although the facts listed about him
may not seem to add up to much, he was, in fact a
tremendously influential person. Along with writers
such as Ralph Waldo Emerson, Mark Twain, and Walt
Whitman, Thoreau helped to create the first literature
and philosophy that most people identify as unique
American.

In 1845, Thoreau built a cabin. Near Walden Pond
and remained there for more than two years, living
alone, fending for himself, and observing the nature
around him. He kept scrupulous notes in his diary,
notes that he later distilled into his most famous work
titled *Walden*.

18. F. NO CHANGE
    G. two years living alone
    H. two solitary years all by himself
    J. a couple of lonely years living in solitude

19. A. NO CHANGE
    B. he is rarely venturing
    C. he has rare ventures
    D. this person was to venture rarely

20. F. NO CHANGE
    G. was Henry David Thoreau and he
    H. was: Henry David Thoreau; and he
    J. was Henry David Thoreau, and he

21. A. NO CHANGE
    B. was, in fact, a
    C. was in fact a
    D. was in fact, a

22. F. NO CHANGE
    G. uniquely
    H. uniqueness
    J. the most unique

23. A. NO CHANGE
    B. cabin. On
    C. cabin, by
    D. cabin near

Walden is read by many literature students today.
   24

[1] To protest slavery, Thoreau refused to pay his taxes in 1846. [2] Thoreau was a firm believer in the abolition of slavery, and he objected to the practice's extension into the new territories of the West. [3] For this act of rebellion, he was thrown in the Concord jail. 25

Thoreau used his writing to spread his message of resistance and activism; he published an essay entitled
                              26
Civil Disobedience (also known as *Resistance to Civil Government*). In it, Thoreau laid out his argument for refusing to obey unjust laws.

Although Thoreau's life was very brief, his works
                                              27
and his ideas continue to touch and influence people. Students all over the country—all over the world—continue to read his essays and hear his unique voice, urging them to lead lives of principle, individuality, and freedom. 28 To be able to live out the ideas that burn in

the heart of a person—surely that is the meaning of
   29
success.

24. F. NO CHANGE
    G. This book is read by many literature students today.
    H. Today, many literature students read *Walden*.
    J. OMIT the underlined portion.

25. What is the most logical order of sentences in this paragraph?
    A. NO CHANGE
    B. 3, 2, 1
    C. 2, 1, 3
    D. 3, 1, 2

26. F. NO CHANGE
    G. activism, he published:
    H. activism, he published
    J. activism, he published,

27. A. NO CHANGE
    B. he's
    C. their
    D. those

28. The purpose of this paragraph is to:
    F. explain why Thoreau was put in jail.
    G. prove a point about people's conception of success.
    H. suggest that Thoreau may be misunderstood.
    J. discuss Thoreau's importance in today's world.

29. A. NO CHANGE
    B. one's heart
    C. the heart and soul of a person
    D. through the heart of a person

GO ON TO THE NEXT PAGE

Question 30 asks about the preceding passage as a whole.

30. By including questions throughout the entire first paragraph, the author encourages the reader to:

   F. answer each question as the passage proceeds.
   G. think about the meaning of success.
   H. assess the quality of Thoreau's work.
   J. form an opinion about greed in modern society.

PASSAGE III

THE SLOTH: SLOW BUT NOT SLOTHFUL

[1]

More than half of the world's <u>currently living plant</u> and
                                          31
animal species live in tropical rain forests. Four square miles of a Central American rain forest can be home to up to 1,500 different species of flowering plants, 700 species of trees, 400 species of birds, and 125 species of mammals. Of these mammals, the sloth is one of the most unusual.

31. A. NO CHANGE
    B. currently existing plant
    C. living plant
    D. plant

[2]

Unlike most mammals, the sloth is usually upside down. A sloth does just about everything upside down, including sleeping, eating, mating, and giving birth. <u>Its' unique</u> anatomy allows the sloth to spend most of
       32
the time hanging from one tree branch or another, high in the canopy of a rain forest tree. About the size of a large domestic <u>cat, the</u> sloth hangs from its unusually
                        33
long limbs and long, hooklike claws.

32. F. NO CHANGE
    G. It's unique
    H. Its unique
    J. Its uniquely

33. A. NO CHANGE
    B. cat; the
    C. cat. The
    D. cat, but the

GO ON TO THE NEXT PAGE

Specially designed for limbs, the sloth's muscles seem to cling to things.
34

34. F. NO CHANGE
G. The sloth's muscles seem to cling to things for specially designed limbs.
H. The muscles in a sloth's limbs seem to be specially designed for clinging to things.
J. OMIT the underlined portion.

[3]

In fact, a sloth's limbs are so specific adapted to
35
upside-down life that a sloth is essentially incapable

35. A. NO CHANGE
B. so specific and
C. so specified
D. so specifically

of walking on the ground. Instead, they must crawl or
36
drag itself with its massive claws. This makes it easy to see why the sloth rarely leaves its home in the trees.

36. F. NO CHANGE
G. Instead, it
H. However, they
J. In addition, it

Because it can not move swiftly on the ground, the sloth
37
is an excellent swimmer.

37. A. NO CHANGE
B. Despite
C. Similarly,
D. Though

[4]

[38] A sloth can hang upside down and, without

38. The author wants to insert a sentence here to help connect paragraph 3 and paragraph 4. Which of the following sentences would best serve that purpose?
F. Of course, many other animals are also excellent swimmers.
G. Another unique characteristic of the sloth is its flexibility.
H. In addition to swimming, the sloth is an incredible climber.
J. Flexibility is a trait that helps the sloth survive.

moving the rest of its body turn its face 180 degrees so
                        39

that it was looking at the ground. A sloth can rotate
           40
its forelimbs in all directions, so it can easily reach the leaves that make up its diet. The sloth can also roll itself

up into a ball in order to protect and defend itself from
                               41

predators. The howler monkey, another inhabitant of
           42
the rain forest, is not as flexible as the sloth.
                       42

[5]

The best defense a sloth has from predators such as jaguars and large snakes, though, is its camouflage. During the rainy season, a sloth's thick brown or gray fur is usually covered with a coat of blue-green algae. Which
                                                  43
helps it blend in with its forest surroundings. Another type of camouflage is the sloth's incredibly slow movement: it often moves less than 100 feet during a 24-hour period.

[6]

It is this slow movement that earned the sloth its name. *Sloth* is also a word for laziness or an aversion to work. But even though it sleeps an average of 15 hours a day, the sloth isn't necessarily lazy. It just moves, upside

39. A. NO CHANGE
    B. body turns
    C. body, it has the capability of turning
    D. body, turn

40. F. NO CHANGE
    G. had been looking
    H. will have the ability to be looking
    J. can look

41. A. NO CHANGE
    B. protect itself and defend itself from
    C. protect itself so it won't be harmed by
    D. protect itself from

42. F. NO CHANGE
    G. Another inhabitant of the rain forest, the howler monkey, is not as flexible as the sloth.
    H. Not as flexible as the sloth is the howler monkey, another inhabitant of the rain forest.
    J. OMIT the underlined portion.

43. A. NO CHANGE
    B. algae, which
    C. algae, being that it
    D. algae

down, at its own slow pace through its world of rain forest trees. 44

44. The author is considering deleting the last sentence of paragraph 6. This change would:

F. diminish the amount of information provided about the habits of the sloth.
G. make the ending of the passage more abrupt.
H. emphasize the slothful nature of the sloth.
J. make the tone of the essay more consistent.

> Question 45 asks about the preceding passage as a whole.

45. The author wants to insert the following description:

   > An observer could easily be tricked into thinking that a sloth was just a pile of decaying leaves.

   What would be the most appropriate placement for this sentence?

   A. After the last sentence of paragraph 1
   B. After the third sentence of paragraph 2
   C. Before the last sentence of paragraph 5
   D. Before the first sentence of paragraph 6

PASSAGE IV

FIRES IN YELLOWSTONE

During the summer of 1988, I watched Yellowstone National Park go up in flames. In June, fires ignited by lightning had been allowed to burn unsuppressed because park officials expected that the usual summer rains would douse the flames. However, the rains never will have come. A plentiful fuel supply of fallen logs and pine needles was available, and winds of up to 100 miles per hour whipped the spreading fires along and carried red-hot embers to other areas, creating new fires. By the time park officials succumbed to the pressure of public opinion and decide to try to extinguish the flames. It's too late. The situation remained out of control in spite of the efforts of 9,000 firefighters who were using state-of-the-art equipment. By September, more than 720,000 acres of Yellowstone had been affected by fire. Nature was only able to curb the destruction; the smoke did not begin to clear until the first snow arrived on September 11.

Being that I was an ecologist who has studied forests for 20 years, I know that this was not nearly the tragedy it seemed to be. Large fires are, after

46. F. NO CHANGE
     G. fires having been ignited by lightning
     H. fires, the kind ignited by lightning,
     J. fires ignited and started by lightning

47. A. NO CHANGE
     B. came
     C. were coming
     D. have come

48. F. NO CHANGE
     G. are deciding
     H. decided
     J. OMIT the underlined portion.

49. A. NO CHANGE
     B. flames, it's
     C. flames, it was
     D. flames; it was

50. F. NO CHANGE
     G. Only curbing the destruction by able nature
     H. Only nature was able to curb the destruction
     J. Nature was able to curb only the destruction

51. A. NO CHANGE
     B. Being that I am
     C. I'm
     D. As

GO ON TO THE NEXT PAGE

all, necessary in order that the continued health in
the forest ecosystem be maintained. Fires thin out overcrowded areas and allow the sun to reach species of plants stunted by shade. Ash fertilizes the soil, and fire smoke kills forest bacteria. In the case of the lodgepole pine, fire is essential to reproduction: the pines' cone open only when exposed to temperatures greater than 112 degrees.

The fires in Yellowstone did result in some loss of wildlife, but overall, the region's animals proved to be fire-tolerant and fire-adaptive. However, large animals such as bison were often seen grazing, and bedding down in meadows near burning forests. Also, the fire posed little threat to the members of any endangered animal species in the park.

My confidence in the natural resilience of the forest has been borne out in the years since the fires ravaged Yellowstone. Judged from recent pictures of the park the forest was not destroyed; it was rejuvenated.

52. F. NO CHANGE
    G. for the continued health of the forest ecosystem to be maintained.
    H. in order to continue the maintenance of the health of the forest ecosystem.
    J. for the continued health of the forest ecosystem.

53. A. NO CHANGE
    B. pines cones'
    C. pine's cones
    D. pine's cone

54. F. NO CHANGE
    G. Clearly,
    H. In fact,
    J. Instead,

55. A. NO CHANGE
    B. grazing; and bedding
    C. grazing: and bedding
    D. grazing and bedding

56. F. NO CHANGE
    G. Recent pictures of the park show that
    H. Judging by the recent pictures of the park,
    J. As judged according to pictures taken of the park recently,

57. A. NO CHANGE
    B. they
    C. the fires
    D. I

Questions 58–59 ask about the preceding passage as a whole.

58. The writer is considering inserting the following true statement after the first sentence of the second paragraph:

    Many more acres of forest burned in Alaska in 1988 than in Yellowstone Park.

    Would this addition be appropriate for the essay?

    F. Yes, the statement would add important information about the effects of large-scale forest fires.
    G. Yes, the statement would provide an informative contrast to the Yellowstone fire.
    H. No, the statement would not provide any additional information about the effect of the 1988 fire in Yellowstone.
    J. No, the statement would undermine the author's position as an authority on the subject of forest fires.

59. Suppose that the writer wishes to provide additional support for the claim that the fire posed little threat to the members of any endangered animal species in the park. Which of the following additions would be most effective?

    A. A list of the endangered animals known to inhabit the park
    B. A discussion of the particular vulnerability of endangered species of birds to forest fires
    C. An explanation of the relative infrequency of such an extensive series of forest fires
    D. A summary of reports of biologists who monitored the activity of endangered species in the park during the fire

PASSAGE V

MY FIRST WHITE-WATER RAFTING TRIP

[1]

White-water rafting <u>being</u> a favorite pastime of mine
for several years. I have drifted down many challenging
North American rivers, including the Snake, the Green,

and the <u>Salmon, and there are many other rivers in</u>
<u>America as well.</u> I have spent some of my best moments
in dangerous rapids, yet nothing has matched the thrill

60. F. NO CHANGE
    G. have been
    H. has been
    J. was

61. A. NO CHANGE
    B. Salmon, just three of many rivers existing in North America.
    C. Salmon; many other rivers exist in North America.
    D. Salmon.

I experienced facing my first, rapids, on the Deschutes River.

[2]

My father and I spent the morning floating down a calm and peaceful stretch of the Deschutes in his wooden MacKenzie river boat. This trip it being the wooden boat's first time down rapids, as well as mine.

Rapids are rated according to a uniform scale of relative difficulty.

[3]

Roaring, I was in the boat approaching Whitehorse Rapids. I felt much like a novice skier peering down her first steep slope: I was scared, but even more excited.

The water churned and covering me with a refreshing spray. My father, toward the stern, controlled the oars. The carefree expression he usually wore on the river had been replaced, and instead he adopted a look of intense concentration as he maneuvered around boulders dotting our path. To release tension, we began to holler

62. F. NO CHANGE
    G. first: rapids on the Deschutes River.
    H. first rapids; on the Deschutes River.
    J. first rapids on the Deschutes River.

63. A. NO CHANGE
    B. it happened that it was
    C. was
    D. being

64. F. NO CHANGE
    G. Rated according to a uniform scale, rapids are relatively difficult.
    H. (Rapids are rated according to a uniform scale of relative difficulty.)
    J. OMIT the underlined portion.

65. A. NO CHANGE
    B. It roared, and the boat and I approached Whitehorse Rapids.
    C. While the roaring boat was approaching Whitehorse Rapids, I could hear the water.
    D. I could hear the water roar as we approached Whitehorse Rapids.

66. F. NO CHANGE
    G. churned, and covering me
    H. churning and covering me
    J. churned, covering me

67. A. NO CHANGE
    B. with
    C. by another countenance altogether:
    D. instead with another expression;

like kids on a roller-coaster, our voices echoing <u>across</u> the water as we lurched violently about.

[4]

Suddenly we came to a jarring halt <u>and we stopped</u>; the left side of the bow was wedged on a large rock. A whirlpool swirled around us; if we capsized, we would be sucked into the undertow. Instinctively, I threw all of my weight toward the right side of the tilting boat. Luckily, <u>it was</u> just enough force to dislodge us, and we continued on downstream to enjoy about 10 more minutes of spectacular rapids.

[5]

Later that day, we went through Buckskin Mary Rapids and Boxcar Rapids. When we pulled up on the bank that evening, we saw that the boat had received its first scar: <u>that scar was a</u> small hole on the upper bow from the boulder we had wrestled with. In the years to come, we went down many rapids and the boat <u>receiving many</u> bruises, but Whitehorse remains the most

68. F. NO CHANGE
    G. throughout
    H. around
    J. from

69. A. NO CHANGE
    B. which stopped us
    C. and stopped
    D. OMIT the underlined portion.

70. F. NO CHANGE
    G. it's
    H. it is
    J. its

71. A. NO CHANGE
    B. that was a
    C. which was a
    D. a

72. F. NO CHANGE
    G. received many
    H. received much
    J. receives many

memorable rapids of all. [73]

73. Which of the following concluding sentences would most effectively emphasize the final point made in this paragraph while retaining the style and tone of the narrative as a whole?

   A. The brutal calamities that it presented the unwary rafter were more than offset by its beguiling excitement.
   B. Perhaps it is true that your first close encounter with white water is your most intense.
   C. Or, if not the most memorable, then at least a very memorable one!
   D. Call me crazy or weird if you want, but white-water rafting is the sport for me.

Questions 74–75 ask about the preceding passage as a whole.

74. The writer has been assigned to write an essay that focuses on the techniques of white-water rafting. Would this essay meet the requirements of that assignment?

   F. No, because the essay's main focus is on a particular experience, not on techniques.
   G. No, because the essay mostly deals with the relationship between father and daughter.
   H. Yes, because specific rafting techniques are the essay's main focus.
   J. Yes, because it presents a dramatic story of a day of white-water rafting.

75. Suppose that the writer wants to add the following sentence to the essay:

   It was such a mild summer day that it was hard to believe dangerous rapids awaited us downstream.

   What would be the most logical placement of this sentence?

   A. After the last sentence of paragraph 1
   B. After the last sentence of paragraph 2
   C. Before the first sentence of paragraph 4
   D. After the last sentence of paragraph 4

MATHEMATICS TEST

60 Minutes—60 Questions

Directions: Solve each problem, choose the correct answer, and then fill in the corresponding oval on your Answer Grid.

Do not linger over problems that take too much time. Solve as many as you can, then return to the others in the time you have left for this test.

You are permitted to use a calculator on this test. You may use your calculator for any problems you choose, but some of the problems may best be done without using a calculator.

1. In a recent survey, 14 people found their mayor to be "very competent." This number is exactly 20% of the people surveyed. How many people were surveyed?

   A. 28
   B. 35
   C. 56
   D. 70
   E. 84

2. A train traveled at a rate of 90 miles per hour for x hours, and then at a rate of 60 miles per hour for y hours. Which expression represents the train's average rate in miles per hour for the entire distance traveled?

   F. $\dfrac{540}{xy}$
   G. $\dfrac{90}{x} \times \dfrac{60}{y}$
   H. $\dfrac{90}{x} + \dfrac{60}{y}$
   J. $\dfrac{90x + 60y}{x + y}$
   K. $\dfrac{150}{x + y}$

3. In a certain string ensemble, the ratio of men to women is 5:3. If there are a total of 24 people in the ensemble, how many women are there?

   A. 8
   B. 9
   C. 10
   D. 11
   E. 12

4. If $x \neq 0$, and $x^2 - 3x = 6x$, then $x = ?$

   F. -9
   G. -3
   H. $\sqrt{3}$
   J. 3
   K. 9

GO ON TO THE NEXT PAGE

5. Two overlapping circles below form three regions, as shown:

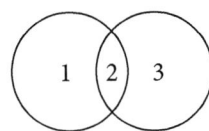

What is the maximum number of regions that can be formed by three overlapping circles?

A. 5
B. 6
C. 7
D. 8
E. 9

6. If $x^2 + 6x + 8 = 4 + 10x$, then x equals which of the following?

F. −2
G. −1
H. 0
J. 1
K. 2

7. Nine less than the number c is the same as the number d, and d less than twice c is 20. Which two equations could be used to determine the value of c and d?

A. $d − 9 = c$
   $d − 2c = 20$
B. $c − 9 = d$
   $2c − d = 20$
C. $c − 9 = d$
   $d − 2c = 20$
D. $9 − c = d$
   $2c − d = 20$
E. $9 − c = d$
   $2cd = 20$

8. An ice cream parlor offers five flavors of ice cream and four different toppings (sprinkles, hot fudge, whipped cream, and butterscotch). There is a special offer that includes one flavor of ice cream and one topping, served in a cup, sugar cone, or waffle cone. How many ways are there to order ice cream with the special offer?

F. 4
G. 5
H. 12
J. 23
K. 60

9. At a recent audition for a school play, 1 out of 3 students who auditioned were asked to come to a second audition. After the second audition, 75% of those asked to the second audition were offered parts. If 18 students were offered parts, how many students went to the first audition?

A. 18
B. 24
C. 48
D. 56
E. 72

10. One number is 5 times another number, and their sum is −60. What is the lesser of the two numbers?

F. −5
G. −10
H. −12
J. −48
K. −50

11. In the following figure, which is composed of equilateral triangles, what is the greatest number of parallelograms that can be found?

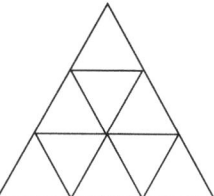

   A. 6
   B. 9
   C. 12
   D. 15
   E. 18

12. The circle in the following figure is inscribed in a square with a perimeter of 16 inches. What is the area of the shaded region?

   F. 4π
   G. $16 - 2\pi$
   H. $16 - 4\pi$
   J. $8 - 2\pi$
   K. $8 - 4\pi$

13. How many positive integers less than 50 are multiples of 4 but *not* multiples of 6?

   A. 4
   B. 6
   C. 8
   D. 10
   E. 12

14. Given that $f(x) = (8 - 3x)(x^2 - 2x - 15)$, what is the value of $f(3)$?

   F. -30
   G. -18
   H. 12
   J. 24
   K. 30

15. A class contains five juniors and five seniors. If one member of the class is assigned at random to present a paper on a certain subject, and another member of the class is randomly assigned to assist him, what is the probability that both will be juniors?

   A. $\dfrac{1}{10}$
   B. $\dfrac{1}{5}$
   C. $\dfrac{2}{9}$
   D. $\dfrac{2}{5}$
   E. $\dfrac{1}{2}$

16. In triangle XYZ shown, $\overline{XS}$ and $\overline{SZ}$ are 3 and 12 units, respectively. If the area of triangle XYZ is 45 square units, how many units long is altitude $\overline{YS}$?

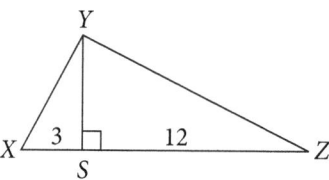

   F. 3
   G. 6
   H. 9
   J. 12
   K. 15

GO ON TO THE NEXT PAGE

17. At which *y*-coordinate does the line described by the equation $6y - 3x = 18$ intersect the *y*-axis?

    A. 2
    B. 3
    C. 6
    D. 9
    E. 18

18. If $x^2 - y^2 = 12$ and $x - y = 4$, what is the value of $x^2 + 2xy + y^2$?

    F. 3
    G. 8
    H. 9
    J. 12
    K. 16

19. What is the area in square units of the following figure?

    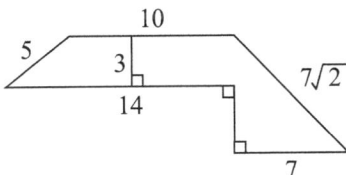

    A. $39 + 7\sqrt{2}$
    B. 60.5
    C. 91
    D. 108.5
    E. 147

20. A carpenter is cutting wood to make a new bookcase with a board that is 12 feet long. If the carpenter cuts off three pieces, each of which is 17 inches long, how many inches long is the remaining fourth and final board? (A foot contains 12 inches.)

    F. 36
    G. 51
    H. 93
    J. 108
    K. 144

21. If $x^2 - 4x - 6 = 6$, what are the possible values for *x* ?

    A. 4, 12
    B. −6, 2
    C. −6, −2
    D. 6, 2
    E. 6, −2

22. If −3 is a solution for the equation $x^2 + kx - 15 = 0$, what is the value of *k* ?

    F. 5
    G. 2
    H. −2
    J. −5
    K. Cannot be determined from the information given.

23. If the lengths of all three sides of a triangle are integers, and one side is 7 inches long, what is the smallest possible perimeter of the triangle, in inches?

    A. 9
    B. 10
    C. 12
    D. 15
    E. 18

24. If $0° < \theta < 90°$ and $\sin\theta = \dfrac{\sqrt{11}}{2\sqrt{3}}$, then $\cos\theta = ?$

   F. $\dfrac{1}{2\sqrt{3}}$

   G. $\dfrac{1}{\sqrt{11}}$

   H. $\dfrac{2}{\sqrt{3}}$

   J. $\dfrac{2\sqrt{3}}{\sqrt{11}}$

   K. $\dfrac{11}{2\sqrt{3}}$

25. Which of the following expressions is equivalent to $\dfrac{\sqrt{3+x}}{\sqrt{3-x}}$ for all x such that $-3 < x < 3$?

   A. $\dfrac{3-x}{3+x}$

   B. $\dfrac{3+x}{3-x}$

   C. $\dfrac{-3\sqrt{3}+x}{\sqrt{3-x}}$

   D. $\dfrac{\sqrt{9-x^2}}{3-x}$

   E. $\dfrac{x^2-9}{3+x}$

26. In a certain cookie jar containing only macaroons and gingersnaps, the ratio of macaroons to gingersnaps is 2 to 5. Which of the following could be the total number of cookies in the cookie jar?

   F. 24
   G. 35
   H. 39
   J. 48
   K. 52

27. What is the sum of $\dfrac{3}{16}$ and 0.175?

   A. 0.3165
   B. 0.3500
   C. 0.3625
   D. 0.3750
   E. 0.3875

28. What is the maximum possible area, in square inches, of a rectangle with a perimeter of 20 inches?

   F. 15
   G. 20
   H. 25
   J. 30
   K. 40

29. $\dfrac{\dfrac{3}{2}+\dfrac{7}{4}}{\left(\dfrac{15}{8}-\dfrac{3}{4}\right)-\left(\dfrac{4+3}{-4+3}\right)} = ?$

   A. $\dfrac{3}{8}$

   B. $\dfrac{2}{5}$

   C. $\dfrac{9}{13}$

   D. $\dfrac{5}{2}$

   E. $\dfrac{8}{3}$

30. If $x - 15 = 7 - 5(x - 4)$, then $x = ?$

   F. 0
   G. 2
   H. 4
   J. 5
   K. 7

GO ON TO THE NEXT PAGE

31. The following sketch shows the dimensions of a flower garden. What is the area of this garden in square meters?

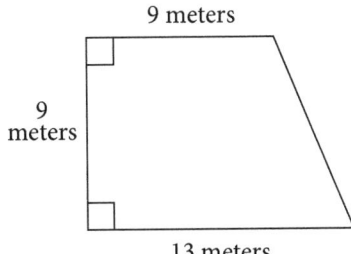

A. 31
B. 85
C. 99
D. 101
E. 117

32. What is the slope of the line described by the equation $6y - 3x = 18$?

F. -2
G. $-\dfrac{1}{2}$
H. $\dfrac{1}{2}$
J. 2
K. 3

33. Line m passes through the point $(4,3)$ in the standard (x,y) coordinate plane and is perpendicular to the line described by the equation $y = -\dfrac{4}{5}x + 6$. Which of the following equations describes line m ?

A. $y = \dfrac{5}{4}x - 2$
B. $y = -\dfrac{5}{4}x + 6$
C. $y = -\dfrac{4}{5}x - 2$
D. $y = -\dfrac{4}{5}x + 2$
E. $y = -\dfrac{5}{4}x - 2$

34. Line t in the standard (x,y) coordinate plane has a y-intercept of -3 and is parallel to the line having the equation $3x - 5y = 4$. Which of the following is an equation for line t ?

F. $y = -\dfrac{3}{5}x + 3$
G. $y = -\dfrac{5}{3}x - 3$
H. $y = \dfrac{3}{5}x + 3$
J. $y = \dfrac{5}{3}x + 3$
K. $y = \dfrac{3}{5}x - 3$

35. If $y = mx + b$, which of the following equations expresses x in terms of y, m, and b ?

A. $x = \dfrac{y - b}{m}$
B. $x = \dfrac{b - y}{m}$
C. $x = \dfrac{y + b}{m}$
D. $x = \dfrac{y}{m} - bx$
E. $x = \dfrac{y}{m} + b$

36. In the following figure, $\overline{AB} = 20$, $\overline{BC} = 15$, and $\angle ADB$ and $\angle ABC$ are right angles. What is the length of $\overline{AD}$?

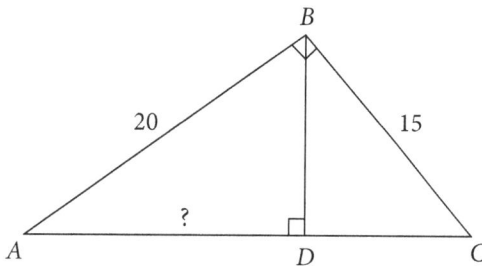

F. 9
G. 12
H. 15
J. 16
K. 25

37. In the standard (x,y) coordinate plane shown in the figure, points A and B lie on line m, and point C lies below it. The coordinates of points A, B, and C are (0,5), (5,5), and (3,3), respectively. What is the shortest possible distance from point C to a point on line m?

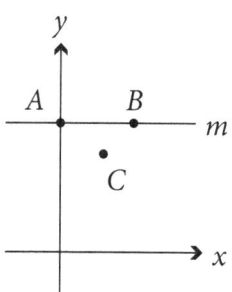

A. 2
B. $2\sqrt{2}$
C. 3
D. $\sqrt{13}$
E. 5

38. For all $x \neq 8$, $\dfrac{x^2 - 11x + 24}{8 - x} = ?$

F. $8 - x$
G. $3 - x$
H. $x - 3$
J. $x - 8$
K. $x - 11$

39. Points A and B lie in the standard (x,y) coordinate plane. The (x,y) coordinates of A are (2,1), and the (x,y) coordinates of B are (−2,−2). What is the distance from A to B?

A. $3\sqrt{2}$
B. $3\sqrt{3}$
C. 5
D. 6
E. 7

40. In the following figure, $\overline{AB}$ and $\overline{CD}$ are both tangent to the circle as shown, and ABCD is a rectangle with side lengths 2x and 5x as shown. What is the area of the shaded region?

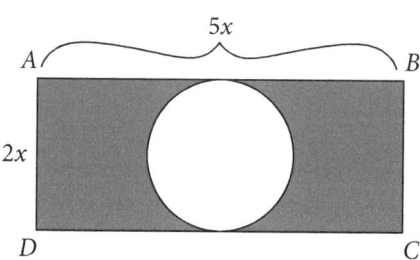

F. $10\pi x^2$
G. $10x^2 - \pi x^2$
H. $10x^2 - 2\pi x$
J. $9\pi x^2$
K. $6\pi x^2$

GO ON TO THE NEXT PAGE

41. If $0° < \theta < 90°$ and $\cos \theta = \dfrac{5\sqrt{2}}{8}$, then $\tan \theta = ?$

    A. $\dfrac{5}{\sqrt{7}}$

    B. $\dfrac{\sqrt{7}}{5}$

    C. $\dfrac{\sqrt{14}}{8}$

    D. $\dfrac{8}{\sqrt{14}}$

    E. $\dfrac{8}{5\sqrt{2}}$

42. Consider fractions of the form $\dfrac{7}{n}$, where n is an integer. How many integer values of n make this fraction greater than 0.5 and less than 0.8 ?

    F. 3
    G. 4
    H. 5
    J. 6
    K. 7

43. The figure below shows two tangent circles. The circumference of circle X is 12π, and the circumference of circle Y is 8π. What is the greatest possible distance between two points, one of which lies on the circumference of circle X and one of which lies on the circumference of circle Y ?

    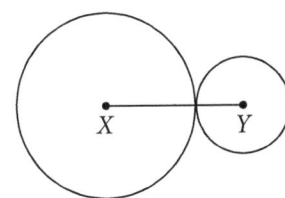

    A. 6
    B. 10
    C. 20
    D. 10π
    E. 20π

44. $\sqrt{(x^2+4)^2} - (x+2)(x-2) = ?$

    F. $2x^2$
    G. $x^2 - 8$
    H. $2(x-2)$
    J. 0
    K. 8

45. If $s = -3$, then $s^3 + 2s^2 + 2s = ?$

    A. -15
    B. -10
    C. -5
    D. 5
    E. 33

46. How many different numbers are solutions for the equation $2x + 6 = (x+5)(x+3)$?

    F. 0
    G. 1
    H. 2
    J. 3
    K. Infinitely many

47. In square $ABCD$ shown, $\overline{AC} = 8$. What is the perimeter of $ABCD$?

    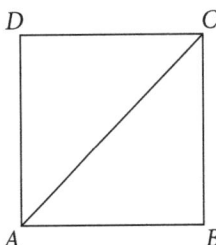

    A. $4\sqrt{2}$
    B. 8
    C. $8\sqrt{2}$
    D. 16
    E. $16\sqrt{2}$

48. The front surface of a fence panel is shown here with the lengths labeled representing inches. The panel is symmetrical along its center vertical axis. What is the surface area of the front surface of the panel in square inches?

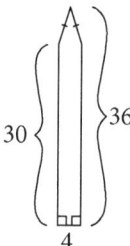

F. 144
G. 132
H. 120
J. 80
K. $64 + 6\sqrt{5}$

49. In the following figure, O is the center of the circle, and C, D, and E are points on the circumference of the circle. If $\angle OCD$ measures 70° and $\angle OED$ measures 45°, what is the measure of $\angle CDE$?

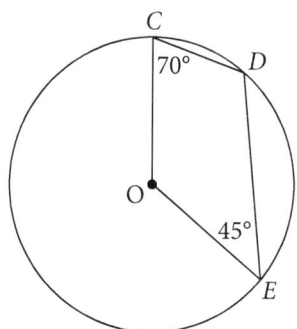

A. 25°
B. 45°
C. 70°
D. 90°
E. 115°

50. Which of the following systems of equations does NOT have a solution?

F. $x + 3y = 19$
$3x + y = 6$

G. $x + 3y = 19$
$x - 3y = 13$

H. $x - 3y = 19$
$3x - y = 7$

J. $x - 3y = 19$
$3x + y = 6$

K. $x + 3y = 6$
$3x + 9y = 7$

51. What is the 46th digit to the right of the decimal point in the decimal equivalent of $\frac{1}{7}$?

A. 1
B. 2
C. 4
D. 7
E. 8

52. Which of the following inequalities is equivalent to $-2 - 4x \leq -6x$?

F. $x \geq -2$
G. $x \geq 1$
H. $x \geq 2$
J. $x \leq -1$
K. $x \leq 1$

GO ON TO THE NEXT PAGE

53. If $x > 0$ and $y > 0$, $\dfrac{\sqrt{x}}{x} + \dfrac{\sqrt{y}}{y}$ is equivalent to which of the following?

A. $\dfrac{2}{xy}$

B. $\dfrac{\sqrt{x} + \sqrt{y}}{\sqrt{xy}}$

C. $\dfrac{x + y}{xy}$

D. $\dfrac{\sqrt{x} + \sqrt{y}}{\sqrt{x + y}}$

E. $\dfrac{x + y}{\sqrt{xy}}$

54. In the following diagram, $\overline{CD}$, $\overline{BE}$, and $\overline{AF}$ are all parallel and are intersected by two transversals as shown. What is the length of $\overline{EF}$?

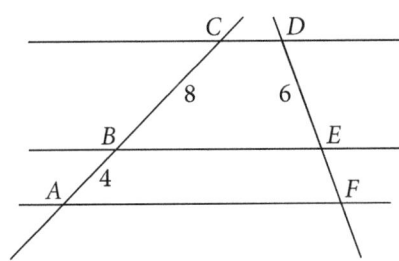

F. 2
G. 3
H. 4
J. 6
K. 9

55. What is the area, in square units, of the square whose vertices are located at the (x,y) coordinate points indicated in the following figure?

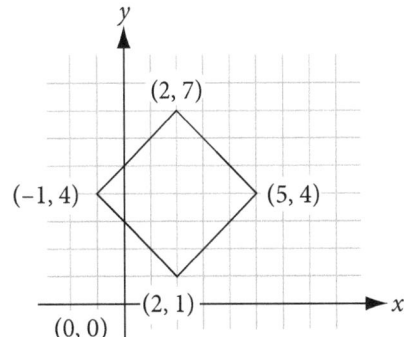

A. 9
B. 12
C. 16
D. 18
E. 24

56. Compared to the graph of $y = \cos \theta$, the graph of $y = 2 \cos \theta$ has:

F. twice the period and the same amplitude.
G. half the period and the same amplitude.
H. twice the period and half the amplitude.
J. half the amplitude and the same period.
K. twice the amplitude and the same period.

57. Brandy has a collection of comic books. If she adds 15 to the number of comic books in her collection and multiplies the sum by 3, the result will be 65 less than 4 times the number of comic books in her collection. How many comic books are in her collection?

    A. 50
    B. 85
    C. 110
    D. 145
    E. 175

58. One empty cylinder has three times the height and twice the diameter of another empty cylinder. How many fillings of the smaller cylinder would be equivalent to one filling of the larger cylinder?

    (Note: The volume of a cylinder of radius r and height h is $\pi r^2 h$.)

    F. 6
    G. $6\sqrt{2}$
    H. 12
    J. 18
    K. 24

59. What is the perimeter of a 30°-60°-90° triangle with a long leg of 12 inches?

    A. $5\sqrt{3} + 12$
    B. $4\sqrt{3} + 18$
    C. $8\sqrt{3} + 18$
    D. $12\sqrt{3} + 12$
    E. $12\sqrt{3} + 18$

60. A baseball team scores an average of x points in its first n games and then scores y points in its next and final game of the season. Which of the following represents the team's average score for the entire season?

    F. $x + \dfrac{y}{n}$
    G. $x + \dfrac{y}{n+1}$
    H. $\dfrac{x + ny}{n+1}$
    J. $\dfrac{nx + y}{n+1}$
    K. $\dfrac{n(x+y)}{n+1}$

IF YOU FINISH BEFORE TIME IS CALLED, YOU MAY CHECK YOUR WORK ON THIS SECTION ONLY. DO NOT TURN TO ANY OTHER SECTION IN THE TEST. **STOP**

READING TEST

35 Minutes—40 Questions

Directions: There are four passages in this test. Each passage is followed by several questions. After reading a passage, choose the best answer to each question and fill in the corresponding oval on your Answer Grid. You may refer to the passages as often as necessary.

PASSAGE I

PROSE FICTION

This passage is adapted from the novel Emma *by Jane Austen. It was originally published in 1815.*

Emma Woodhouse, handsome, clever, and rich, with a comfortable home and happy disposition, seemed to unite some of the best blessings of existence. She had lived
(5) nearly twenty-one years in the world with very little to distress or vex her. She was the youngest of the two daughters of a most affectionate, indulgent father, and had, in consequence of her sister's marriage, been
(10) mistress of his house from a very early period. Her mother had died too long ago for her to have more than an indistinct remembrance of her caresses, and her place had been taken by an excellent governess
(15) who had fallen little short of a mother in affection.

Sixteen years had Miss Taylor been in Mr. Woodhouse's family, less as a governess than a friend, very fond of both daughters,
(20) but particularly of Emma. Between them it was more the intimacy of sisters. Even before Miss Taylor had ceased to hold the nominal office of governess, the mildness of her temper had hardly allowed her
(25) to impose any restraint. The shadow of authority being now long passed away, they had been living together as friend and friend very mutually attached, and Emma doing just what she liked, highly esteeming Miss
(30) Taylor's judgment, but directed chiefly by her own. The real evils, indeed, of Emma's situation were the power of having rather too much her own way, and a disposition to think a little too well of herself; these were
(35) the disadvantages which threatened alloy to her many enjoyments. The danger, however, was at present so unperceived, that they did not by any means rank as misfortunes with her.

(40) Sorrow came—a gentle sorrow—but not at all in the shape of any disagreeable consciousness. Miss Taylor married. It was Miss Taylor's loss which first brought grief. It was on the wedding-day of this beloved
(45) friend that Emma first sat in mournful thought of any continuance. The wedding over, and the bride-people gone, she and her father were left to dine together, with no prospect of a third to cheer a long evening.
(50) Her father composed himself to sleep after dinner, as usual, and she had then only to sit and think of what she had lost.

The marriage had every promise of happiness for her friend. Mr. Weston was
(55) a man of unexceptionable character, easy fortune, suitable age, and pleasant manners. There was some satisfaction in considering with what self-denying, generous friendship she had always wished and promoted the
(60) match, but it was a black morning's work for her. The want of Miss Taylor would be felt every hour of every day. She recalled her past kindness—the kindness, the affection of sixteen years—how she had taught her
(65) and how she had played with her from five years old—how she had devoted all her

powers to attach and amuse her in health—
and how she had nursed her through the
various illnesses of childhood. A large
(70) debt of gratitude was owing here, but the
intercourse of he last seven years, the equal
footing and perfect unreserve which had
soon followed Isabella's marriage, on their
being left to each other, was yet a dearer,
(75) tenderer recollection. She had been a friend
and companion such as few possessed:
intelligent, well-informed, useful, gentle,
knowing all the ways of the family, interested
in all its concerns, and peculiarly
(80) interested in her, in every pleasure, every
scheme of hers—one to whom she could
speak every thought as it arose, and who
had such an affection for her as could never
find fault.
(85) How was she to bear the change? It was
true that her friend was going only half a
mile from them, but Emma was aware that
great must be the difference between a Mrs.
Weston, only half a mile from them, and
(90) a Miss Taylor in the house. With all her
advantages, natural and domestic, she was
now in great danger of suffering from intellectual
solitude.

1. According to the passage, what are the greatest disadvantages facing Emma?
   A. Her father is not a stimulating conversationalist, and she is bored.
   B. She is lonely and afraid that Mrs. Weston will not have a happy marriage.
   C. She is used to having her way too much, and she thinks too highly of herself.
   D. She misses the companionship of her mother, her sister, and Miss Taylor.

2. The name of Emma's sister is:
   F. Mrs. Weston.
   G. Isabella.
   H. Miss Taylor.
   J. Mrs. Woodhouse.

3. As described in the passage, Emma's relationship with Miss Taylor can be characterized as:
   A. similar to a mother-daughter relationship.
   B. similar to the relationship of sisters or best friends.
   C. weaker than Emma's relationship with her sister.
   D. stronger than Miss Taylor's relationship with her new husband.

4. As used in line 33, *disposition* can most closely be defined as:
   F. a tendency.
   G. control.
   H. placement.
   J. transfer.

5. Which of the following are included in Emma's memories of her relationship with Miss Taylor?
   I. Miss Taylor taking care of Emma during childhood illnesses
   II. Miss Taylor entertaining Emma
   III. Miss Taylor teaching her mathematics
   IV. Miss Taylor scolding her for being selfish

   A. I, III, and IV only
   B. I and III only
   C. II, III, and IV only
   D. I and II only

6. It is most reasonable to infer from Emma's realization that "great must be the difference between a Mrs. Weston, only half a mile from them, and a Miss Taylor in the house" (lines 88–90) that:

   F. Miss Taylor will no longer be a part of Emma's life.
   G. Emma is happy about the marriage because now she will have more freedom.
   H. Emma regrets that her relationship with Miss Taylor will change.
   J. Emma believes that her relationship with Miss Taylor will become stronger.

7. Based on the passage, Emma could best be described as:

   A. sweet and naïve.
   B. self-centered and naïve.
   C. self-centered and headstrong.
   D. unappreciative and bitter.

8. The passage suggests that the quality Emma values most in a friend is:

   F. charisma.
   G. devotion.
   H. honesty.
   J. intelligence.

9. How does Emma view Mr. Weston?

   A. She thinks that he is an excellent match, and it required considerable self-sacrifice not to pursue him herself.
   B. She considers him to be a respectable if somewhat average match for her friend.
   C. She sees him as an intruder who has carried away her best friend in "a black morning's work" (line 60).
   D. She believes he is an indulgent, easily swayed man, reminiscent of her father.

10. From the passage, it can be inferred that Emma is accustomed to:

    F. behaving according to the wishes of her affectionate father.
    G. taking the advice of Miss Taylor when faced with deciding upon a course of action.
    H. doing as she pleases without permission from her father or governess.
    J. abiding by strict rules governing her behavior.

PASSAGE II

SOCIAL SCIENCE

The period of active experimentation to develop the airplane began in the 1890s. Many scientists and engineers attempted to solve the problem in the decade following, but with limited progress until Orville and Wilbur Wright made the first successful powered, heavier-than-air flight in 1903. Both of the passages below discuss aspects of the Wright brothers' invention.

PASSAGE A

What about the method used by the Wright brothers allowed them to succeed where so many scientists, engineers, and crackpots had failed to make progress for a dozen years? In
(5) the decade leading up to their success, there had been so many unsuccessful attempts that newspaper reporters became jaded, tired of investigating each yokel who claimed to have made an airplane. In fact, the reporter present
(10) at that historical first flight didn't even bother to take his camera out of its bag, deciding that two unassuming brothers from Ohio without college educations would be two more in a long line. Instead, the Wrights, quite systematically
(15) and without much fuss or outside assistance, changed the world dramatically in 1903. What made Orville and Wilbur so different from the rest of the pack?

GO ON TO THE NEXT PAGE

Most inventors of the time were working on their planes with a fairly simple and logical approach: They would design an airplane, build it, test it in the field, and then use the results of that test to tinker with their designs in an attempt to improve the next model. The problem with this method, though, was that the field test of a new airplane only provided information about whether it flew or not, for how long, and how high. There was no way of knowing whether the wings were good but the engine was bad, or the shape was right but the materials were too heavy. With no way of discerning which parts worked and which parts didn't, inventors' second attempts often flew worse than their initial ones, because their creators had inadvertently removed design features that were effective and exaggerated features that were not.

The Wright brothers proved to be adept scientists. With their keen analytical insight and love of engineering and all things mechanical, they were able to escape that endless loop of misguided "improvements." They worked on their machine one aspect at a time. After familiarizing themselves with all the published literature on flight, they began working on a method of control. They theorized that twisting the wings one way or another would steer a craft. Instead of building an entire airplane to test their theory, they built a five-foot biplane kite. Sure enough, twisting the wings controlled the craft laterally. Having settled that aspect of the craft's design, they turned to wing shape.

After building two failed gliders based on their original design, the brothers realized that it was too expensive and time consuming to continue designing and making whole machines. As an alternative, they invented the first wind tunnel with instruments capable of quantifying the lift and drag of wing segments. In this wind tunnel, they could test wings alone for their efficiency and aerodynamics. In the process of testing 80 to 200 wing shapes in this way, they disproved a commonly accepted theory of lift (called "Smeaton's coefficient") and settled on a new and highly efficient wing shape for their craft.

The Wrights returned to the wind tunnel to perfect designs for their propeller and then designed an effective four-cylinder engine to power the craft. When the time came to marry all of these carefully designed components into a complete craft, there was no guesswork involved. The Wright brothers knew they had built an airplane, and they knew that each piece was beautifully designed and perfectly functioning. That first historic flight was merely proof of their scientific genius.

PASSAGE B

Few people recognize that the Wright brothers are tragic figures in American history. Today, they are hailed as great inventors, but during their lives they were scorned and discredited publicly, even though the entire world copied their successful designs. The prevailing opinion among those who made airplanes was that two rustic, uneducated fellows from Ohio could never have accomplished such a historic feat, let alone deliberately marry the disparate components of air travel that are required for successful flight. They hadn't paid their dues to the scientific community. The French aviation community especially mocked the brothers, and the secrecy of Orville and Wilbur during the years in which they prepared their patents only fueled derision of and doubts about their accomplishments.

The Wright brothers finally received a U.S. patent for their system of lateral control, perhaps their most important contribution to aviation, in May of 1906. Manufacturers unwilling to pay the modest fee the brothers asked for use of their system launched a vast and sadly successful smear campaign against the brothers, impugning the importance of their contribution to flight. Some European countries simply refused to issue the brothers

a patent, and as a result airplane manufacturers
(110) in those countries could legally copy the
Wrights' technology unchecked.

In the midst of the legal battle over rights
and license fees against several airplane manufacturers, Wilbur sadly succumbed to typhoid
(115) fever. He was thus deprived of seeing his claims
vindicated in court, and, though Orville was
accorded a tidy sum, this small victory was
hardly commensurate with the enormous
contribution the two brothers had made. The
(120) court case also did nothing to compensate the
brothers for the taxing and unfair period of ridicule and doubt and the obstinate refusal by much
of the world to acknowledge their achievements.
Perhaps most tellingly, the Smithsonian Museum
(125) didn't display the brothers' historic craft until
1948, when it finally bestowed on them the
title of the first men to fly in a heavier-than-air
craft. Sadly, this was too little, too late, as the
brothers had both passed away.

Questions 11–13 ask about Passage A.

11. The main purpose of Passage A is to:
    A. describe how the Wright brothers were regarded.
    B. emphasize the process of designing the airplane.
    C. criticize the attitude of other inventors.
    D. explore the practical application of science.

12. What does Passage A suggest about the method used by most inventors at the time of the Wright brothers?
    F. They did not take Smeaton's coefficient into account.
    G. They scorned the methods used by the Wright brothers.
    H. They weren't able to learn effectively from previous failures.
    J. They didn't believe it was possible to build an airplane.

13. Passage A suggests that the wind tunnel played what role in the Wright brothers' research?
    A. It provided more reliable data than their experiments with kites.
    B. It allowed them to isolate single aspects of design from other considerations.
    C. It helped them develop a method of twisting the wings to control the plane laterally.
    D. It confirmed the accuracy of Smeaton's coefficient.

Questions 14–16 ask about Passage B.

14. In Passage B, the author mentions a "legal battle" (line 112) in order to:
    F. emphasize the poor way in which the Wright brothers were treated.
    G. illustrate the dangers of publicizing new knowledge.
    H. help explain why the Wright brothers' discovery was of little importance.
    J. suggest a reason for Wilbur's fatal illness.

15. What does Passage B suggest about the Smithsonian Museum's choice to display the brothers' historic craft in 1948?
    A. It was a small victory for Orville, who lost his brother Wilbur to typhoid fever.
    B. It was a direct result of the obstinate refusal by much of the world to acknowledge their achievements.
    C. While it was a great honor, it did not fully atone for the poor treatment of the brothers.
    D. The historic craft would have been displayed sooner if European countries had issued the brothers a patent.

GO ON TO THE NEXT PAGE

16. In Passage B, the statement "They hadn't paid their dues to the scientific community" (lines 92–93) is presented as the opinion of:

   F. the French aviation community.
   G. the Wright brothers.
   H. the author.
   J. those who made airplanes.

Questions 17–20 ask about both passages.

17. The author of Passage B would likely agree that the "inventors of the time" (line 19) mentioned in Passage A:

   A. thought that the Wright brothers didn't actually make the first airplane.
   B. didn't believe that the Wright brothers deserved credit for the magnitude of their achievement.
   C. were grateful for the breakthrough that the Wrights had engineered.
   D. felt the Wright brothers had likely copied the design from a more accomplished inventor.

18. In lines 72 and 90, "marry" most nearly means:

   F. prove.
   G. test rigorously.
   H. bring together.
   J. satisfy.

19. According to Passage A, while the brothers "hadn't paid their dues to the scientific community" (lines 92–93), as mentioned in Passage B, they were indeed skilled inventors because:

   A. they designed an airplane, built it, tested it in the field, and then used the results of that test to adjust their designs.
   B. they used analytical insight to work on machines one aspect at a time to perfect their design.
   C. they invented the first wind tunnel, which was a greater accomplishment than inventing the first successful aircraft.
   D. their claims were eventually vindicated in court, and Orville received monetary reimbursement.

20. Both passages provide support for the idea that the Wright brothers:

   F. used a method of scientific inquiry that was different from everyone else's.
   G. were poorly treated following their discovery.
   H. were exceptional scientists.
   J. should have protected the rights to their discovery more carefully.

PASSAGE III

HUMANITIES

This passage is excerpted from A History of Women Artists, *© 1975 by Hugo Munsterberg; Clarkson N. Potter (a division of Random House, Inc.), publisher. Reprinted by permission of the author's family.*

There can be little doubt that women artists have been most prominent in photography and that they have made their greatest contribution in this field. One reason for
(5) this is not difficult to ascertain. As several

historians of photography have pointed out, photography, being a new medium outside the traditional academic framework, was wide open to women and offered them
(10) opportunities that the older fields did not....

All these observations apply to the first woman to have achieved eminence in photography, and that is Julia Margaret Cameron....Born in 1815 in Calcutta into an
(15) upper-middle-class family and married to Charles Hay Cameron, a distinguished jurist and member of the Supreme Court of India, Julia Cameron was well-known as a brilliant conversationalist and a woman of personality
(20) and intellect who was unconventional to the point of eccentricity. Although the mother of six children, she adopted several more and still found time to be active in social causes and literary activities. After
(25) the Camerons settled in England in 1848 at Freshwater Bay on the Isle of Wight, she became the center of an artistic and literary circle that included such notable figures as the poet Alfred Lord Tennyson and the
(30) painter George Frederick Watts. Pursuing numerous activities and taking care of her large family, Mrs. Cameron might have been remembered as still another rather remarkable and colorful Victorian lady had it not
(35) been for the fact that, in 1863, her daughter presented her with photographic equipment, thinking her mother might enjoy taking pictures of her family and friends. Although forty-eight years old, Mrs. Cameron took
(40) up this new hobby with enormous enthusiasm and dedication. She was a complete beginner, but within a very few years she developed into one of the greatest photographers of her period and a giant in the
(45) history of photography. She worked ceaselessly as long as daylight lasted and mastered the technical processes of photography, at that time far more cumbersome than today, turning her coal house into a darkroom
(50) and her chicken house into a studio. To her, photography was a "divine art," and in it she found her vocation. In 1864, she wrote triumphantly under one of her photographs, "My First Success," and from then until her
(55) death in Ceylon in 1874, she devoted herself wholly to this art.

Working in a large format (her portrait studies are usually about 11 inches by 14 inches) and requiring a long exposure
(60) (on the average five minutes), she produced a large body of work that stands up as one of the notable artistic achievements of the Victorian period. The English art critic Roger Fry believed that her portraits were
(65) likely to outlive the works of artists who were her contemporaries. Her friend Watts, then a very celebrated portrait painter, inscribed on one of her photographs, "I wish I could paint such a picture as this."...Her
(70) work was widely exhibited, and she received gold, silver, and bronze medals in England, America, Germany, and Austria. No other female artist of the nineteenth century achieved such acclaim, and no other woman
(75) photographer has ever enjoyed such success.

Her work falls into two main categories on which her contemporaries and people today differ sharply. Victorian critics were particularly impressed by her allegorical
(80) pictures, many of them based on the poems of her friend and neighbor Tennyson.... Contemporary taste much prefers her portraits and finds her narrative scenes sentimental and sometimes in bad taste. Yet,
(85) not only Julia Cameron, but also the painters of that time loved to depict subjects such as *The Five Foolish Virgins* or *Pray God, Bring Father Safely Home*. Still, today her fame rests upon her portraits for, as she herself
(90) said, she was intent upon representing not only the outer likeness but also the inner greatness of the people she portrayed. Working with the utmost dedication, she produced photographs of such eminent
(95) Victorians as Tennyson, Browning, Carlyle, Trollope, Longfellow, Watts, Darwin, Ellen Terry, Sir John Herschel, who was a close friend of hers, and Mrs. Duckworth, the mother of Virginia Woolf.

21. Which of the following conclusions can be reasonably drawn from the passage's discussion of Julia Margaret Cameron?

   A. She was a traditional homemaker until she discovered photography.
   B. Her work holds a significant place in the history of photography.
   C. She was unable to achieve in her lifetime the artistic recognition she deserved.
   D. Her eccentricity has kept her from being taken seriously by modern critics of photography.

22. According to the passage, Cameron is most respected by modern critics for her:

   F. portraits.
   G. allegorical pictures.
   H. use of a large format.
   J. service in recording the faces of so many twentieth century figures.

23. The author uses which of the following methods to develop the second paragraph (lines 11–56)?

   A. A series of anecdotes depicting Cameron's energy and unconventionality
   B. A presentation of factual data demonstrating Cameron's importance in the history of photography
   C. A description of the author's personal acquaintance with Cameron
   D. A chronological account of Cameron's background and artistic growth

24. As it is used in the passage, *cumbersome* (line 48) most closely means:

   F. difficult to manage.
   G. expensive.
   H. intense.
   J. enjoyable.

25. When the author says that Cameron had found "her vocation" (line 52), his main point is that photography:

   A. offered Cameron an escape from the confines of conventional social life.
   B. became the main interest of her life.
   C. became her primary source of income.
   D. provided her with a way to express her religious beliefs.

26. The main point of the third paragraph is that Cameron:

   F. achieved great artistic success during her lifetime.
   G. is the greatest photographer who ever lived.
   H. was considered a more important artist during her lifetime than she is now.
   J. revolutionized photographic methods in the Victorian era.

27. According to the passage, the art of photography offered women artists more opportunities than did other art forms because it:

   A. did not require expensive materials.
   B. allowed the artist to use family and friends for subject matter.
   C. was nontraditional.
   D. required little artistic skill.

28. *The Five Foolish Virgins* and *Pray God, Bring Father Safely Home* are examples of:

   F. portraits of celebrated Victorians.
   G. allegorical subjects of the sort that were popular during the Victorian era.
   H. photographs in which Cameron sought to show a subject's outer likeness and inner greatness.
   J. photographs by Cameron that were scoffed at by her contemporaries.

GO ON TO THE NEXT PAGE

29. According to the passage, which of the following opinions of Cameron's work was held by Victorian critics but is NOT held by modern critics?

   A. Photographs should be based on poems.
   B. Her portraits are too sentimental.
   C. Narrative scenes are often in bad taste.
   D. Her allegorical pictures are her best work.

30. The author's treatment of Cameron's development as a photographer can best be described as:

   F. admiring.
   G. condescending.
   H. neutral.
   J. defensive.

PASSAGE IV

NATURAL SCIENCE

This passage discusses aspects of the harbor seal's sensory systems.

The harbor seal, *Phoca vitulina*, lives amphibiously along the northern Atlantic and Pacific coasts. This extraordinary mammal, which does most of its fishing at
(5) night when visibility is low and in places where noise levels are high, has developed several unique adaptations that have sharpened its acoustic and visual acuity. The need for such adaptations has been
(10) compounded by the varying behavior of sound and light in each of the two habitats of the harbor seal—land and water.

While the seal is on land, its ear operates much like the human ear, with sound waves
(15) traveling through air and entering the inner ear through the auditory canal. The directions from which sounds originate are distinguishable because the sound waves arrive at each inner ear at different times.
(20) In water, however, where sound waves travel faster than they do in air, the ability of the brain to differentiate arrival times between each ear is severely reduced. Yet it is crucial for the seal to be able to pinpoint the exact
(25) origins of sound in order to locate both its offspring and its prey. Therefore, the seal has developed an extremely sensitive quadraphonic hearing system, composed of a specialized band of tissue that extends
(30) down from the ear to the inner ear. In water, sound is conducted to the seal's inner ear by this special band of tissue, making it possible for the seal to identify the exact origins of sounds.

(35) The eye of the seal is also uniquely adapted to operate in both air and water. The human eye, adapted to function primarily in air, is equipped with a cornea, which aids in the refraction and focusing
(40) of light onto the retina. As a result, when a human eye is submerged in water, light rays are further refracted and the image is blurry. The seal's cornea, however, refracts light as water does. Therefore, in water, light
(45) rays are transmitted by the cornea without distortion and are clearly focused on the retina. In air, however, the cornea is astigmatic, resulting in a distortion of incoming light rays. The seal compensates for this by
(50) having a stenopaic pupil, which constricts into a vertical slit. Since the astigmatism is most pronounced in the horizontal plane of the eye, the vertical pupil serves to minimize its effect on the seal's vision.

(55) Since the harbor seal hunts for food under conditions of low visibility, some scientists believe it has echolocation systems akin to those of bats, porpoises, and dolphins. This kind of natural radar involves
(60) the emission of high-frequency sound pulses that reflect off obstacles such as predators, prey, or natural barriers. The reflections are received as sensory signals by the brain, which processes them into an image. The

(65) animal, blinded by unfavorable lighting conditions, is thus able to perceive its surroundings. Such echolocation by harbor seals is suggested by the fact that they emit "clicks," high-frequency sounds produced in
(70) short, fast bursts that occur mostly at night, when visibility is low.
   Finally, there is speculation that the seal's whiskers, or vibrissae, which are unusually well developed and highly
(75) sensitive to vibrations, act as additional sensory receptors. Scientists speculate that the vibrissae may sense wave disturbances produced by nearby moving fish, allowing the seal to home in on and capture prey.

31. The harbor seal's eye compensates for the distortion of light rays on land by means of its:
   A. vibrissae.
   B. cornea.
   C. stenopaic pupil.
   D. echolocation.

32. The passage implies that a harbor seal's vision is:
   F. inferior to a human's vision in the water, but superior to it on land.
   G. superior to a human's vision in the water, but inferior to it on land.
   H. inferior to a human's vision both in the water and on land.
   J. equivalent to a human's vision both in the water and on land.

33. According to the passage, scientists think vibrissae help harbor seals to catch prey by:
   A. improving underwater vision.
   B. sensing vibrations in the air.
   C. camouflaging predator seals.
   D. detecting underwater movement.

34. According to the passage, the speed of sound in water is:
   F. faster than the speed of sound in air.
   G. slower than the speed of sound in air.
   H. the same as the speed of sound in air.
   J. unable to be determined exactly.

35. According to the passage, which of the following have contributed to the harbor seal's need to adapt its visual and acoustic senses?
   I. Night hunting
   II. The need to operate in two habitats
   III. A noisy environment

   A. I and II only
   B. II and III only
   C. I and III only
   D. I, II, and III

36. Which of the following claims expresses the writer's opinion and not a fact?
   F. The human eye is adapted to function primarily in air.
   G. When the seal is on land, its ear operates like a human ear.
   H. The "clicks" emitted by the harbor seal mean it uses echolocation.
   J. The need for adaptation is increased if an animal lives in two habitats.

37. The passage suggests that the harbor seal lives in:
   A. cold ocean waters with accessible coasts.
   B. all areas with abundant fish populations.
   C. most island and coastal regions.
   D. warm coastlines with exceptionally clear waters.

38. According to the passage, a special band of tissue extending from the ear to the inner ear enables the harbor seal to:

    F. make its distinctive "clicking" sounds.
    G. find prey by echolocation.
    H. breathe underwater.
    J. determine where a sound originated.

39. The author compares harbor seal sensory organs to human sensory organs primarily in order to:

    A. point out similarities among mammals.
    B. explain how the seal's sensory organs function.
    C. prove that seals are more adaptively successful than humans.
    D. prove that humans are better adapted to their environment than seals.

40. According to the passage, one way in which seals differ from humans is:

    F. that sound waves enter a seal's inner ear through the auditory canal.
    G. the degree to which their corneas refract light.
    H. that seal's eyes focus light rays on the retina.
    J. that seals have adapted to live in a certain environment.

SCIENCE TEST

45 Minutes—40 Questions

Directions: There are several passages in this test. Each passage is followed by several questions. After reading a passage, choose the best answer to each question and fill in the corresponding oval on your Answer Grid. You may refer to the passages as often as necessary. You are NOT permitted to use a calculator on this test.

PASSAGE I

The following table contains some physical properties of common optical materials. The refractive index of a material is a measure of the amount by which light is bent upon entering the material. The transmittance range is the range of wavelengths over which the material is transparent.

Table 1

Physical Properties of Optical Materials				
Material	Refractive index for light of 0.589 µm	Transmittance range (µm)	Useful range for prisms (µm)	Chemical resistance
Lithium fluoride	1.39	0.12–6	2.7–5.5	Poor
Calcium fluoride	1.43	0.12–12	5–9.4	Good
Sodium chloride	1.54	0.3–17	8–16	Poor
Quartz	1.54	0.20–3.3	0.20–2.7	Excellent
Potassium bromide	1.56	0.3–29	15–28	Poor
Flint glass*	1.66	0.35–2.2	0.35–2	Excellent
Cesium iodide	1.79	0.3–70	15–55	Poor

*Flint glass is lead oxide–doped quartz.

1. According to the table, which material(s) will transmit light at 25 µm?

   A. Potassium bromide only
   B. Potassium bromide and cesium iodide
   C. Lithium fluoride and cesium iodide
   D. Lithium fluoride and flint glass

2. A scientist hypothesizes that any material with poor chemical resistance would have a transmittance range wider than 10 µm. The properties of which of the following materials contradicts this hypothesis?

   F. Lithium fluoride
   G. Flint glass
   H. Cesium iodide
   J. Quartz

3. When light travels from one medium to another, total internal reflection can occur if the first medium has a higher refractive index than the second. Total internal reflection could occur if light were traveling from:

   A. lithium fluoride to flint glass.
   B. potassium bromide to cesium iodide.
   C. quartz to potassium bromide.
   D. flint glass to calcium fluoride.

4. Based on the information in the table, how is the transmittance range related to the useful prism range?

   F. The transmittance range is always narrower than the useful prism range.
   G. The transmittance range is narrower than or equal to the useful prism range.
   H. The transmittance range increases as the useful prism range decreases.
   J. The transmittance range is wider than and includes within it the useful prism range.

5. The addition of lead oxide to pure quartz has the effect of:

   A. decreasing the transmittance range and the refractive index.
   B. decreasing the transmittance range and increasing the refractive index.
   C. increasing the transmittance range and the useful prism range.
   D. increasing the transmittance range and decreasing the useful prism range.

6. Which of the following materials would provide the greatest range of transmittance as well as the greatest useful range for prisms?

   F. Lithium fluoride
   G. Sodium chloride
   H. Quartz
   J. Flint glass

PASSAGE II

Osmosis is the diffusion of a solvent (often water) across a semipermeable membrane from the side of the membrane with a lower concentration of dissolved material to the side with a higher concentration of dissolved material. The result of osmosis is an equilibrium—an even distribution—on both sides of the membrane. In order to prevent osmosis, external pressure must be applied to the side with the higher concentration of dissolved material. *Osmotic pressure* is the external pressure required to prevent osmosis. The apparatus shown was used to measure osmotic pressure in the following experiments.

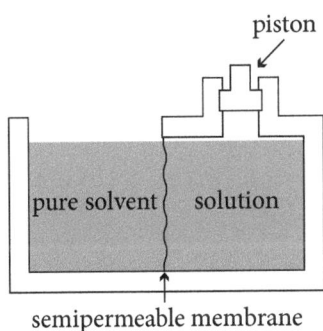

EXPERIMENT 1

Aqueous (water-based) solutions containing different concentrations of sucrose were placed in the closed side of the apparatus. The open side was filled with water. The sucrose solutions also contained a blue dye that binds to sucrose. The osmotic pressure created by the piston was measured for each solution at various temperatures. The results are given in Table 1.

Table 1

Concentration of sucrose solution (mol/L)	Temperature (K)	Osmotic pressure (atm)
1.00	298.0	24.47
0.50	298.0	12.23
0.10	298.0	2.45
0.05	298.0	1.22
1.00	348.0	28.57
0.50	348.0	14.29
0.10	348.0	2.86
0.05	348.0	1.43

EXPERIMENT 2

Sucrose solutions of four different organic solvents were investigated in the same manner as in Experiment 1 with all trials at 298 K. The results are shown in Table 2.

Table 2

Solvent	Concentration of sucrose solution (mol/L)	Osmotic pressure (atm)
Ethanol	0.50	12.23
Ethanol	0.10	2.45
Acetone	0.50	12.23
Acetone	0.10	2.45
Diethyl ether	0.50	12.23
Diethyl ether	0.10	2.45
Methanol	0.50	12.23
Methanol	0.10	2.45

7. Osmotic pressure can be calculated using the formula $\Pi = MRT$, where Π represents the calculated osmotic pressure, M = mol/L, R is a constant equal to 0.0821 and T is temperature in Kelvins. Which of the following can be inferred from the data in Table 1?

   I. In order to maintain osmotic pressure, temperature must stay constant.
   II. Temperature and volume must have an inverse relationship in order to maintain a constant osmotic pressure.
   III. Osmotic pressure will increase as volume and temperature increase.

   A. I only
   B. II only
   C. III only
   D. II and III only

8. According to the experimental results, osmotic pressure is dependent upon the:

   F. solvent and temperature only.
   G. solvent and concentration only.
   H. temperature and concentration only.
   J. solvent, temperature, and concentration.

9. According to Experiment 2, if methanol was used as a solvent, what pressure must be applied to a 0.5 mol/L solution of sucrose at 298 K to prevent osmosis?

   A. 1.23 atm
   B. 2.45 atm
   C. 12.23 atm
   D. 24.46 atm

GO ON TO THE NEXT PAGE

10. A 0.10 mol/L aqueous sucrose solution is separated from an equal volume of pure water by a semipermeable membrane. If the solution is at a pressure of 1 atm and a temperature of 298 K:

    F. water will diffuse across the semipermeable membrane from the sucrose solution side to the pure water side.
    G. water will diffuse across the semipermeable membrane from the pure water side to the sucrose solution side.
    H. water will not diffuse across the semipermeable membrane.
    J. water will diffuse across the semipermeable membrane, but the direction of diffusion cannot be determined.

11. In Experiment 1, the scientists investigated the effect of:

    A. solvent and concentration on osmotic pressure.
    B. volume and temperature on osmotic pressure.
    C. concentration and temperature on osmotic pressure.
    D. temperature on atmospheric pressure.

12. Which of the following conclusions can be drawn from the experimental results?

    I. Osmotic pressure is independent of the solvent used.
    II. Osmotic pressure is only dependent upon the temperature of the system.
    III. Osmosis occurs only when the osmotic pressure is exceeded.

    F. I only
    G. III only
    H. I and II only
    J. I and III only

13. What was the most likely purpose of the dye placed in the sucrose solutions in Experiments 1 and 2?

    A. The dye showed when osmosis was completed.
    B. The dye showed the presence of ions in the solutions.
    C. The dye was used to make the experiment more colorful.
    D. The dye was used to make the onset of osmosis visible.

PASSAGE III

A series of experiments was performed to study the environmental factors affecting the size and number of leaves on the *Cycas* plant.

EXPERIMENT 1

Five groups of 25 *Cycas* seedlings, all 2–3 cm tall, were allowed to grow for 3 months, each group at a different humidity level. All of the groups were kept at 75°F and received 9 hours of sunlight a day. The average leaf lengths, widths, and densities are given in Table 1.

Table 1

% Humidity	Average length (cm)	Average width (cm)	Average density* (leaves/cm)
15	5.6	1.6	0.13
35	7.1	1.8	0.25
55	9.8	2.0	0.56
75	14.6	2.6	0.61
95	7.5	1.7	0.52

*Number of leaves per 1 cm of plant stalk

EXPERIMENT 2

Five new groups of 25 seedlings, all 2–3 cm tall, were allowed to grow for three months, each group receiving different amounts of sunlight at a constant humidity of 55%. All other conditions were the same as in Experiment 1. The results are listed in Table 2.

Table 2

Sunlight (hrs/day)	Average length (cm)	Average width (cm)	Average density* (leaves/cm)
0	5.3	1.5	0.32
3	12.4	2.4	0.59
6	11.2	2.0	0.56
9	8.4	1.8	0.26
12	7.7	1.7	0.19

*Number of leaves per 1 cm of plant stalk

EXPERIMENT 3

Five new groups of 25 seedlings, all 2–3 cm tall, were allowed to grow at a constant humidity of 55% for three months at different daytime and nighttime temperatures. All other conditions were the same as in Experiment 1. The results are shown in Table 3.

Table 3

Day/night temperature (°F)	Average length (cm)	Average width (cm)	Average density* (leaves/cm)
85/85	6.8	1.5	0.28
85/65	12.3	2.1	0.53
65/85	8.1	1.7	0.33
75/75	7.1	1.9	0.45
65/65	8.3	1.7	0.39

*Number of leaves per 1 cm of plant stalk

14. Based on the data in Experiment 3, which day/night temperatures produced the smallest leaves?

   F. 85/85
   G. 85/65
   H. 75/75
   J. 65/85

15. Which of the following conclusions can be made based on the results of Experiment 2 alone?

   A. The seedlings do not require long daily periods of sunlight to grow.
   B. The average leaf density is independent of the humidity the seedlings receive.
   C. The seedlings need more water at night than during the day.
   D. The average length of the leaves increases as the amount of sunlight increases.

16. Seedlings grown at a 40% humidity level under the same conditions as in Experiment 1 would have average leaf widths closest to:

    F. 1.6 cm.
    G. 1.9 cm.
    H. 2.2 cm.
    J. 2.5 cm.

17. According to the experimental results, under which set of conditions would a *Cycas* seedling be most likely to produce the largest leaves?

    A. 95% humidity and 3 hours of sunlight
    B. 75% humidity and 3 hours of sunlight
    C. 95% humidity and 6 hours of sunlight
    D. 75% humidity and 6 hours of sunlight

18. Which variable remained constant throughout all of the experiments?

    F. The number of seedling groups
    G. The percent of humidity
    H. The daytime temperature
    J. The nighttime temperature

19. It was assumed in the design of the three experiments that all of the *Cycas* seedlings were:

    A. more than 5 cm tall.
    B. equally capable of germinating.
    C. equally capable of producing flowers.
    D. equally capable of further growth.

20. As a continuation of the three experiments listed, it would be most appropriate to next investigate:

    F. how many leaves over 6.0 cm long there are on each plant.
    G. which animals consume *Cycas* seedlings.
    H. how the mineral content of the soil affects the leaf size and density.
    J. what time of year the seedlings have the darkest coloring.

PASSAGE IV

The resistance (*R*) of a conductor is the extent to which it opposes the flow of electricity. Resistance depends not only on the conductor's resistivity (ρ) but also on the conductor's length (*L*) and cross-sectional area (*A*). The resistivity of a conductor is a physical property of the material that varies with temperature.

A research team designing a new appliance was researching the best type of wire to use in a particular circuit. The most important consideration was the wire's resistance. The team studied the resistance of wires made from four metals—gold (Au), aluminum (Al), tungsten (W), and iron (Fe). Two lengths and two gauges (diameters) of each type of wire were tested at 20°C. The results are recorded in the following table.

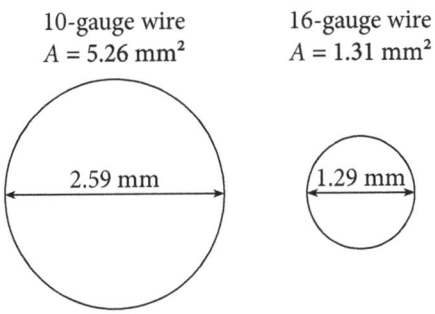

Note: area of circle = πr^2

Table 1

Material	Resistivity (mV–cm)	Length (cm)	Cross-sectional area (mm²)	Resistance (mV)
Au	2.44	1.0	5.26	46.4
Au	2.44	1.0	1.31	186.0
Au	2.44	2.0	5.26	92.8
Au	2.44	2.0	1.31	372.0
Al	2.83	1.0	5.26	53.8
Al	2.83	1.0	1.31	216.0
Al	2.83	2.0	5.26	107.6
Al	2.83	2.0	1.31	432.0
W	5.51	1.0	5.26	105.0
W	5.51	1.0	1.31	421.0
W	5.51	2.0	5.26	210.0
W	5.51	2.0	1.31	842.0
Fe	10.00	1.0	5.26	190.0
Fe	10.00	1.0	1.31	764.0
Fe	10.00	2.0	5.26	380.0
Fe	10.00	2.0	1.31	1,528.0

21. Of the wires tested, resistance increases for any given material as which parameter is decreased?

   A. Length
   B. Cross-sectional area
   C. Resistivity
   D. Gauge

22. Given the data in the table, which of the following best expresses resistance in terms of resistivity (ρ), cross-sectional area (A), and length (L)?

   F. $\dfrac{\rho^A}{L}$

   G. $\dfrac{\rho^L}{A}$

   H. $\rho A L$

   J. $\dfrac{AL}{\rho}$

23. Which of the following wires would have the highest resistance?

   A. A 1-cm aluminum wire with a cross-sectional area of 0.33 mm²
   B. A 2-cm aluminum wire with a cross-sectional area of 0.33 mm²
   C. A 1-cm tungsten wire with a cross-sectional area of 0.33 mm²
   D. A 2-cm tungsten wire with a cross-sectional area of 0.33 mm²

24. According to the information given, which of the following statements is (are) correct?

   I. 10-gauge wire has a larger diameter than 16-gauge wire.
   II. Gold has a higher resistivity than tungsten.
   III. Aluminum conducts electricity better than iron.

   F. I only
   G. II only
   H. III only
   J. I and III only

GO ON TO THE NEXT PAGE

25. Which of the following graphs best represents the relationship between the resistivity of a tungsten wire and its length?

A.
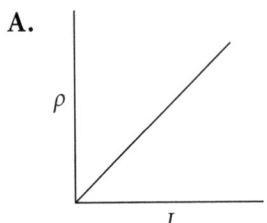

B.
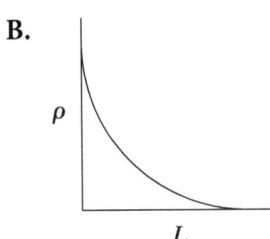

C.
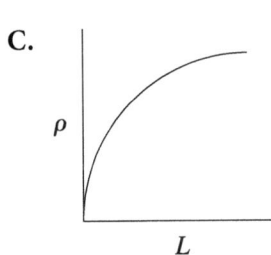

D.
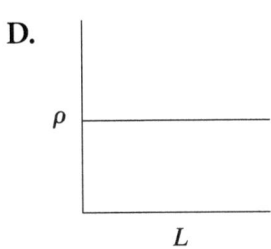

26. If the length of the wires were increased to 4 cm, what could be expected in terms of resistance?

F. Resistance would increase, but only with a 10 gauge wire.
G. Resistance would decrease, but only with a 16 gauge wire.
H. Resistance would not change because 2 cm is the maximum length that affects resistance.
J. Resistance would increase on both the 10 and 16 gauge wires.

PASSAGE V

How does evolution occur? Two views are presented here.

SCIENTIST 1

Evolution occurs by natural selection. Random mutations are continually occurring in a species as it propagates. A number of these mutations result in traits that help the species adapt to environmental changes. Because these mutant traits are advantageous, the members of the species who possess them tend to survive and pass on their genes more often than those who do not have these traits. Therefore, the percentage of the population with an advantageous trait increases over time. Long necks evolved in giraffes by natural selection. The ancestors of giraffes had necks of various sizes; however, their average neck length was much shorter than the average neck length of modern-day giraffes. Since the food supply was limited, the individuals with necks on the long range of the spectrum had access to more food (the leaves of trees) and therefore were more likely to survive and pass on their traits than individuals with shorter necks. Therefore, the proportion of the individuals with long necks was slightly greater in each subsequent generation.

SCIENTIST 2

Evolution occurs by the inheritance of acquired characteristics. Characteristics that are acquired by an individual member of a species during its lifetime are passed on to its offspring. Therefore, each generation's traits are partially accounted for by all the changes that occurred in the individuals of the previous generation. This includes changes that occurred as a result of accidents, changes in the environment, overuse of muscles, etc. The evolution of long necks of giraffes is an example. Ancestors of giraffes had short necks and consequently had to stretch their necks to reach the leaves of trees that were their main source of food. This repeated stretching of their necks caused them to elongate

GO ON TO THE NEXT PAGE

slightly. This trait was passed on, so that the individuals of the next generation had slightly longer necks. Each subsequent generation also stretched their necks to feed; therefore, each generation had slightly longer necks than the previous generation.

27. Both scientists agree that:

    A. the environment affects evolution.
    B. the individuals of a generation have identical traits.
    C. acquired characteristics are inherited.
    D. random mutations occur.

28. How would the two hypotheses be affected if it were found that all of the offspring of an individual with a missing leg due to an accident were born with a missing leg?

    F. It would support Scientist 1's hypothesis, because it is an example of random mutations occurring within a species.
    G. It would refute Scientist 1's hypothesis, because it is an example of random mutations occurring within a species.
    H. It would support Scientist 2's hypothesis, because it is an example of an acquired characteristic being passed on to the next generation.
    J. It would support Scientist 2's hypothesis, because it is an example of random mutations occurring within a species.

29. Which of the following characteristics can be inherited according to Scientist 2?

    I. Fur color
    II. Bodily scars resulting from a fight with another animal
    III. Poor vision

    A. I only
    B. II only
    C. I and III only
    D. I, II, and III

30. Scientist 1 believes that the evolution of the long neck of the giraffe:

    F. is an advantageous trait that resulted from overuse of neck muscles over many generations.
    G. is an advantageous trait that resulted from a random mutation.
    H. is an advantageous trait that resulted from a mutation that occurred in response to a change in the environment.
    J. is a disadvantageous trait that resulted from a random mutation.

31. The fundamental point of disagreement between the two scientists is whether:

    A. giraffes' ancestors had short necks.
    B. evolved traits come from random mutations or from the previous generation.
    C. the environment affects the evolution of a species.
    D. the extinction of a species could be the result of random mutations.

32. Suppose evidence was found that suggested that before the discovery of fire, human skin lacked the nerve endings necessary to detect extreme heat. Which of the following pieces of information, if true, would most seriously weaken the hypothesis of Scientist 2?

   F. Human skin is capable of generating nerve endings with new functions during life.
   G. The total number of nerve endings in the skin of a human is determined at birth and remains constant until death.
   H. An excess of nerve endings that are sensitive to extreme heat is a relatively common human mutation.
   J. No evidence exists to suggest that an excess of nerve endings that are sensitive to heat could be acquired through mutation.

33. The average height of a full-grown person today is significantly greater than was the average height of a full-grown person 1,000 years ago. If it was proven that the increase in average height was due only to evolutionary changes, how would Scientist 1 most likely explain this increase?

   A. People genetically prone to growing taller have been more likely to produce offspring over the last 1,000 years.
   B. Over the last 1,000 years, improvements in nutrition and medicine have led to greater average growth over a person's lifetime, and this growth has been passed from one generation to the next.
   C. Increased height is not a trait that can be acquired through mutation.
   D. Measurements of average height were less accurate 1,000 years ago than they are today.

PASSAGE VI

Bovine spongiform encephalopathy (BSE) is caused by the spread of a misfolded protein that eventually kills infected cattle. BSE is diagnosed postmortem from the diseased cavities that appear in brain tissue and is associated with the use in cattle feed of ground-up meat from scrapie-infected sheep. A series of experiments was performed to determine the mode of transmission of BSE. The results of both experiments are provided in Table 1.

EXPERIMENT 1

Sixty healthy cows were divided into two equal groups. Group A's feed included meat from scrapie-free sheep; and Group B's feed included meat from scrapie-infected sheep. Eighteen months later, the two groups were slaughtered and their brains examined for BSE cavities.

EXPERIMENT 2

Researchers injected ground-up sheep brains directly into the brains of two groups of 30 healthy cows. The cows in Group C received brains from scrapie-free sheep. The cows in Group D received brains from scrapie-infected sheep. Eighteen months later, both groups were slaughtered and their brains examined for diseased cavities.

Table 1

Group	Mode of transmission	Scrapie present	Number of cows infected with BSE*
A	feed	no	1
B	feed	yes	12
C	injection	no	0
D	injection	yes	3

*As determined visually by presence/absence of spongiform encephalopathy

34. Based on the information provided in Table 1, a cow is at greatest risk for contracting BSE if the cow:

    F. consumes meat from scrapie-free sheep.
    G. consumes meat from scrapie-infected sheep.
    H. is injected with ground-up sheep brains from scrapie-free sheep.
    J. is injected with ground-up sheep brains from scrapie-infected sheep.

35. Which of the following hypotheses was investigated in Experiment 1?

    A. The injection of scrapie-infected sheep brains into cows' brains causes BSE.
    B. The ingestion of wild grasses causes BSE.
    C. The ingestion of scrapie-infected sheep meat causes scrapie.
    D. The ingestion of scrapie-infected sheep meat causes BSE.

36. What is the purpose of Experiment 2?

    F. To determine whether BSE can be transmitted by injection
    G. To determine whether BSE can be transmitted by ingestion
    H. To determine whether ingestion or injection is the primary mode of BSE transmission
    J. To determine the healthiest diet for cows

37. Which of the following assumptions is made by the researchers in Experiments 1 and 2?

    A. Cows do not suffer from scrapie.
    B. A year and a half is a sufficient amount of time for BSE to develop in a cow.
    C. Cows and sheep suffer from the same diseases.
    D. Cows that eat scrapie-free sheep meat will not develop BSE.

38. A researcher wishes to determine whether BSE can be transmitted through scrapie-infected goats. Which of the following experiments would best test this?

    F. Repeating Experiment 1, using a mixture of sheep and goat meat in Group C's feed
    G. Repeating Experiments 1 and 2, replacing sheep with healthy goats
    H. Repeating Experiments 1 and 2, replacing healthy sheep with healthy goats and scrapie-infected sheep with scrapie-infected goats
    J. Repeating Experiment 2, replacing healthy cows with healthy goats

39. What is the control group in Experiment 1?

    A. Group A
    B. Group B
    C. Group C
    D. Group D

40. Which of the following conclusions can be drawn based on the results of the experiments?

    I. Cows that are exposed to scrapie-infected sheep are more likely to develop BSE than cows that are not.
    II. BSE is only transmitted by eating scrapie-infected sheep meat.
    III. A cow that eats scrapie-infected sheep meat is more likely to develop BSE than a cow that is injected with scrapie-infected sheep brains.

    F. II only
    G. III only
    H. I and III only
    J. II and III only

WRITING TEST

40 Minutes—1 Question

Directions: This is a test of your writing skills. You will have forty (40) minutes to write an essay in English. Before you begin planning and writing your essay, read the writing prompt carefully to understand exactly what you are being asked to do. Your essay will be evaluated on the evidence it provides of your ability to do the following:

- Express judgments by evaluating the three perspectives given in the prompt, taking a position on an issue, and explaining the relationship among all four ideas
- Develop a position by using logical reasoning and by supporting your ideas
- Maintain a focus on the topic throughout the essay
- Organize ideas in a logical way
- Use language clearly and effectively according to the conventions of standard written English

You may use a separate piece of paper to plan your essay. *You must write your essay in pencil on the lined pages provided after the prompt.* Your writing on those lined pages will be scored. You may not need all the lined pages, but to ensure you have enough room to finish, do NOT skip lines. You may write corrections or additions neatly between the lines of your essay, but do NOT write in the margins of the lined pages. *Illegible essays cannot be scored, so you must write (or print) clearly.*

DO NOT OPEN THIS BOOKLET UNTIL TOLD TO DO SO.

CAREER READINESS PROGRAMS

High school curricula are designed to ready students for future career paths, many of which include higher education. Whether or not students choose to attend college, a comprehensive high school education provides an essential foundation. Some educators argue that high schools have an obligation to provide career readiness training for students who do not intend to pursue a college degree. Should high schools invest time and money to develop programs for students who do not wish to continue their education beyond 12th grade? Given the many factors that students weigh when considering if, where, and when to attend college, it is prudent for educators to explore programs that contribute to a better-skilled workforce.

Read and carefully consider these perspectives. Each offers suggestions regarding high school–based career readiness programs.

Perspective One	Perspective Two	Perspective Three
Rather than concentrating solely on students who may not pursue higher education, high schools should help all students develop valuable skills for the workforce. Requiring students to complete classes that focus on key cognitive strategies, content knowledge, and relevant skills and techniques will help them enter the workforce, either immediately after high school or later in their lives.	Career-readiness training should be provided for students who do not wish to pursue college, and it should be particularly targeted at students who are at risk for dropping out. When their high school experience is reframed as training for successful careers rather than government-mandated learning, students can succeed where they may previously have failed.	Students who do not want to pursue higher education should not be given additional accommodations in high school, because they should not be provided any incentives to not attend college. College is the best way to learn how to be productive in the workforce, and students should be encouraged to attend since it is in their best interest.

ESSAY TASK

Write a unified, coherent essay in which you evaluate multiple perspectives on high school–based career readiness programs. In your essay, be sure to:

- analyze and evaluate the perspectives given
- state and develop your own perspective on the issue
- explain the relationship between your perspective and those given

Your perspective may be in full agreement with any of the others, in partial agreement, or wholly different. Whatever the case, support your ideas with logical reasoning and detailed, persuasive examples.

PLANNING YOUR ESSAY

You may wish to consider the following as you think critically about the task:

Strengths and weaknesses of the three given perspectives
- What insights do they offer, and what do they fail to consider?
- Why might they be persuasive to others, or why might they fail to persuade?

Your own knowledge, experience, and values
- What is your perspective on this issue, and what are its strengths and weaknesses?
- How will you support your perspective in your essay?

IF YOU FINISH BEFORE TIME IS CALLED, YOU MAY CHECK YOUR WORK ON THIS SECTION ONLY. DO NOT TURN TO ANY OTHER SECTION IN THE TEST.

STOP

Practice Test
ANSWER KEY

ENGLISH TEST

1. C	11. C	21. B	31. D	41. D	51. D	61. D	70. F
2. F	12. G	22. G	32. H	42. J	52. J	62. J	71. D
3. D	13. B	23. D	33. A	43. B	53. C	63. C	72. G
4. F	14. H	24. J	34. H	44. G	54. H	64. J	73. B
5. D	15. C	25. C	35. D	45. C	55. D	65. D	74. F
6. G	16. H	26. F	36. G	46. F	56. G	66. J	75. B
7. B	17. B	27. A	37. D	47. B	57. A	67. B	
8. J	18. G	28. J	38. G	48. H	58. H	68. F	
9. A	19. A	29. B	39. D	49. C	59. D	69. D	
10. J	20. J	30. G	40. J	50. H	60. H		

MATHEMATICS TEST

1. D	9. E	17. B	25. D	33. A	41. B	49. E	57. C
2. J	10. K	18. H	26. G	34. K	42. H	50. K	58. H
3. B	11. D	19. B	27. C	35. A	43. C	51. E	59. D
4. K	12. H	20. H	28. H	36. J	44. K	52. K	60. J
5. C	13. C	21. E	29. B	37. A	45. A	53. B	
6. K	14. H	22. H	30. K	38. G	46. G	54. G	
7. B	15. C	23. D	31. C	39. C	47. E	55. D	
8. K	16. G	24. F	32. H	40. G	48. G	56. K	

READING TEST

1. C	6. H	11. B	16. J	21. B	26. F	31. C	36. H
2. G	7. C	12. H	17. B	22. F	27. C	32. G	37. A
3. B	8. G	13. B	18. H	23. D	28. G	33. D	38. J
4. F	9. B	14. F	19. B	24. F	29. D	34. F	39. B
5. D	10. H	15. C	20. H	25. B	30. F	35. D	40. G

SCIENCE TEST

1. B	6. G	11. C	16. G	21. B	26. J	31. B	36. F
2. F	7. D	12. F	17. B	22. G	27. A	32. G	37. B
3. D	8. H	13. D	18. F	23. D	28. H	33. A	38. H
4. J	9. C	14. F	19. D	24. J	29. D	34. G	39. A
5. B	10. G	15. A	20. H	25. D	30. G	35. D	40. G

ANSWERS AND EXPLANATIONS

ENGLISH TEST

PASSAGE I

1. C
Category: Punctuation
Difficulty: Medium
Getting to the Answer: Choice (C) is the correct and most concise answer choice. Choice A uses an unnecessary comma. Choice B is unnecessarily wordy. Choice D is redundant—if the societies created the legends, there is no need to describe the legends as "original."

2. F
Category: Writing Strategy
Difficulty: High
Getting to the Answer: The question stem gives an important clue to the best answer: The purpose of the inserted sentence is "to describe the different kinds" of stories. Choice (F) is the only choice that does this. Choice G explains how the stories were told. Choice H explains why more is not known about the stories. Choice J describes the length of some stories.

3. D
Category: Connections
Difficulty: Medium
Getting to the Answer: Choices A, B, and C create run-on sentences. Choice (D) describes a relationship that makes sense between our "many more permanent ways of handing down our beliefs" and the fact that "we continue to create and tell legends." It also creates a complete sentence.

4. F
Category: Verb Tenses
Difficulty: Low
Getting to the Answer: Choices H and J are ungrammatical after a colon. Choice G is unnecessarily wordy.

5. D
Category: Wordiness
Difficulty: Medium
Getting to the Answer: Choices A, B, and C are redundant or unnecessarily wordy. Because the contrasting word *but* is already used, *however* is repetitive and should be eliminated.

6. G
Category: Wordiness
Difficulty: Low
Getting to the Answer: Choices F, H, and J are all redundant. The word *conclusion* is unnecessary because the word *ending* has already been used.

7. B
Category: Verb Tenses
Difficulty: Medium
Getting to the Answer: Choice (B) is the only choice that is consistent with the verb tense established by *knew* and *decided*.

8. J
Category: Verb Tenses
Difficulty: Medium
Getting to the Answer: Choice F creates a run-on sentence and also makes it seem that the hunter, not the deer, "was only temporarily knocked unconscious by the car." Choices G and H use incorrect verb tenses.

9. A
Category: Punctuation
Difficulty: High
Getting to the Answer: Choice B is incorrect because the words preceding the semicolon could not be a complete sentence on their own. Choice C would create a sentence fragment. Choice D would create a run-on sentence.

10. J
Category: Wordiness
Difficulty: Medium
Getting to the Answer: Regardless of the sequence of the words, the information provided in F, G, and H is irrelevant to the passage's topic of urban legends.

11. C
Category: Verb Tenses
Difficulty: Medium
Getting to the Answer: The subject of the sentence is *One*, so the verb must be singular. Choices B and D use incorrect verb tenses.

12. G
Category: Word Choice
Difficulty: Low
Getting to the Answer: Choice F creates a sentence that does not make sense. Choices H and J use the plural *women* instead of the singular *woman*.

13. B
Category: Sentence Sense
Difficulty: Medium
Getting to the Answer: Choice (B) most clearly expresses the idea that several websites research "the validity of commonly told urban legends." Because this information is relevant to the topic of urban legends, "OMIT the underlined portion" is not the best answer.

14. H
Category: Writing Strategy
Difficulty: High
Getting to the Answer: Paragraph 4 describes an urban legend that is "humorous in nature." Paragraph 5 describes a rather frightening legend: alligators living underneath the city in the sewer system. The sentence "Other urban legends seem to be designed to instill fear" is an appropriate topic sentence for paragraph 5, and it also serves as a needed transition between paragraph 4 and paragraph 5.

15. C
Category: Writing Strategy
Difficulty: Medium
Getting to the Answer: Although paragraph 1 provides *some* general information about the purpose and topics of the myths and legends of primitive societies, no specifics are given. This makes (C) the best answer.

PASSAGE II

16. H
Category: Verb Tenses
Difficulty: Medium
Getting to the Answer: Correct choices here could be *do you* or *does one*. The latter appears in (H).

17. B
Category: Punctuation
Difficulty: Medium
Getting to the Answer: Choice A incorrectly uses a colon. Choices C and D are grammatically incorrect.

18. G
Category: Wordiness
Difficulty: Medium
Getting to the Answer: *Solitary* and *alone* are redundant in the same sentence. Choices H and J also have redundancy.

19. A
Category: Word Choice
Difficulty: Low
Getting to the Answer: The underlined portion is clearest the way it is written.

20. J
Category: Punctuation
Difficulty: Medium
Getting to the Answer: The colon is incorrect, so eliminate F and H. Because this sentence is a compound sentence, a comma is needed before *and*.

21. B
Category: Sentence Sense
Difficulty: Medium
Getting to the Answer: *In fact* is nonessential—it should be set off by commas.

22. G
Category: Word Choice
Difficulty: Medium
Getting to the Answer: *American* (an adjective) is the word being modified. Therefore, the adverb form of *unique—uniquely—* is needed.

23. D
Category: Sentence Sense
Difficulty: Low
Getting to the Answer: "Near Walden Pond..." is a long sentence fragment. The best way to fix the error is to simply combine the sentences by eliminating the period.

24. J
Category: Sentence Sense
Difficulty: Medium
Getting to the Answer: This paragraph and the ones that immediately follow outline Thoreau's life. His influence on the people of today is not discussed until the end of the essay. Therefore, the underlined sentence does not belong here.

25. C
Category: Organization
Difficulty: High
Getting to the Answer: Sentence 3 logically follows sentence 1. Choice (C) is the only choice that lists this correct order.

26. F
Category: Punctuation
Difficulty: Medium
Getting to the Answer: There is one independent clause on each side of the semicolon, so the sentence is punctuated correctly. Choice G would need *and* after the comma to be correct. Choices H and J create run-on sentences.

27. A
Category: Word Choice
Difficulty: Low
Getting to the Answer: A possessive pronoun is needed because the works belong to Thoreau. Eliminate B and D. Choice C relates to more than one person, so it is incorrect as well.

28. J
Category: Writing Strategy
Difficulty: Medium
Getting to the Answer: This paragraph discusses Thoreau's impact on modern society; only (J) expresses the correct topic.

29. B
Category: Wordiness
Difficulty: Medium
Getting to the Answer: Choices A, C, and D are excessively wordy.

30. G
Category: Writing Strategy
Difficulty: High
Getting to the Answer: The use of questions prompts a reader to think about the answers to those questions. Choice F is too literal, and J is too broad for the topic of the essay. Choice H is incorrect because the author establishes the quality of Thoreau's work.

PASSAGE III

31. D
Category: Wordiness
Difficulty: Medium
Getting to the Answer: Because the word *live* is used later in the sentence, A, B, and C contain redundant information.

32. H
Category: Word Choice
Difficulty: Low
Getting to the Answer: In this sentence, the *its* must be possessive because the "unique anatomy" belongs to the sloth. The word describing *anatomy* must be an adjective, not an adverb.

33. A
Category: Punctuation
Difficulty: Medium
Getting to the Answer: The comma is correctly used in (A) to separate the nonessential descriptive phrase "about the size of a large domestic cat" from the rest of the sentence.

34. H
Category: Sentence Sense
Difficulty: Medium
Getting to the Answer: The information about the sloth's limbs is relevant to the topic, so it should not be omitted. Choice (H) clearly and directly expresses how the sloth's muscles are designed to allow this animal to cling to things.

35. D
Category: Word Choice
Difficulty: Medium
Getting to the Answer: *Adapted* needs to be modified by an adverb, so (D) is the best choice.

36. G
Category: Connections
Difficulty: Medium
Getting to the Answer: *Instead* describes the right relationship between the two sentences. The pronouns must be consistent, and because *its* is already used in the sentence, (G) is the best choice.

37. D
Category: Connections
Difficulty: Low
Getting to the Answer: Choice (D) is the only choice that correctly establishes the relationship between the sloth's inability to "move swiftly on the ground" and its ability to swim.

38. G
Category: Writing Strategy
Difficulty: High
Getting to the Answer: Choice (G) connects the sloth's unique characteristics discussed in paragraph 3 with the description of its flexibility in paragraph 4.

39. D
Category: Punctuation
Difficulty: Medium
Getting to the Answer: Choice (D) correctly uses the second comma necessary to separate the phrase "without moving the rest of its body" from the rest of the sentence. Choice C can be eliminated because it is unnecessarily wordy.

40. J
Category: Verb Tenses
Difficulty: Medium
Getting to the Answer: Choice (J) is the only choice that contains a verb tense consistent with the sentence.

41. D
Category: Wordiness
Difficulty: Low
Getting to the Answer: Choices A, B, and C contain redundant information.

42. J
Category: Wordiness
Difficulty: Medium
Getting to the Answer: This information about the howler monkey is irrelevant to the topic of the passage.

43. B
Category: Sentence Sense
Difficulty: Medium
Getting to the Answer: Choice A creates a sentence fragment. Choice C is unnecessarily wordy and awkward. Choice D creates a run-on sentence.

44. G
Category: Writing Strategy
Difficulty: Medium
Getting to the Answer: The last sentence aptly concludes the entire passage, and removing it would make the ending more abrupt.

45. C
Category: Organization
Difficulty: High
Getting to the Answer: The description of the sloth's "camouflage" is in paragraph 5.

PASSAGE IV

46. F
Category: Verb Tenses
Difficulty: Medium
Getting to the Answer: The underlined portion is best left as is. The other answer choices make the sentence unnecessarily wordy.

47. B
Category: Verb Tenses
Difficulty: Low
Getting to the Answer: The verb tense must agree with the tense that has been established up to this point. The passage is in the past tense, so (B) is correct.

48. H
Category: Verb Tenses
Difficulty: Medium
Getting to the Answer: As with the answer to the previous question, the simple past tense is correct.

49. C
Difficulty: Medium
Category: Verb Tenses
Getting to the Answer: Choice A creates a sentence fragment and uses an incorrect verb tense. Choice B also uses the wrong verb tense. Choice D incorrectly uses a semicolon, as the words preceding the semicolon do not constitute an independent clause.

50. H
Category: Sentence Sense
Difficulty: High
Getting to the Answer: In the context of the rest of the passage, only (H) makes sense. The firefighters' attempts to extinguish the flames failed; *only* nature could stop the fire with the first snowfall.

51. D
Category: Wordiness
Difficulty: Medium
Getting to the Answer: Choices A and B are unnecessarily wordy and awkward. Choice C creates a run-on sentence.

52. J
Category: Wordiness
Difficulty: Medium
Getting to the Answer: All of the other answer choices are unnecessarily wordy and/or repetitive.

53. C
Category: Verb Tenses
Difficulty: High
Getting to the Answer: From the plural verb *open*, you can determine that the best answer will contain *cones*. This makes (C) the only possible answer, as the apostrophe is incorrectly used in B.

54. H
Category: Connections
Difficulty: Medium
Getting to the Answer: This is the only choice that makes sense in the context of the passage. The sighting of the large animals near burning forests

is used as evidence that the animals of the region were "fire-tolerant and fire-adaptive."

55. D
Category: Punctuation
Difficulty: Medium
Getting to the Answer: The comma in A is unnecessary because the sentence has a list of only two examples, not three. The semicolon in B is incorrectly used because "and bedding down" does not begin an independent clause. The colon in C is incorrectly used because it is not being used to introduce or emphasize information.

56. G
Category: Sentence Sense
Difficulty: High
Getting to the Answer: The problem with "judging from recent pictures of the park" is that the phrase is modifying *forest*, and a forest obviously can't judge anything. The phrase would have been correct if the sentence had read "judging from the recent pictures of the park, I think that the forest was not destroyed." In this case, the phrase would modify *I*, the author, who is capable of judging. Choice (G) takes care of the problem by rewriting the sentence to eliminate the modifying phrase.

57. A
Category: Word Choice
Difficulty: Low
Getting to the Answer: The pronoun refers to *forest*.

58. H
Category: Writing Strategy
Difficulty: Medium
Getting to the Answer: The introduction of information about fires in Alaska is unwarranted, so F and G can be eliminated. Choice J is incorrect because the additional information would actually uphold the author's position as an authority.

59. D
Category: Writing Strategy
Difficulty: High
Getting to the Answer: The reports mentioned in (D) directly substantiate the author's claims much more than do any of the other answer choices.

PASSAGE V

60. H
Category: Verb Tenses
Difficulty: Medium
Getting to the Answer: Choice F creates a sentence fragment, and G incorrectly uses a plural verb with a singular subject. The verb tense of the paragraph makes (H) a better choice than J.

61. D
Category: Wordiness
Difficulty: Medium
Getting to the Answer: The final part of the sentence "…and there are many other rivers in America as well" is completely irrelevant to the rest of the sentence and the paragraph, in which the author discusses white-water rafting and the rivers she's rafted.

62. J
Category: Punctuation
Difficulty: Medium
Getting to the Answer: Choice F is wrong because *rapids* is essential information and should not be set off by commas. Choice G is wrong because what follows the colon is not an explanation. Choice H is incorrect because what follows the semicolon cannot stand alone as a sentence.

63. C
Category: Wordiness
Difficulty: Low
Getting to the Answer: Choices A and D create sentence fragments, and B is extremely awkward.

64. J
Category: Wordiness
Difficulty: Medium
Getting to the Answer: This sentence is irrelevant to the topic of the passage.

65. D
Category: Word Choice
Difficulty: Medium
Getting to the Answer: This sentence makes it sound as though the author were roaring, not the rapids; *roaring* is a misplaced modifier. Choice B doesn't fix the problem because the reader has no idea what *it* refers to. Choice C has *the boat* roaring. Choice (D) is the clearest choice.

66. J
Category: Sentence Sense
Difficulty: Medium
Getting to the Answer: Either the word *cover* must be in past tense, or the structure of the sentence must change. Choice (J) does the latter.

67. B
Category: Wordiness
Difficulty: Medium
Getting to the Answer: Choice (B) is the simplest, most concise way of expressing the idea. Replacing "and instead he adopted" with "with" and removing the comma make the sentence much less awkward.

68. F
Category: Word Choice
Difficulty: Low
Getting to the Answer: Choices G and J make it sound as though the author were in the water. Choice (F) expresses the idea more accurately than H does.

69. D
Category: Wordiness
Difficulty: High
Getting to the Answer: The phrase "and we stopped" is redundant because "we came to a jarring halt" says the same thing much more expressively. Omit the underlined portion.

70. F
Category: Word Choice
Difficulty: Low
Getting to the Answer: "It was" is fine here because the author is telling her story in the past tense. Choices G and H are in the present tense, and J incorrectly introduces the possessive form.

71. D
Category: Wordiness
Difficulty: Medium
Getting to the Answer: The other answer choices are unnecessarily wordy; the simplest choice, (D), is the best.

72. G
Category: Verb Tenses
Difficulty: Medium
Getting to the Answer: The participle *receiving* has to be changed into a verb in the past tense, *received*, in order to be consistent with *went*. Choice (G) is correct as opposed to H, because the number of bruises something has can be counted, necessitating *many* bruises, not *much* bruises.

73. B
Category: Writing Strategy
Difficulty: Medium
Getting to the Answer: Choice A wouldn't work as a concluding sentence because its style and tone are off; nowhere in the passage does the writer use language such as "brutal calamities" and "beguiling excitement." Also, the writer and her father were not "unwary rafters." Choice C contradicts the writer's main theme that nothing was as memorable as her first ride through the rapids. This is also a sentence fragment. The tone in D, "call me crazy or weird…," is much different from the writer's. Choice (B) closely matches the author's style and tone while restating the main theme of the passage.

74. F
Category: Writing Strategy
Difficulty: Medium
Getting to the Answer: This essay relates a personal experience of the writer: her first time rafting down a rapids. There is very little mention of the techniques of white-water rafting, so the essay would not meet the requirements of the assignment. Choice G is incorrect because the essay does not focus on the relationship between father and daughter but on their first rafting experience together.

75. B
Category: Organization
Difficulty: High
Getting to the Answer: The sentence foreshadows things to come, so it must appear toward the beginning of the essay. That eliminates C and D. The second paragraph is about the peaceful setting, so (B) is the most sensible answer.

MATHEMATICS TEST

1. D
Category: Proportions and Probability
Difficulty: Medium
Getting to the Answer: You know that 14 people are 20% of the total, and you need to find 100% of the total. You could set up an equation, or you could multiply 14 by 5, because 100% is 5 times as much as 20%. The number of people surveyed is 14×5, or 70.

2. J
Category: Proportions and Probability
Difficulty: Medium
Getting to the Answer: One safe way to answer this question is by Picking Numbers. For instance, if you let $x = 2$ and $y = 3$, the train would have traveled $90 \times 2 + 60 \times 3 = 360$ miles in 5 hours, or $\frac{360}{5} = 72$ miles per hour. If you then plug $x = 2$ and $y = 3$ into the answer choices, it's clear that the correct answer is (J). No other answer choice equals 72 when $x = 2$ and $y = 3$.

3. B
Category: Proportions and Probability
Difficulty: High
Getting to the Answer: If the ratio of men to women is 5:3, then the ratio of women to the total is $3:(3 + 5) = 3:8$. Because you know the total number of string players is 24, you can set up the equation $\frac{3}{8} = \frac{x}{24}$ to find that $x = 9$. Also, without setting up the proportion, you could note that the total number of players is 3 times the ratio total, so the number of women will be 3 times the part of the ratio that represents women.

4. K
Category: Variable Manipulation
Difficulty: Medium
Getting to the Answer: In a pinch, you could Backsolve on this question, but this one is fairly easy to solve algebraically:

$$x^2 - 3x = 6x$$
$$x^2 = 9x$$

Now you can divide both sides by x because $x \neq 0$:

$$\frac{x^2}{x} = \frac{9x}{x}$$
$$x = 9$$

5. C
Category: Patterns, Logic, and Data
Difficulty: Medium
Getting to the Answer: With visual perception problems such as this one, the key is to play around with possibilities as you try to draw a solution. Eventually, you should be able to come up with a picture like this:

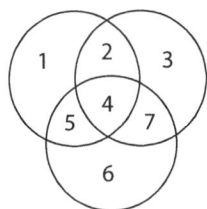

6. K
Category: Variable Manipulation
Difficulty: High
Getting to the Answer: This problem could be solved algebraically, but look at the answer choices. They are all simple numbers, making this a great opportunity for Backsolving. Begin with H.

Plugging in 0, you get:

$(0)^2 + 6(0) + 8 = 4 + 10(0)$

$8 = 4$

Because 8 does not equal 4, you know this isn't the correct answer. But it is difficult to know which answer to try next. Should you aim higher or lower? If you're unsure of which direction to go, just try whatever looks easiest. Choice J, 1, looks like a good candidate:

$(1)^2 + 6(1) + 8 = 4 + 10(1)$

$1 + 6 + 8 = 4 + 10$

$15 = 14$

So J doesn't work either, but it looks like the numbers are getting closer, so you're going in the right direction. Try (K) just to be sure.

$(2)^2 + 6(2) + 8 = 4 + 10(2)$

$4 + 12 + 8 = 4 + 20$

$24 = 24$

Choice (K) is the correct answer.

7. B
Category: Variable Manipulation
Difficulty: Medium
Getting to the Answer: Translate piece by piece:

"Nine less than c" indicates subtraction: $c - 9$.

"Nine less than c is the same as the number d": $c - 9 = d$. There's one equation. The answer is either (B) or C.

"d less than" also indicates subtraction: $- d$.

"d less than twice c is 20": $2c - d = 20$. There's the second equation.

Choice (B) matches what you found.

8. K
Category: Proportions and Probability
Difficulty: Medium
Getting to the Answer: To determine the total number of possible arrangements on a question like this one, simply determine the number of possibilities for each component and then multiply them together. There are three ways of serving the ice cream, five flavors, and four toppings. Therefore, there are $3 \times 5 \times 4 = 60$ ways to order ice cream, and (K) is correct.

9. E
Category: Proportions and Probability
Difficulty: High
Getting to the Answer: Backsolving is a great technique to use for this problem. Start with C. The director asked 1 out of 3 students to come to the second audition and $\frac{1}{3}$ of 48 is 16, so 16 students were invited to a second audition. Then 75% of 16, which is $\frac{3}{4}(16) = 12$ students, were offered parts. The question states that 18 students were offered parts, so you already know that C is too small. (You can also, thus, eliminate A and B.) Because

the director invited $\frac{1}{3}$ of the students to a second audition, the number of students at the first audition must be divisible by 3. (You can't have a fraction of a student.) That eliminates D, leaving only (E).

10. K
Category: Variable Manipulation
Difficulty: Medium
Getting to the Answer: Begin by translating the English into math: $x + 5x = -60$, $6x = -60$, so $x = -10$, and the two numbers are -10 and -50. Thus, the lesser number is -50.

By the way, this is where most people mess up. They forget that the lesser of two negative numbers is the negative number with the larger absolute value (because *less* means *to the left of* on the number line):

11. D
Category: Patterns, Logic, and Data
Difficulty: High
Getting to the Answer: You're looking for the total number of parallelograms that can be found among the triangles, and parallelograms could be formed two ways from these triangles, either from two adjacent triangles or from four adjacent triangles, like so:

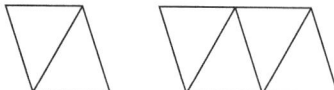

Begin by looking for the smaller parallelograms. If you look for parallelograms leaning in the same direction as the one we drew, you'll find 3. But there are two other possible orientations for the smaller parallelogram; it could be flipped horizontally, or it could be rotated 90 degrees so that one triangle sits atop the other in the form of a diamond; both of these orientations also have 3 parallelograms, for a total of 9 smaller parallelograms.

Now look for larger parallelograms. Perhaps the easiest way to count these is to look along the sides of the larger composite triangle. You should be able to spot 2 of the larger parallelograms along each side, one originating at each vertex, for a total of 6 larger parallelograms.

Thus, there are a total of $9 + 6 = 15$ parallelograms in all.

12. H
Category: Plane Geometry
Difficulty: Medium
Getting to the Answer: The square has a perimeter of 16 inches, so each side of the square is 4 inches; the area of the square is, therefore, 16 square inches. If the side of the square is 4 inches, then the diameter of the circle is also 4 inches. The radius of the circle is then 2 inches, making the area of the circle 4π square inches. The area of the shaded region is then $16 - 4\pi$ square inches.

13. C
Category: Number Properties
Difficulty: Medium
Getting to the Answer: The safest strategy is simply to list out the possibilities. It's also helpful to realize that multiples of both 4 and 6 are multiples of 12 (the least common multiple between the two), so skip over all multiples of 12:

4, 8, ~~12~~, 16, 20, ~~24~~, 28, 32, ~~36~~, 40, 44, ~~48~~

So there are 8 in all.

14. H
Category: Variable Manipulation
Difficulty: Medium
Getting to the Answer: Don't be intimidated by the expression $f(x)$. In this case, you should just plug in the number that appears in the parentheses for the x in the expression the question has given you. So, if $f(x) = (8 - 3x)(x^2 - 2x - 15)$, $f(3) = [8 - 3(3)][(3)^2 - 2(3) - 15]$.

Once you get to this point, just remember PEMDAS.

$[8 - 3(3)][(3)^2 - 2(3) - 15] = (8 - 9)(9 - 6 - 15) = (-1)(-12) = 12$, (H).

15. C
Category: Proportions and Probability
Difficulty: Medium
Getting to the Answer: A class contains five juniors and five seniors. If one member of the class is assigned at random to present a paper on a certain subject, and another member of the class is randomly assigned to assist him, then:
The probability that the first student picked will be a

$$\text{junior} = \frac{\text{\# of juniors}}{\text{Total \# of students}} = \frac{5}{10} = \frac{1}{2}.$$

Given that the first student picked was a junior, the probability that the second student picked will be a

$$\text{junior} = \frac{\text{\# of juniors remaining}}{\text{Total \# of students remaining}}.$$

So the probability that both students will be

$$\text{juniors} = \frac{1}{2} \times \frac{4}{9} = \frac{2}{9}.$$

16. G
Category: Plane Geometry
Difficulty: Medium
Getting to the Answer: Because the formula to find the area of a triangle is $\frac{1}{2}$(base)(height), you can plug in the base and area to find the height. You know that the area of this triangle is 45 units and that the base is $3 + 12 = 15$. Let x be the length of altitude $\overline{YS}$. Plug these into the area formula to get $45 = \frac{15x}{2}$. Solve for x to get $x = 6$.

17. B
Category: Coordinate Geometry
Difficulty: Medium
Getting to the Answer: The y-coordinate is the point at which the x value is zero, so plug $x = 0$ into the equation:

$$6y - 3(0) = 18$$
$$6y = 18$$
$$y = 3$$

18. H
Category: Variable Manipulation
Difficulty: High
Getting to the Answer: This question involves common quadratics, so the key is to write these quadratic expressions in their other forms. For instance, $x^2 - y^2 = 12$, so $(x + y)(x - y) = 12$. Because $x - y = 4$, $(x + y)(4) = 12$, so $x + y = 3$. Finally, $x^2 + 2xy + y^2 = (x + y)^2 = (3)^2 = 9$.

19. B
Category: Plane Geometry
Difficulty: High
Getting to the Answer: This shape must be divided into three simple shapes. By drawing two perpendicular line segments down from the endpoints of the side that is 10 units long, you are left with a 3 × 10 rectangle, a triangle with a base of 4 and a height of 3, and a triangle with a base of 7 and a hypotenuse of $7\sqrt{2}$. The rectangle has an area of 3 × 10 = 30 square units. The smaller triangle has an area of $\frac{4 \times 3}{2} = 6$ square units. The larger triangle is a 45°-45°-90° triangle, so the height must be 7. Therefore, it has an area of $\frac{7 \times 7}{2} = 24.5$ square units. The entire shape has an area of $6 + 30 + 24.5 = 60.5$ square units.

20. H
Category: Operations
Difficulty: High
Getting to the Answer: Although Backsolving is certainly possible with this problem, it's probably quicker to solve with arithmetic. The board is 12 feet long, which means it is $12 \times 12 = 144$ inches. The carpenter cuts off $3 \times 17 = 51$ inches. That leaves $144 - 51 = 93$ inches.

21. E
Category: Variable Manipulation
Difficulty: Low
Getting to the Answer: To answer this question, begin by setting the right side of the equation equal to zero:

$x^2 - 4x - 6 = 6$

$x^2 - 4x - 12 = 0$

Now use reverse-FOIL to factor the left side of the equation:

$(x - 6)(x + 2) = 0$

Thus, either $x - 6 = 0$ or $x + 2 = 0$, so $x = 6$ or -2.

22. H
Category: Variable Manipulation
Difficulty: Medium
Getting to the Answer: Here's another question that tests your understanding of FOIL, but you have to be careful. The question states that -3 is a possible solution for the equation $x^2 + kx - 15 = 0$, so in its factored form, one set of parentheses with a factor inside must be $(x + 3)$. Because the last term in the equation in its expanded form is -15, that means that the entire factored equation must read $(x + 3)(x - 5) = 0$, which in its expanded form is $x^2 - 2x - 15 = 0$. Thus, $k = -2$.

23. D
Category: Plane Geometry
Difficulty: Medium
Getting to the Answer: To solve this problem, you need to understand the triangle inequality theorem, which states: The sum of the lengths of any two sides of a triangle is always greater than the length of the third side. Therefore, the other sides of this triangle must add up to more than 7. You know from the problem that every side must be an integer. That means that the sides must add up to at least 8 inches (4 inches and 4 inches, or 7 inches and 1 inch, for example). The smallest possible perimeter is $7 + 8 = 15$.

24. F
Category: Trigonometry
Difficulty: Medium
Getting to the Answer: It's time to use SOHCAH-TOA, and drawing a triangle might help as well. If the sine of θ (opposite side over hypotenuse) is $\dfrac{\sqrt{11}}{2\sqrt{3}}$, then one of the legs of the right triangle is $\sqrt{11}$, and the hypotenuse is $2\sqrt{3}$. Now apply the Pythagorean theorem to come up with the other (adjacent) leg: $\left(\sqrt{11}\right)^2 + (n)^2 = \left(2\sqrt{3}\right)^2$, so $11 + n^2 = 12$, which means that $n^2 = 1$, and $n = 1$. Thus, cosine (adjacent side over hypotenuse) θ is $\dfrac{1}{2\sqrt{3}}$.

25. D
Category: Operations
Difficulty: Medium
Getting to the Answer: Take a quick look at the answer choices before simplifying an expression like this one. Notice that only one of these choices contains a radical sign in its denominator. So when you simplify the expression, try to eliminate that radical sign. Your calculations should look something like this:

$$\frac{\sqrt{3+x}}{\sqrt{3-x}} \times \frac{\sqrt{3-x}}{\sqrt{3-x}} = \frac{\sqrt{(3+x)(3-x)}}{\sqrt{(3-x)^2}} =$$

$$\frac{\sqrt{9 - 3x + 3x - x^2}}{3 - x} = \frac{\sqrt{9 - x^2}}{3 - x}$$

So (D) is correct.

26. G
Category: Proportions and Probability
Difficulty: Low
Getting to the Answer: If the ratio of the parts is 2:5, then the ratio total is 2 + 5 = 7. Thus, the actual total number of cookies must be a multiple of 7. The only choice that's a multiple of 7 is (G), 35.

27. C
Category: Number Properties
Difficulty: Medium
Getting to the Answer: This question is a great opportunity to use your calculator. Notice that all your choices are decimals. In order to solve, convert $\frac{3}{16}$ into a decimal and add that to 0.175: $\frac{3}{16} = 0.1875$, so the sum equals 0.1875 + 0.175 = 0.3625. Thus, (C) is correct.

28. H
Category: Plane Geometry
Difficulty: Low
Getting to the Answer: Remember that if you are given a perimeter for a rectangle, the rectangle with the greatest area for that perimeter will be a square. So you are looking for the area of a square with a perimeter of 20. The perimeter of a square equals $4s$, where s is the length of one side of the square. If $4s = 20$, then $s = 5$. The area of the square equals $s^2 = 5^2 = 25$, (H).

29. B
Category: Operations
Difficulty: High
Getting to the Answer: Be careful on this one. You can't start plugging numbers into your calculator without paying attention to the order of operations. This one is best solved on your own.

$$\frac{\frac{3}{2} + \frac{7}{4}}{\frac{15}{8} - \frac{3}{4}} - \frac{4 + 3}{-4 + 3} =$$

$$\frac{\frac{3}{2} + \frac{7}{4}}{\frac{9}{8} - \frac{7}{-1}} = \frac{\frac{13}{4}}{\frac{65}{8}} = \frac{13}{4} \times \frac{8}{65} = \frac{2}{5}$$

30. K
Category: Variable Manipulation
Difficulty: Medium
Getting to the Answer: You could solve this algebraically for x as follows:

$$x - 15 = 7 - 5(x - 4)$$
$$x - 15 = 7 - 5x + 20$$
$$x - 15 = -5x + 27$$
$$6x = 42$$
$$x = 7$$

Remember also that if you are ever stuck, you can Backsolve using the answer choices. Here, if you try them all out, only 7 works:

$$7 - 15 = 7 - 5(7 - 4)$$
$$-8 = 7 - 5(3)$$
$$-8 = 7 - 15$$
$$-8 = -8$$

31. C

Category: Plane Geometry

Difficulty: Medium

Getting to the Answer: Break strange figures like this one up into shapes that are more familiar and easier to handle. In this case, the quadrilateral can be split into a square and a right triangle. The square is 9 × 9, so the area of that part of the figure is 81 square meters. The right triangle has a height of 9 and a base of 4, so the area of the triangle would be

$$\frac{1}{2}bh = \frac{1}{2}(4 \times 9) = \frac{1}{2}(36) = 18$$

square meters. Therefore, the total area of the figure is (81 + 18) square meters = 99 square meters, (C).

32. H

Category: Coordinate Geometry

Difficulty: Medium

Getting to the Answer: The easiest way to solve this question is to put it in the form $y = mx + b$, where m equals the slope. In other words, you want to isolate y:

$$6y - 3x = 18$$
$$6y = 3x + 18$$
$$y = \frac{3x + 18}{6}$$
$$y = \frac{1}{2}x + 3$$

So the slope equals $\frac{1}{2}$.

33. A

Category: Coordinate Geometry

Difficulty: Low

Getting to the Answer: To answer this question, you have to know that perpendicular lines on the standard (x, y) coordinate plane have slopes that are negative reciprocals of each other. In other words, the line described by the equation $y = -\frac{4}{5}x + 6$ has a slope of $-\frac{4}{5}$, so a line perpendicular to it has a slope of $\frac{5}{4}$. This eliminates all choices but (A). However, if you want to double-check, you can plug the coordinates you're given (4, 3) into the equation found in (A).

$$3 = \frac{5}{4}(4) - 2$$
$$3 = 5 - 2$$
$$3 = 3$$

34. K

Category: Coordinate Geometry

Difficulty: Medium

Getting to the Answer: Because the problem gives you the y-intercept, it is easy to look at the answer choices and rule out F, H, and J. Put the equation from the question in slope-intercept form to find its slope:

$$3x - 5y = 4$$
$$-5y = -3x + 4$$
$$y = \frac{-3x + 4}{-5}$$
$$y = \frac{3}{5}x - \frac{4}{5}$$

Because line t is parallel, it has the same slope. This matches (K).

35. A

Category: Variable Manipulation

Difficulty: Low

Getting to the Answer: To solve for x in the equation $y = mx + b$, isolate x on one side of the equation. Begin by subtracting b from both sides. You will be left with $y - b = mx$. Then divide both sides by m, and you will be left with $x = \frac{y - b}{m}$, (A).

36. J

Category: Plane Geometry

Difficulty: Medium

Getting to the Answer: In this figure, there are many right triangles and many similar triangles. If you know to be on the lookout for 3-4-5 triangles, it should be easy to spot that triangle ABC has sides of 15-20-25, so $\overline{AC}$ is 25. Now turn your attention to triangle ABD. Because it's a right triangle that shares ∠BAC with triangle ABC, it too must be a 3-4-5 triangle. So if the hypotenuse is 20, the shorter leg ($\overline{BD}$) must have a length of 12, and the longer leg ($\overline{AD}$) must have a length of 16.

37. A

Category: Coordinate Geometry

Difficulty: High

Getting to the Answer: The shortest distance to line m will be a line perpendicular to m. So the distance will be the difference between the y-coordinates of point C and the nearest point on line m. Because every point on m has a y-coordinate of 5, and point C has a y-coordinate of 3, the difference is 2.

38. G

Category: Variable Manipulation

Difficulty: Medium

Getting to the Answer: While you could try factoring the numerator, you'll find that you can't easily cancel out the denominator by doing so. Perhaps the easiest approach here is to Pick Numbers. Pick a simple number such as $x = 2$. Thus,

$$\frac{x^2 - 11x + 24}{8 - x} = \frac{(2)^2 - 11(2) + 24}{6} = \frac{4 - 22 + 24}{6} = \frac{6}{6} = 1.$$

So 1 is your target number. When you plug $x = 2$ into the choices, the only choice that gives you 1 is (G).

39. C

Category: Coordinate Geometry

Difficulty: Medium

Getting to the Answer:

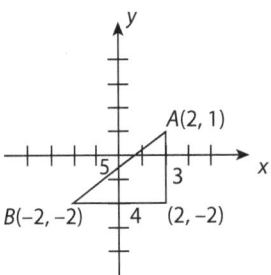

The textbook method for this problem would be to use the distance formula, but that's time-consuming. Instead, it may help to draw a picture. Draw a right triangle on the coordinate plane as shown above. Note that the distance between the two points represents the hypotenuse of the triangle. The legs of the triangle have lengths of 3 and 4, so the distance between the two points must be 5, (C).

40. G

Category: Plane Geometry

Difficulty: Medium

Getting to the Answer: To find the area of the shaded region, you must subtract the area of the circle from the area of the rectangle. Because the sides of the rectangle are 2x and 5x, it has an area of $2x \times 5x = 10x^2$. By examining the diagram, you can see that the circle has a diameter of 2x, so it has a radius of x. Its area is, therefore, πx^2. Thus, the shaded region has an area of $10x^2 - \pi x^2$.

41. B

Category: Trigonometry

Difficulty: High

Getting to the Answer: Because you are not given a diagram for this problem, it's best to draw a quick sketch of a right triangle to help keep the sides separate in your mind. Mark one of the acute angles θ. Because $\cos \theta = \frac{5\sqrt{2}}{8}$, mark the adjacent side $5\sqrt{2}$ and the hypotenuse as 8. (Remember SOHCAHTOA.) Use the Pythagorean theorem to find that the side opposite θ is $\sqrt{14}$. The problem asks you to find tan θ. Tangent = $\frac{\text{opposite}}{\text{adjacent}}$, so $\tan θ = \frac{\sqrt{14}}{5\sqrt{2}}$, which can be simplified to $\frac{\sqrt{7}}{5}$.

42. H
Category: Proportions and Probability
Difficulty: Medium
Getting to the Answer: This question is one where your calculator can come in handy. Divide 7 by integer values for *n*, and look for values between 0.5 and 0.8. Begin by looking for the integer values of *n* where $\frac{7}{n}$ is greater than 0.5. If *n* = 14, then $\frac{7}{n} = 0.5$, so *n* must be less than 14. Work through values of *n* until you get to the point where $\frac{7}{n}$ + 0.8. When *n* = 9, $\frac{7}{n}$ = 0.778, but when *n* = 8, $\frac{7}{n} = 0.875$. So the integer values that work in this case are *n* = 9, 10, 11, 12, and 13. Five integer values work, making (H) correct.

43. C
Difficulty: Medium
Category: Plane Geometry
Getting to the Answer: The points are as far apart as possible when separated by a diameter of *X* and a diameter of *Y*.

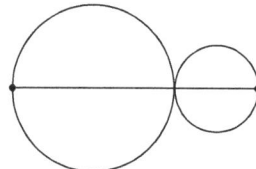

The circumference of a circle is π × (diameter), so the diameter of circle *X* is 12, and the diameter of circle *Y* is 8. The greatest possible distance between points then is 12 + 8 = 20.

44. K
Category: Variable Manipulation
Difficulty: Medium
Getting to the Answer: Begin by getting rid of the square root sign. If *y* ≥ 0, then $\sqrt{y^2} = y$, so $\sqrt{(x^2 + 4)^2} = x^2 + 4$. Then (*x* + 2)(*x* − 2) = x^2 − 4, so you now have (x^2 + 4) − (x^2 − 4) = ? Get rid of the parentheses, and you have x^2 + 4 − x^2 + 4 = x^2 − x^2 + 4 + 4 = 8.

45. A
Category: Variable Manipulation
Difficulty: Medium
Getting to the Answer: Here, you need to substitute −3 for *s* and solve. That gives you the expression $(−3)^3 + 2(−3)^2 + 2(−3)$, which equals −27 + 18 − 6, or −15. If you missed this problem, you probably made a mistake with the signs of the numbers.

46. G
Category: Variable Manipulation
Difficulty: High
Getting to the Answer: Be careful on this one. Begin by simplifying the equation by FOILing one side:

$2x + 6 = (x + 5)(x + 3)$

$2x + 6 = x^2 + 8x + 15$

Then get the right side of the equation to equal zero: $x^2 + 6x + 9 = 0$.

The left side of this equation is the perfect square $(x + 3)^2$, so $(x + 3)^2 = 0$, which has only one solution, *x* = −3. Choice (G) is correct.

47. E
Category: Pythagorean Theorem
Difficulty: Low
Getting to the Answer: The textbook method for this would be to use the Pythagorean theorem to find the length of a side and then multiply that by 4, but there's an easier way: eyeball it! The perimeter is greater than $\overline{AC}$, so you can get rid of A and B.

It appears to be quite a bit greater than $\overline{AC}$, more than twice as great, so C and D are out as well. That only leaves (E).

If you wanted to solve this the conventional way, because the perimeter is the sum of the lengths of all the sides of the square, you need to find the length of the square's sides. Let the length of each of the square's sides be x. $\overline{AC}$ divides the square into two right triangles, so you can apply the Pythagorean theorem: $\overline{AB}^2 + \overline{BC}^2 = \overline{AC}^2$. Because $\overline{AB}$ and $\overline{BC}$ are sides of the square, they have the same length. You can write that as $x^2 + x^2 = \overline{AC}^2$. $\overline{AC} = 8$, so $2x^2 = 8^2$, $2x^2 = 64$, $x^2 = 32$, $x = \sqrt{32} = \sqrt{16 \times 2} = 4\sqrt{2}$.

So each side of the square is $4\sqrt{2}$, and the perimeter of the square is $4 \times 4\sqrt{2} = 16\sqrt{2}$.

48. G
Category: Plane Geometry
Difficulty: Medium
Getting to the Answer: To find the area of this complex shape, you could divide it into two simple shapes by drawing a line 30 inches up, parallel to the horizontal base. This leaves you with a 4 × 30 rectangle and a triangle with height of 6 and a base of 4. The rectangle has an area of $4 \times 30 = 120$ square inches, and the triangle has an area of $\frac{4 \times 6}{2} = 12$ square inches. That makes a total of $120 + 12 = 132$ square inches.

49. E
Category: Plane Geometry
Difficulty: Medium
Getting to the Answer: Triangles are the secret to solving this one. Drawing $\overline{OD}$ divides quadrilateral $OCDE$ into two triangles, OCD and ODE. Both triangles are isosceles because $\overline{OC}$, $\overline{OD}$, and $\overline{OE}$ are all radii of circle O. Angles ODC and OCD have equal measures, because they're opposite equal sides, so $\angle ODC$ measures 70°. Similarly, $\angle ODE$ measures 45°.

Together, angles ODC and ODE make up $\angle CDE$, so its measure is 70° + 45° = 115°.

50. K
Category: Coordinate Geometry
Difficulty: High
Getting to the Answer: Remember that lines intersect at the point that is a solution to both equations. So equations with no common solution don't intersect—they have the same slope and are parallel. To solve this problem, search through the answer choices to find the pair of equations representing lines with the same slope. If you write the equations in (K) in slope-intercept form, you'll get

$$y = -\frac{1}{3}x + 2, y = -\frac{1}{3}x + \frac{7}{9},$$

so the slope is clearly the same for both equations.

51. E
Category: Number Properties
Difficulty: Medium
Getting to the Answer: To solve a repeating decimal question, begin by determining the pattern of the decimal on your calculator: $\frac{1}{7} = 0.142857142857\ldots$ so you know that this fraction repeats every six decimal places. Because you are looking for the 46th decimal place, you need to determine where in the six-term pattern you would be at the 46th place. Divide 46 by 6 and look for the remainder. The remainder in this case is 4, so you are looking for the 4th term in the sequence, which is 8, (E).

52. K
Category: Variable Manipulation
Difficulty: Medium
Getting to the Answer: Remember that you treat an inequality exactly like an equality, except that you need to flip the sign when you multiply or divide by a negative number. In this problem, you start with the inequality $-2 - 4x \leq -6x$. Add $4x$ to

both sides to get $-2 \leq -2x$. Divide by -2 and flip the sign to get $1 \geq x$, which matches (K).

53. B
Category: Operations
Difficulty: High
Getting to the Answer: For this problem, it would probably be easiest to Pick Numbers. Because you will be taking the square root of the numbers, it's easiest to pick perfect squares, like 4 and 9:

$$\frac{\sqrt{4}}{4} + \frac{\sqrt{9}}{9} = \frac{2}{4} + \frac{3}{9} = \frac{1}{2} + \frac{1}{3} = \frac{5}{6}$$

When you plug 4 and 9 into the answer choices, only (B) gives you $\frac{5}{6}$.

54. G
Category: Plane Geometry
Difficulty: Medium

Getting to the Answer: When transversals intersect parallel lines, corresponding line segments on the transversals are proportional. In other words, $\frac{\overline{DE}}{\overline{CB}} = \frac{\overline{EF}}{\overline{BA}}$. Thus, $\frac{6}{8} = \frac{\overline{EF}}{4}$, so $EF = 3$.

55. D
Category: Coordinate Geometry
Difficulty: High
Getting to the Answer: Divide the square into two right triangles by drawing the diagonal from (2, 7) to (2, 1). Remember that the area of each triangle is half its base times its height. Treat the diagonal as the base of a triangle. Its length is the distance from (2, 7) to (2, 1). Because the x-coordinates are the same, that distance is simply the difference between the y-coordinates, 7 − 1, or 6. The diagonal bisects the square, so the height of the triangle is half the distance from (−1, 4) to (5, 4). You already know that a diagonal of this square is 6, so half the distance is 3. Therefore, the base and height of either triangle are 6 and 3, making the area of each triangle $\frac{6 \times 3}{2}$, or 9 square units. The square is made up of two such triangles and so has twice the area, or 18 square units.

Alternatively, you could use the Distance Formula to find the length of one side and square that side to find the area.

56. K
Category: Trigonometry
Difficulty: Medium
Getting to the Answer: Compared to the graph of $y = \cos \theta$, the graph of $y = 2 \cos \theta$ would have twice the amplitude and the same period, (K). Here you are doubling y, which represents the vertical coordinates, but the θ coordinates stay the same. The amplitude of a trigonometric equation refers to how high or low the curve moves from the horizontal axis. The period refers to the distance required to complete a single wave along the horizontal axis.

57. C
Category: Variable Manipulation
Difficulty: Medium
Getting to the Answer: To solve this problem with algebra, you need to translate each phrase into mathematics. Translated, the problem is $3(x + 15) = 4x − 65$. Solve for x to get 110. Alternatively, you could Backsolve starting with the middle value:

$$3(110 + 15) = 4(110) − 65$$
$$3(125) = 440 − 65$$
$$375 = 375$$

Because the two sides are equal, (C) is correct.

58. H
Category: Proportions and Probability
Difficulty: Medium
Getting to the Answer: You're given the formula for the volume of a cylinder in the equation so you can find the volume of both cylinders described. Then this becomes a ratio problem in which you're comparing the volumes of both cylinders. Pick Numbers to make this question more concrete and plug them into this volume formula.

Let's say the smaller cylinder has a height of 1 and a radius of 1 (diameter of 2), for a volume of $\pi(1)^2 \times 1 = \pi$. The larger cylinder would then have a height of 3 and a radius of 2 (diameter of 4), for a volume of $\pi(2)^2 \times 3 = 12\pi$. Thus, it would take 12 fillings of the smaller cylinder to fill the larger cylinder.

59. D
Category: Plane Geometry
Difficulty: High
Getting to the Answer: Draw a picture of the triangle and carefully apply your knowledge of the ratio of the lengths of the sides of a 30°-60°-90° triangle ($x : x\sqrt{3} : 2x$). If the longer leg has a length of 12, the shorter leg has a length of

$$\frac{12}{\sqrt{3}} = \frac{12\sqrt{3}}{\sqrt{3} \times \sqrt{3}} = \frac{12\sqrt{3}}{3} = 4\sqrt{3}.$$

Then, the hypotenuse is twice this, or $8\sqrt{3}$. Finally, the perimeter is the sum of the three sides, or

$$4\sqrt{3} + 12 + 8\sqrt{3} = 12\sqrt{3} + 12.$$

60. J
Category: Proportions and Probability
Difficulty: Medium
Getting to the Answer: Remember the average formula on this one. The average formula states,

$$\text{Average} = \frac{\text{Sum of the terms}}{\text{Number of the terms}}.$$

So to find the total average, find the total sum and divide it by the total number of terms. If a team averages x points in n games, then it scored nx points in n games. In the final game of the season, it scored y points. So the total sum of points for the season is $nx + y$, and the total number of games is $n + 1$. So the team's average score for the entire season is $\frac{nx + y}{n + 1}$, (J).

READING TEST

PASSAGE I

1. C
Category: Detail
Difficulty: Medium
Getting to the Answer: The answer can be found in lines 31–36: "The real evils, indeed, of Emma's situation were the power of having rather too much her own way, and a disposition to think a little too well of herself; these were the disadvantages which threatened alloy to her many enjoyments."

2. G
Category: Detai
Difficulty: High
Getting to the Answer: Isabella's name is given in line 73.

3. B
Category: Detail
Difficulty: Medium
Getting to the Answer: The answer can be found in lines 20–21: "Between them it was more the intimacy of sisters."

4. F
Category: Vocab-in-Context
Difficulty: Low
Getting to the Answer: As it is used in the sentence, *disposition* means "tendency" or "inclination." It would not make sense for Emma to have G, control; H, placement; or J, transfer "to think a little too well of herself" (lines 33–34).

5. D
Category: Detail
Difficulty: High
Getting to the Answer: The answer can be found in lines 62–69: "She recalled her past kindness—the

kindness, the affection of sixteen years—how she had taught her and…how she had devoted all her powers to attach and amuse her in health—and how she had nursed her through the various illnesses of childhood."

6. H
Category: Inference
Difficulty: Medium
Getting to the Answer: Miss Taylor will continue to be a part of Emma's life, but they will not be as close because Miss Taylor no longer lives with Emma and because Miss Taylor will be primarily concerned with her husband's, not Emma's, well-being.

7. C
Category: Inference
Difficulty: Medium
Getting to the Answer: Emma is self-centered, as evidenced by her description of her relationship with Miss Taylor. Among Miss Taylor's admirable qualities, Emma includes the fact that Miss Taylor was "interested in her, in every pleasure, every scheme of hers—one to whom she could speak every thought as it arose, and who had such an affection for her as could never find fault" (lines 80–84). Emma is also clearly headstrong. She is described as "having rather too much her own way" (lines 32–33).

8. G
Category: Generalization
Difficulty: Medium
Getting to the Answer: Emma's description of her friendship with Miss Taylor suggests that Emma most highly values devotion in her friends.

9. B
Category: Detail
Difficulty: Medium
Getting to the Answer: The description of Mr. Weston is in lines 53–56: "The marriage had every promise of happiness for her friend. Mr. Weston was a man of unexceptionable character, easy fortune, suitable age, and pleasant manners." None of the other choices match this description.

10. H
Category: Inference
Difficulty: Low
Getting to the Answer: The answer to the question is in lines 28–31: "Emma doing just what she liked, highly esteeming Miss Taylor's judgment, but directed chiefly by her own."

PASSAGE II

11. B
Category: Generalization
Difficulty: Medium
Getting to the Answer: Passage A discusses the Wright brothers' process for designing a successful airplane; (B) is correct. Although the passage mentions how the Wright brothers were regarded, A, this information appears in the first paragraph only, and is not the main focus of the passage. The passage discusses the approaches used by other inventors, but the author does not criticize them, as represented in C. The practical application of science, D, is too broad to be correct.

12. H
Category: Inference
Difficulty: High
Getting to the Answer: According to paragraph 2, most inventors would design an airplane, build it, and test it, but not know specifically what caused a plane to succeed or fail, (H). Choice F is opposite because Smeaton's coefficient was commonly accepted during that time in history. There's no indication that they considered the methods and rejected them, G. Choice J is opposite; people who were trying to build an airplane likely believed it was possible.

13. B
Category: Inference
Difficulty: High
Getting to the Answer: The passage says that the Wright brothers invented the wind tunnel as an alternative to building and testing "whole machines." They tested only parts of their design in the tunnel, such as wing shape. You can infer that the wind tunnel made it possible for them to deal with their airplane design one piece at a time. The author never implies that the data from the kites, A, was inaccurate. To work on controlling the plane laterally, they used a five-foot biplane kite rather than the wind tunnel, which rules out C. Choice D is opposite; they disproved a commonly-accepted theory of lift (called Smeaton's coefficient).

14. F
Category: Function
Difficulty: High
Getting to the Answer: Passage B deals mainly with how the Wright brothers were treated publicly following their discovery. The "legal battle" is mentioned as another example of how the brothers didn't receive the money and respect they deserved for their important contribution, (F). The author does not imply that it is unwise to publicize knowledge, G. Choice H is opposite; the author feels that their discovery was quite important. Choice J isn't directly related to the court case.

15. C
Category: Inference
Difficulty: Medium
Getting to the Answer: In the last paragraph, the author states that "this was too little, too late," so the author would agree that the honor did not properly compensate for the poor treatment of the brothers, (C). It was not a victory for Orville, A, because both brothers had passed away by 1948. The Smithsonian's choice was not a result of a refusal to recognize the brothers' achievements, B, because it was a great honor. There is no evidence to suggest that the craft would have been displayed sooner if European countries had issued the brothers a patent, D.

16. J
Category: Detail
Difficulty: High
Getting to the Answer: This Detail question requires very careful reading. The previous sentence talks about how "those who made airplanes" thought little of the Wright brothers' accomplishments. The following sentence is a continuation of that thought, and so it is "those who made airplanes," (J), who are expressing this opinion. The discussion of "the French aviation community" begins a new thought, ruling out F. The Wright brothers, G, didn't have a poor view of themselves. The author, H, has a positive view of the Wright brothers.

17. B
Category: Inference
Difficulty: Medium
Getting to the Answer: The passage says "the prevailing opinion among those who made airplanes was that two rustic, uneducated fellows from Ohio could never have accomplished such an historic feat except by accident." From this, you can infer that those who made airplanes didn't think that the Wright brothers were exceptional; in their eyes, the brothers' discovery must have been sheer luck, not the result of scientific experimentation. Eliminate A because the passage never says that they thought the Wrights hadn't made a working airplane, only that they thought little of the accomplishment. Choice C is opposite; they had a negative opinion the Wrights' breakthrough. Choice D is a distortion; they felt the brothers were lucky, not dishonest.

18. H
Category: Vocab-in-Context
Difficulty: Low
Getting to the Answer: The authors state that the Wrights were able to "marry all of these carefully designed components into a complete craft" (lines 72–73) and "deliberately marry the disparate components of air travel that are required for successful flight" (line 90–93). So, the Wright brothers brought together all the separate pieces into a whole airplane. Predict that "marry" means "bring together,"

(H). The airplane did prove, F, that the components worked when together, but it doesn't make sense to say that the brothers were able to deliberately prove the components. The Wright brothers had already rigorously tested each component separately, so G is incorrect. Airplane components can't be satisfied, so J won't work.

19. B
Category: Detail
Difficulty: Medium
Getting to the Answer: At the beginning of paragraph 3, Passage A states, "The Wright brothers proved to be adept scientists. With their keen analytical insight and love of engineering and all things mechanical, they were able to escape that endless loop of misguided 'improvements.'" This matches perfectly with (B). Choice A describes the approach that other, unsuccessful inventors used. Passage A does not provide evidence that the invention of the wind tunnel was a greater accomplishment than the airplane, C. The court case cited in D is included in Passage B, not in Passage A.

20. H
Category: Detail
Difficulty: Low
Getting to the Answer: Wrong answer choices for this type of question are commonly those that are true for one passage but not the other. Both passages agree that the Wright brothers did something great that no one else was capable of at the time, which is reflected in (H). The brothers' method of inquiry, F, is discussed in Passage A only. Choices G and J are included in Passage B, but not in Passage A.

PASSAGE III

21. B
Category: Inference
Difficulty: Medium
Getting to the Answer: In lines 11–13, Julia Margaret Cameron is described as "the first woman to have achieved eminence in photography." The other answer choices contradict information supplied in the passage.

22. F
Category: Detail
Difficulty: Low
Getting to the Answer: The answer to this question can be found in lines 82–83, "Contemporary taste much prefers her portraits…," and in lines 88–89, "today her fame rests upon her portraits…."

23. D
Category: Detail
Difficulty: High
Getting to the Answer: The dates used in the passage tell you that this is a chronological account; the author begins with Cameron's birth in 1815, tells of her marriage and then her move to England in 1848, points out that she received her first photographic equipment in 1863, describes one of her photographs from 1864, and then concludes the paragraph with her death in 1874.

24. F
Category: Vocab-in-Context
Difficulty: Medium
Getting to the Answer: The dictionary definition of *cumbersome* is "difficult to handle because of weight or bulk." Choice (F) most closely fits this definition, and it is the only answer choice that makes sense within the context of the sentence.

25. B
Category: Inference
Difficulty: Medium
Getting to the Answer: Lines 55–56 describe how Cameron "devoted herself wholly to this art," which matches (B). Choice A contradicts information from the passage, which suggests that Cameron led anything but a conventional life. Neither the money that Cameron earned as a photographer nor her religious beliefs are discussed in the passage, making C and D incorrect.

26. F
Category: Generalization
Difficulty: Medium
Getting to the Answer: Lines 60–63 say, "she produced a large body of work that stands up as one of the notable artistic achievements of the Victorian period." To say that she is "the greatest photographer who ever lived" goes beyond anything stated or implied in the passage. The third paragraph does not compare her importance as an artist during her lifetime to her importance today. The passage also does not state that she "revolutionized" any photographic methods.

27. C
Category: Detail
Difficulty: Medium
Getting to the Answer: The answer to this question can be found in lines 7–10: "photography, being a new medium outside the traditional academic framework, was wide open to women and offered them opportunities that the older fields did not…"

28. G
Category: Detail
Difficulty: Low
Getting to the Answer: These titles refer to allegorical pictures, as described in lines 78–81: "Victorian critics were particularly impressed by her allegorical pictures, many of them based on the poems of her friend and neighbor Tennyson…."

29. D
Category: Detail
Difficulty: Medium
Getting to the Answer: The answer to this question can be found in lines 82–84: "Contemporary taste much prefers her portraits and finds her narrative scenes sentimental and sometimes in bad taste."

30. F
Category: Inference
Difficulty: Low
Getting to the Answer: The author says that Cameron "achieved eminence" (line 12) in her field, that she "devoted herself wholly to this art" (lines 55–56), and that "no other woman photographer has ever enjoyed such success" (lines 74–75). Only (F) fits these descriptions.

PASSAGE IV

31. C
Category: Detail
Difficulty: Low
Getting to the Answer: For details about the eye, look at paragraph 3. Only the cornea and stenopaic pupil are relevant, eliminating A and D. But the cornea, B, is helpful underwater, not on land.

32. G
Category: Inference
Difficulty: Medium
Getting to the Answer: The eye is covered in paragraph 3. The seal's cornea improves vision in the water (note the comparison to human underwater vision), but it distorts light moving through the air. Another adaptation was then needed to *minimize* (line 53) distortion, but that doesn't mean distortion is completely eliminated, so the seal's vision in the air is distorted, (G).

33. D
Category: Detail
Difficulty: Low
Getting to the Answer: The vibrissae are discussed only in the last paragraph. They sense wave disturbances made by nearby moving fish, so (D) is correct. Choice B, by using the phrase "in the air," distorts information in the passage.

34. F
Category: Detail
Difficulty: Low
Getting to the Answer: This is stated in the second paragraph, where the seal's hearing is discussed.

35. D
Category: Detail
Difficulty: Medium
Getting to the Answer: This appears in the first paragraph, which introduces the influences on the seal's adaptations. They include that the seal "does most of its fishing at night," that "noise levels are high," and that these factors are compounded by the seal's "two habitats."

36. H
Category: Detail
Difficulty: Medium
Getting to the Answer: Locating each of these claims in the passage, you find that (H) is *suggested* (line 68) and the subject of speculation, rather than stated as fact. All of the other choices are given in support of claims.

37. A
Category: Inference
Difficulty: High
Getting to the Answer: You learn in the first paragraph that they live along the northern Atlantic and Pacific coasts. Because they live both on the land and in the water, the coastlines must be accessible. You can infer that the waters are cold rather than warm, eliminating D. Choices B and C are too broad.

38. J
Category: Detail
Difficulty: Medium
Getting to the Answer: This feature is mentioned at the end of paragraph 2. It shouldn't be confused with echolocation, which is discussed in paragraph 4 but not associated with any particular sensory organ.

39. B
Category: Function
Difficulty: Medium
Getting to the Answer: The entire passage is about how the seal's sensory organs have adapted to life on land and in the water, making (B) the best choice. Generally, you are told about differences, not similarities, between the sensory organs of humans and harbor seals, eliminating A. The relative success of human and seal adaptation to their environments isn't discussed, thus eliminating C and D.

40. G
Category: Detail
Difficulty: Medium
Getting to the Answer: In paragraph 3, we see that human corneas refract light badly in water, while the seal's corneas perform well.

SCIENCE TEST

PASSAGE I

1. B
Category: Figure Interpretation
Difficulty: Medium
Getting to the Answer: To answer this question, you have to examine the third column of the table, transmittance range. For a material to transmit light at a wavelength of 25 μm, its transmittance range—the range of wavelengths over which the material is transparent—must include 25 μm. Only potassium bromide (0.3–29 μm) and cesium iodide (0.3–70 μm) have transmittance ranges that include 25 μm, so (B) is correct.

2. F
Category: Figure Interpretation
Difficulty: Medium
Getting to the Answer: The material that contradicts this hypothesis is going to have poor chemical resistance but a transmittance range less than 10 μm. Lithium fluoride, (F), fits the bill: Its chemical

resistance is poor, and its transmittance range is less than 6 μm wide. Choices G and J are wrong because both flint glass and quartz have excellent chemical resistance. Choice H is out because cesium iodide has a transmittance range nearly 70 μm wide.

3. D
Category: Scientific Reasoning
Difficulty: High
Getting to the Answer: The correct answer is a pair of materials in which the refractive index of the first material is greater than that of the second. In A, B, and C, the refractive index of the first material is less than that of the second. In (D), however, flint glass has a refractive index of 1.66 while calcium fluoride's refractive index is only 1.43. That makes (D) the correct answer.

4. J
Category: Scientific Reasoning
Difficulty: Medium
Getting to the Answer: The easiest way to answer this question is to use the first couple materials and test each hypothesis on them. Choices F and G are incorrect because the transmittance range of lithium fluoride is wider than its useful prism range. Comparing the data on lithium fluoride and calcium fluoride rules out H because transmittance range does NOT increase as useful prism range decreases. In fact, looking down the rest of the table, you see that transmittance range seems to decrease as useful prism range decreases. Choice (J) is the only one left, and the data on lithium fluoride and calcium fluoride as well as all the other materials confirm that the transmittance range is always wider than, and includes within it, the useful prism range.

5. B
Category: Figure Interpretation
Difficulty: Medium
Getting to the Answer: According to the footnote to the table, quartz infused with lead oxide is flint glass. Comparison of the properties of pure quartz and flint glass shows that the transmittance range of flint glass is narrower than that of quartz but its refractive index is greater. This supports (B).

6. G
Category: Scientific Reasoning
Difficulty: Medium
Getting to the Answer: Begin this question by looking at the answer choices and finding the transmittance range and useful range for prisms for lithium fluoride, sodium chloride, quartz, and flint glass. A quick glance at the chart shows that the ranges for lithium flouride (for transmittance and prisms, respectively) are slightly below 6 and 2. Sodium chloride shows ranges of just under 17 and 8. Quartz has ranges of less than 3 and 2, while flint glass has ranges of less than 2 for both categories. Therefore, sodium chloride, (G), is the correct answer.

PASSAGE II

7. D
Category: Scientific Reasoning
Difficulty: High
Getting to the Answer: Begin by looking at the equation in the question. Given that osmotic pressure is already isolated on one side, using some basic rules of math will make this question go much faster. R is a constant and therefore does not factor into the answer choices. Because temperature and osmotic pressure increase together, you can eliminate roman numeral I as well as A. Statement II describes what happens to Π when M and T are inversely related. The statement says that as one goes up and the other goes down, Π remains constant. That is true: Because both M and T are on the same side of the equation, the only way to keep Π constant and still vary M and T is to have an inverse relationship between the latter two variables. Statement II is correct, so you can eliminate C. For statement III, you can look at the equation and recognize that because M, R, and T are all multiplied together,

Π must increase if even one of those increases. Because statement III is also true, (D) is correct.

8. H
Category: Scientific Reasoning
Difficulty: Medium
Getting to the Answer: Use the results of both experiments to answer this question. The answer choices all involve temperature, concentration, and solvent in different combinations. To determine whether osmotic pressure is dependent upon a variable, look for a pair of trials in which all conditions except for that variable are identical. In doing so, you see that temperature and concentration affect osmotic pressure, but solvent does not.

9. C
Category: Figure Interpretation
Difficulty: High
Getting to the Answer: Find methanol at 0.5 mol/L, which is in Table 2. The text above the table states that all the trials were conducted under the same temperature (298 K). Therefore, simply look across the row that you identified. The osmotic pressure is 12.23, (C).

10. G
Category: Scientific Reasoning
Difficulty: High
Getting to the Answer: To figure out whether or not the sucrose solution will diffuse across the membrane under the conditions described in the question, go back to the definition of osmotic pressure given in the introduction. Once the external pressure reaches the osmotic pressure, osmosis will not occur. In order for osmosis to occur, the external pressure must be less than the osmotic pressure of the solution. The solution in this question is a 0.1 mol/L aqueous sucrose solution at 298 K; those conditions correspond to an osmotic pressure of 2.45 atm. Because the external pressure is 1 atm, which is less than the osmotic pressure, osmosis will occur. From the definition of osmosis in the passage, it is clear that the solution will diffuse from the side of the membrane with a lower concentration of dissolved material, in this case pure water, to the side with a higher concentration, in this case sucrose solution. Choice (G) is correct.

11. C
Category: Figure Interpretation
Difficulty: Medium
Getting to the Answer: To determine what the scientists investigated in Experiment 1, look at what they varied and what they measured. In Experiment 1, the scientists varied the concentration and the temperature of sucrose solutions, and they measured the osmotic pressure. Therefore, they were investigating the effect of concentration and temperature on osmotic pressure, (C). Watch out for A: It states what was investigated in Experiment 2, not Experiment 1.

12. F
Category: Patterns
Difficulty: Low
Getting to the Answer: The results in Table 2 indicate that osmotic pressure doesn't depend on the solvent, as discussed in the explanation to question 6. So Statement I is a valid conclusion, and G can be eliminated. Statement II is false. The results in Table 1 indicate that osmotic pressure is dependent on concentration as well as temperature. So H can be ruled out. Now consider Statement III. It is not a valid conclusion because osmotic pressure is the pressure required to prevent osmosis, so osmosis occurs only if the external pressure is less than the osmotic pressure.

13. D
Category: Scientific Reasoning
Difficulty: Medium
Getting to the Answer: To answer questions that ask about the design of an experiment, look at what the scientists are trying to measure. You're told that osmotic pressure is the pressure required to prevent osmosis. In order to measure the osmotic pressure

of a solution, scientists need to be able to tell when osmosis begins. If you have two clear solutions with sucrose dissolved in one of them, how can you tell when there's any movement of solvent between the two of them? If the sucrose is dyed, the blue solution will become paler when osmosis starts, i.e., when solvent moves across the membrane to create an equilibrium. Therefore, (D) is correct.

PASSAGE III

14. F
Category: Figure Interpretation
Difficulty: Low
Getting to the Answer: The question refers to Experiment 3, so look at Table 3. You see that when the temperature is 85 during the day and 85 at night, the leaves have the smallest measurements. Choice (F) is correct.

15. A
Category: Scientific Reasoning
Difficulty: Low
Getting to the Answer: The question refers to Experiment 2 only, so the correct answer will involve sunlight. Table 2 shows that the average length of the leaves increased from 5.3 cm to 12.4 cm as the amount of sunlight increased from 0 to 3 hours per day. But as the amount of sunlight increased further, leaf size decreased. Therefore, D is incorrect. Neither humidity, B, nor water, C, is relevant to Experiment 2.

16. G
Category: Figure Interpretation
Difficulty: Low
Getting to the Answer: Table 1 gives leaf widths at 35% and 55% humidity at 1.8 cm and 2.0 cm, respectively. The leaf width at 40% humidity would most likely be between those two figures. Choice (G) is the only choice within that range.

17. B
Category: Scientific Reasoning
Difficulty: Medium
Getting to the Answer: All the answer choices involve humidity and sunlight, which were investigated in Experiments 1 and 2, respectively. In Table 1, leaf length and width were greatest at 75% humidity. In Table 2, they were greatest at three hours per day of sunlight. Combining those two conditions, as in (B), would probably produce the largest leaves.

18. F
Category: Scientific Reasoning
Difficulty: Medium
Getting to the Answer: This question relates to the method of the study. Each experiment begins with a statement that five groups of seedlings were used. Therefore, (F) is correct. The other choices list variables that were manipulated.

19. D
Category: Scientific Reasoning
Difficulty: High
Getting to the Answer: Choice (D) is an assumption that underlies the design of all three experiments. If the seedlings were not equally capable of further growth, then changes in leaf size and density could not be reliably attributed to researcher-controlled changes in humidity, sunlight, and temperature. Choice A is incorrect because all the seedlings were 2–3 cm tall. The seedlings' abilities to germinate, B, or to produce flowers, C, were not mentioned in the passage.

20. H
Category: Scientific Reasoning
Difficulty: Medium
Getting to the Answer: Each of the three experiments investigated a different factor related to leaf growth. To produce the most useful new data, researchers would probably vary a fourth condition. Soil mineral content would be an appropriate factor to examine. None of the other choices relate directly

to the purpose of the experiments as expressed in paragraph 1 of the passage.

PASSAGE IV

21. B
Category: Figure Interpretation
Difficulty: Medium
Getting to the Answer: According to the table, decreasing the cross-sectional area of a given wire always increases resistance, so (B) is correct. Choice C is incorrect because resistivity, displayed in the second column, is constant for each material and thus cannot be responsible for variations in resistance for any given material. Gauge varies inversely with cross-sectional area, so D is incorrect.

22. G
Category: Patterns
Difficulty: High
Getting to the Answer: Because resistance varies inversely with cross-sectional area A, as discussed in the previous explanation, the correct answer to this question must place A in the denominator. The only choice that does so is (G).

23. D
Category: Patterns
Difficulty: Medium
Getting to the Answer: Compare the choices two at a time. The wires in A and B are made of the same material and have the same cross-sectional area; only their length is different. Doubling the length doubles the resistance, so B would have a higher resistance than A. By similar reasoning, (D) would have a higher resistance than C. The only difference between B and (D) is the material. Even though the research team didn't test wire with a 0.33 mm^2 cross-sectional area, Table 1 shows that tungsten wire has higher levels of resistance than aluminum wire across all factors.

24. J
Category: Scientific Reasoning
Difficulty: Medium
Getting to the Answer: The larger circle represents 10-gauge wire; its diameter is 2.59 mm. The smaller circle has a diameter of only 1.29 mm, but it represents 16-gauge wire, so Statement I is true, and you can eliminate G and H without even checking Statements II or III. To check Statement III, the table shows that the resistance of an iron (Fe) wire is much higher than that of an aluminum (Al) wire with the same length and cross-sectional area. The first sentence of paragraph 1 defined the resistance of a conductor as "the extent to which it opposes the flow of electricity." Because iron has a higher resistance than aluminum, iron must not conduct electricity as well. Therefore, Statement III is true, and (J) is correct.

25. D
Category: Patterns
Difficulty: Medium
Getting to the Answer: The data indicate that the resistivity of a material doesn't change when wire length changes. Therefore, the graph of resistivity versus length for tungsten (or any other) wire is a horizontal line.

26. J
Category: Patterns
Difficulty: Medium
Getting to the Answer: Refer to Table 1 to see the effect that wire length has on resistance. Regardless of wire gauge, resistance increases for each material when length is increased. Choice (J) is correct.

PASSAGE V

27. A
Category: Scientific Reasoning
Difficulty: Medium
Getting to the Answer: To answer this question, you have to refer to the examples presented by the scientists to find a point of agreement. Both use the

example of giraffes to show how scarcity of food and the need to reach higher and higher branches led to the evolution of long necks; thus, they both agree that environment affects evolution.

28. H
Category: Scientific Reasoning
Difficulty: Medium
Getting to the Answer: This Principle question requires that you figure out how new evidence affects the two hypotheses. To answer it, all you have to consider are the hypotheses of the two scientists. Scientist 2 believes that characteristics acquired by an individual over a lifetime are passed on to its offspring, a theory that would be supported by this finding.

29. D
Category: Scientific Reasoning
Difficulty: Low
Getting to the Answer: This question requires some reasoning. Scientist 2 states that all of the changes that occur in an individual's life can be passed on to offspring. Because he believes that any characteristic can undergo change, he must also believe that any characteristic can be inherited.

30. G
Category: Scientific Reasoning
Difficulty: Medium
Getting to the Answer: You don't need any information other than the hypothesis of Scientist 1 to answer this question. He believes that random mutations continually occur within a species as it propagates and that advantageous mutations, such as long necks on giraffes, help the species adapt to environmental changes and thus become more prevalent within the species. This is what (G) states.

31. B
Category: Scientific Reasoning
Difficulty: Low
Getting to the Answer: Here, you don't need any information other than the hypotheses of the two scientists. The crux of their disagreement is over how evolution occurs—whether through random mutations or through the inheritance of acquired characteristics.

32. G
Category: Scientific Reasoning
Difficulty: High
Getting to the Answer: Recall that Scientist 2 states that evolution occurs through the inheritance of acquired characteristics. In order to account for humans possessing nerve endings now that were not present before the discovery of fire, Scientist 2 would have to believe that new nerve endings could be acquired during a single lifetime. Choice (G) directly contradicts this idea and would therefore refute the hypothesis.

33. A
Category: Scientific Reasoning
Difficulty: Medium
Getting to the Answer: Recall that Scientist 1 explains that evolution occurs as a result of random mutation, while Scientist 2 credits the inheritance of acquired characteristics. Choice B can then be eliminated, because it is related to the explanation of the wrong scientist. Choice C would actually refute Scientist 1's hypothesis, and D is irrelevant. Only (A) provides a valid explanation for the increase in average height based on the random mutations described by Scientist 1.

PASSAGE VII

34. G
Category: Figure Interpretation
Difficulty: Low
Getting to the Answer: According to Figure 1, Group B had the greatest number of cows infected with BSE. Group B was fed meat from scrapie-infected sheep, which matches (G).

35. D
Category: Figure Interpretation
Difficulty: Medium
Getting to the Answer: In Experiment 1, the researchers vary what is fed to the cows by giving them meat from scrapie-free sheep and from scrapie-infected sheep. The cows are later examined for signs of BSE. One common type of incorrect answer choice for Experiment questions are choices, such as B for this question, that include factors that are outside the parameters of the experiment.

36. F
Category: Figure Interpretation
Difficulty: Medium
Getting to the Answer: In Experiment 2, the researchers vary what is injected into cows' brains. Any answer choice that discusses ingestion as a focus of this experiment is incorrect. This eliminates G, H, and J. Often, incorrect answer choices for Experiment questions, such as G for this question, will include the appropriate information from the wrong experiment.

37. B
Category: Scientific Reasoning
Difficulty: Medium
Getting to the Answer: By examining the method used in a given experiment, one can determine the assumptions the researchers made in carrying out the experiment and the sources of error. Often, an error enters the experiment because of the assumptions researchers make. In Experiments 1 and 2, the researchers examined the brains of cows a year and a half after the cows were fed scrapie-infected sheep meat or were injected with scrapie-infected sheep brains. If a year and a half is not a sufficient amount of time for BSE to develop, some of the cows that were counted as not infected might have developed BSE if they had been given more time.

38. H
Category: Scientific Reasoning
Difficulty: Low
Getting to the Answer: To answer this question, you need to determine how to test whether BSE can be transmitted via scrapie-infected goats. To test this, one would compare the effects of feeding cows scrapie-free goat meat with the effects of feeding cows scrapie-infected goat meat and compare the effects of injecting cows with scrapie-free goat brains with the effects of injecting them with scrapie-infected goat brains.

39. A
Category: Scientific Reasoning
Difficulty: Medium
Getting to the Answer: Remember that control groups are used as standards of comparison. The control group used in Experiment 1 is the group that is fed scrapie-free sheep meat. If the same proportion of Group A developed BSE as that of Group B, then the researchers would not have any evidence to support the hypothesis that the ingestion of scrapie-infected sheep meat causes BSE.

40. G
Category: Scientific Reasoning
Difficulty: High
Getting to the Answer: Because the proportion of the group of cows that ate scrapie-infected sheep meat and developed BSE was greater than the proportion of the group that were injected with scrapie-infected sheep brains and developed BSE, one can conclude that a cow that eats scrapie-infected sheep meat is more likely to develop BSE than a cow that is injected with scrapie-infected sheep brains. Mere exposure to scrapie-infected sheep, as opposed to ingestion of it, is never studied in either experiment, so conclusion I can be eliminated.

WRITING TEST

MODEL ESSAY

Below is an example of what a high-scoring essay might look like. Notice that the author states her position clearly in the introductory paragraph and supports that position with evidence in the following paragraphs. This essay also uses transitions, some advanced vocabulary, and an effective "hook" to draw in the reader.

Children are often asked, "What do you want to be when you grow up?" Little do they know, whether or not they go to college has a huge impact on their career choices. The issue under discussion is whether or not schools should develop dual curricula to serve both those students who are college bound and those who intend to forego college, instead entering a career directly after high school graduation. The fundamental concern is how to best serve all students, which I believe should be through two curricula working together.

The first point of view supports having all students pursue the same curriculum, one primarily directed at college-bound students. It essentially states that an academic-only curriculum is valuable for all students, regardless of their future plans. It is true that the ability to think critically, have a wide range of content knowledge, and be adept at the skills and techniques required to live a full and productive life are important to all students. A well-rounded person is able to take advantage of many more opportunities than those with limited skills. Furthermore, should a career-bound student change his mind and decide to go to college, he will have the basic requirements for a successful college experience. However, if a student is determined to start his career directly after high school, the college curriculum could be a waste of his time, and he would be better served by taking courses that prepare him for his career. I am in partial agreement with option one, since a broad, basic education is important for all students. However, it is similarly important to prepare students for their future lives, which may begin immediately after high school.

The second option supports career-readiness education. As stated above, it is important to recognize that some students are set on a embarking on a career after high school rather than on going to college. High school is the place to prepare these students, since it can offer the courses that are most applicable to them. Furthermore, students in danger of dropping out of high school are generally those who are uninterested in or bored by the academic curriculum. Such students would be more engaged and successful if they were able to take classes that fit their goals and interests, and they would be more likely not only to stay in school but also to be well-prepared for their careers. This option purposes a dual curriculum, one for the college bound and one for career readiness, and thus provides the best education for both. On the assumption that non-college-bound students are also taking an adequate number of general education classes, and supplementing them with courses designed to provide them with the skills they need for their careers, these students will now have a solid academic foundation as well as career skills. College-bound students will still have the option to take more academic classes. Thus, I support this option because it provides the best solution for both groups.

Those who agree that students who are not planning on going to college should not be offered career-centered classes are denying the fact that not all students go to college, even if given incentives to do so.

This option does not take into consideration the numerous facts that can affect whether or not a student goes to college. Some students cannot afford college fees, even with scholarships; some have a low GPA that would prohibit their acceptance at college; and some do poorly on pre-college tests such as the ACT. Encouraging students to go to college is not enough to ensure that they will. Though it may be true that college teaches how to be productive in the workforce, it is also true that being a fully qualified mechanic or electrician after high school is extremely productive for those who choose these careers. This option is an elitist one that would disregard those for whom college is not a goal, and it is one with which I completely disagree.

It is vital to all students that high schools prepare them for their future, whatever that may be. Those who choose college are well-served by an intensive academic curriculum that gives them a solid foundation for college. On the other hand, for those who choose, or are forced by circumstances, to forego college in favor of immediate entry into the workforce, it is important that, along with a sufficient academic foundation, they also receive training in their intended careers. Thus the second perspective, that of providing both an academic and a career-oriented curriculum, serves the needs of both and is the most effective one for all students.

You can evaluate your essay and the model essay based on the following criteria, covered in the Scoring section of ACT Writing Test:

- Does the author discuss all three perspectives provided in the prompt?
- Is the author's own perspective clearly stated?
- Does the body of the essay assess and analyze each perspective?
- Is the relevance of each paragraph clear?
- Does the author start a new paragraph for each new idea?
- Is each sentence in a paragraph relevant to the point made in that paragraph?
- Are transitions clear?
- Is the essay easy to read? Is it engaging?
- Are sentences varied?
- Is vocabulary used effectively? Is college-level vocabulary used?

Part 8

Busy Resources

Busy Summaries

STEP ONE SUMMARY

What This Book Will Teach You:

- The ACT Test Format
    — The same kinds of questions and the same concepts and skills appear every time the ACT is given.
- Test Strategies
    — The ACT tests problem-solving and memory skills, so test-smart strategies and techniques are extremely beneficial to learn.
- The Concepts Tested
    — The ACT tests certain skills that are learned in high school and will be needed for college.

Format:

- A three-hour exam taken for the college admission process that tests problem-solving skills in:
    — English
    — Math
    — Reading
    — Science
    — Writing (1 optional essay)

ACT Writing Test:

- Certain colleges and universities require this test.
- It consists of a 40-minute essay in which students write a response to a prompt.

Scoring:

- A raw score is calculated and then converted into a scaled score (composite score).
- ACT scaled scores range from 1–36.
- The ACT is only one of several factors that college admission officers take into consideration.
- The composite score is the most important score.

Guessing on the ACT:

- The ACT score is based on the number of questions answered correctly, and there is no wrong-answer penalty.

Retaking the Test:

- You can take the ACT as many times as you would like.

- Caveat: Don't automatically designate colleges to receive your ACT scores when you are registering. It is better to wait until you have received your score to then make the decision.

STEP TWO SUMMARY

The English Test:

- 45 minutes long, 75 questions

- Most common format: a word, phrase, or sentence in a passage is underlined and you are given four options:
    — Leave the underlined portion alone (NO CHANGE).
    — Replace it with one of three alternatives.

- Tricks/Key Tips to Remember:
    — Trust your ears; if it sounds right, it probably is.

The Math Test:

- 60 minutes long, 60 questions

- Format: multiple-choice questions with five possible choices

- Tricks/Key Tips to Remember:
    — Directions may state "Figures not drawn to scale" when in fact, many of them are—which can help when answering questions.

The Reading Test:

- 35 minutes long, 40 questions

- Format:
    — Four different categories of passages:
        - Social Science
        - Natural Science
        - Humanities
        - Prose Fiction
    — Three different categories of Reading questions:
        - Detail questions
        - Inference questions
        - Big Picture questions

- Tricks/Key Tips to Remember:
    — Skim the passages.

The Science Test:

- 35 minutes long, 40 questions
- Format: three types of questions:
  — Data Representation questions
  — Experiment questions
  — Principle questions
- Tricks/Key Tips to Remember:
  — You don't need to be a science expert; all that's required is common sense and general knowledge.

The Writing Test:

- 40 minutes long, 1 essay
- Students are required to write a persuasive essay in which they take a stance on a specific issue and support it with evidence.
- Tricks/Key Tips to Remember:
  — Find out if the college you're applying to requires this test.

STEP THREE SUMMARY

Do Question Triage:

- Make a quick decision about how hard and time-consuming each problem looks:
  — If the question looks comprehensible, answer it right away.
  — If the question looks tough and time-consuming, skip it and come back later.
  — If the question looks impossible, guess and move on.
- Kaplan's Two-Pass Plan
  — Make two passes through each group of questions: a *triage pass* and then a *cleanup pass*.

Put the Material into a Form You Can Understand:

- Reword the questions so that you can figure out what they are really asking.
- Draw diagrams to put material into a usable form.

Ignore Irrelevant Issues:

- Just because an issue looks interesting doesn't make it important or relevant.

Check Back:

- On the Reading and Science tests, always refer to the place in the passage where the answer can be found.

Answer the Right Question:

- Beware, because often the correct answers to different questions are included among the wrong answers to a question.

Look for the Hidden Answer:

- Many questions have more than one possible solution but only one correct answer choice is given (usually the less obvious of the possible answers).

Guess Intelligently:

- There are two kinds of guessing:
  — Blind guessing on questions that are too hard or time-consuming
  — Considered guessing on questions that you have done some work on

Be Careful with the Answer Grid:

- Gridding the answers in groups rather than one question at a time works best.

Use the Letters of the Answer Choices to Stay on Track:

- Pay attention to the letter in the answer [even-numbered questions have F, G, H, J (and K in math) as answer choices, rather than A, B, C, D (and E in math)].

Keep Track of Time:

- On average, English, Reading, and Science questions should take about 30 seconds each.
- English and Reading passages should take about nine minutes each.
- Science passages should average about five minutes.
- Math questions should average less than one minute each.

STEP FOUR SUMMARY

Kaplan's Three-Step Method for ACT English:

- Step 1. Read until you have enough information to identify the issue.
- Step 2. Eliminate choices that do NOT address the issue.
- Step 3. Plug in the remaining choices, and choose the one that is most correct, concise, and relevant.
  — Grammatical errors will most likely sound wrong to your ear, so trust your instinct.
  — Don't concentrate solely on the technical rules of grammar and punctuation.

Skimming English Passages:

- Prior to immediately correcting the prose on the English passage, start by skimming the complete passage to understand its context first.

Economy Questions:

- Remember that the longer answer is not always the better choice.

- When in doubt, take it out.

The Three Rules of Economy:

- *Redundancy*: The text in a sentence should never repeat itself.
- *Verbosity*: Write concisely, as long as it is grammatically correct.
- *Irrelevance*: Omit complete ideas that are not directly related to the purpose of the passage.

Sense Questions:

- Good grammar makes good sense.
  — *Completeness*: Every sentence should consist of an entire thought.
  — *Sentence structure*: Avoid both fragments and run-ons.
  — *Modifiers*: Modifiers should be as close as possible to the things they modify.
  — *Idiom*: Make sure words in the sentence are used in the correct manner.
  — *Pronouns*: Make it explicit to whom or to what the pronoun refers.
  — *Logic*: Structural clues must be logical.
  — *Verb usage*: Make sure verbs match their subject and the tense of the surrounding context.
  — *Tone*: The tone of the text should be kept consistent.

Nonstandard Format Questions:

- Judging the passage
  — Look at the passage in its entirety and make sure that your answer continues the passage's logical flow.

STEP FIVE SUMMARY

Twelve Classic Grammar Errors:

1. *It* and *They* (Singulars and Plurals): Singular nouns must match with singular verbs and pronouns, and plural nouns must match with plural verbs and pronouns.

2. Commas or Dashes (Parenthetical Phrases): Parenthetical phrases must begin and end with the same punctuation mark.

3. Run-Ons and Comma Splices: Usually only one thing should happen in each sentence, but more than one event can be connected by a comma and a conjugation, a semicolon, or by "subordinating" one event to the other in a clause.

4. Fragments: Look for sentence fragments which consist of writing that could be a subordinate part of a sentence but not a whole sentence itself.

5. Misunderstood Punctuation Marks:
   - Comma (,): Represents pause; often a comma is optional.

- Semicolon (;): Separates two complete but closely related thoughts.
- Colon (:): Connects two equivalent things; usually used to begin a list.
- Dash (—): Can be used for any kind of pause, usually a long one or one indicating a significant shift in thought.

6. *-ly* Endings (Adverbs and Adjectives): Nouns and pronouns must be modified by adjectives while verbs and adjectives themselves must be modified by adverbs.

7. *Its* and *It's* (Apostrophe Use): Apostrophes are used with possessives and contractions.
    - *It's* is a contraction for *it is*, while *its* shows possession.

8. *There*, *Their*, *They're* and *Are*, *Our* (Proper Word Usage):
    - *They're* is a contraction for *they are*. *There* is spelled like *here* because both indicate location. *Their* means "of or belonging to them." *Are* is a verb and *our* is a possessive.

9. *Sang*, *Sung*, *Brang*, *Brung*, etc. (Verb Forms):
    - When considering different forms of the same verb ask yourself: Who did it and when did they do it?
    - For regular verbs:
       — Add *-s* when the subject is *he*, *she*, or *it* and the time is present tense.
       — Add *-ed* for times in the past.
       — For times in the future or several steps back in the past, use *will*, *will have*, *have*, and *had*.
    - Irregular verbs should be learned separately.
       — We say *sang* rather than *singed* and *have sung* rather than *have singed* or *have sang*.

10. *-er* and *-est*, *More* and *Most* (Comparatives and Superlatives):
    - Words with *-er* or with *more* should compare only two things. If more than two things are being compared, use *-est* or *most*.
    - Don't use *more* or *most* if you can use *-er* and *-est* endings instead.

11. Confusing *Between* and *Among*:
    - Use *between* only when two things are involved or when comparisons in a larger group are made between pairs of things.
    - Use *among* when more than two things are involved.

12. Confusing *Less* and *Fewer*:
    - Make sure that you use the word *less* only for uncountable things; when things can be counted, use *fewer*.

STEP SIX SUMMARY

Question Breakdown for ACT Math:

- 24 pre-algebra and elementary algebra questions
- 9 intermediate algebra questions
- 9 coordinate geometry questions
- 14 plane geometry questions
- 4 trigonometry questions

Kaplan's Four-Step Method for ACT Math:

Step 1. What is the question?
— Focus on the question stem by rephrasing it or reading it twice before focusing on the answer choices.

Step 2. What information am I given?
— Look for patterns and shortcuts to find the creative solutions that will get you more right answers in less time.
— Try solving the problems without focusing on the answer choices.

Step 3. What can I do with the information?
— Picking Numbers
— Backsolving
— Straightforward math
— Guess strategically

Step 4. Am I finished?
— Double-check that you have answered the question you identified in Step 1. Once you get an answer, or once you are stuck, look at the answer choices.

Important Math Concepts:

- Integers include 0 and negative whole numbers.
- Evens and odds include 0 and negative whole numbers.
- Prime numbers do not include 1.
- Remainders are integers.
- The $\sqrt{}$ symbol represents the positive square root only.
- Rectangles include squares.

Kaplan's Two-Pass Plan for ACT Math:

- *First pass*: Examine each problem in order, and complete every problem that you understand. You should spend approximately 45 minutes on this.
- *Second pass*: Spend the last 15 minutes going back to the questions that you had trouble with the first time.

What to Do When You're Stuck:

- *Guesstimate*: If you understand a problem but cannot figure out how to solve it, then make a "ballpark estimate" or an educated guess.
- *Eyeballing*: When in doubt, use your eyes on diagram questions.

STEP SEVEN SUMMARY

Think before You Calculate:

- You are permitted to use a calculator on the ACT Math test; however, it is not mandatory that you use a calculator to answer questions on the ACT.
- If a problem seems to need a lot of calculation, look for a quicker way.

Calculators—The Game Plan:

- Practice using your calculator.
- Come to the exam with a fresh set of batteries.
- Calculators can help you in *Backsolving* (plugging the answer choices back into the question stem) and *Picking Numbers* (substituting numbers for the variables in the question).

STEP EIGHT SUMMARY

Complex Algebra and Coordinate Geometry Questions:

- To solve these problems, use one of the four "shake-it-up" techniques:
  — *Restate the problem*: Change your perspective and restate expressions that don't make immediate sense. Think of how you would handle an easy problem that tests the same principle.
  — *Remove the disguise*: A complex problem is often just an easier problem in disguise, so try to find the creative solution.
  — *Pick Numbers*: Make abstract problems more concrete by substituting numbers for the variables in the question.
  — *Backsolve*: Plug the answer choices back into the question. When using this approach, start with the middle choice.

Story Questions:

- Percent problems: Part = Percent × Whole
- Percent change problems:
  — To increase a number by a certain percent, calculate that percent of the original number and add it on.
  — To decrease a number by a certain percent, calculate that percent of the original number and subtract.

- Don't just add and subtract percents; pick 100 as the original number and work from there.
- Weighted average problems:
  - To get a combined average, it's usually wrong just to average the averages.
  - As with regular average problems, the key is to use the sum.
- Probability problems:
  - The probability of what will happen is not affected by what has happened already.

STEP NINE SUMMARY

Textbook Geometry Questions:

- *Area of a square or other rectangle*: Area = $l \times w$
- *Area of a circle*: Area = $(\pi)r^2$
- *Area of a trapezoid*: Area = $\left(\dfrac{b_1 + b_2}{2}\right)h$
- *Pythagorean theorem*: $a^2 + b^2 = c^2$
- *Area of a triangle*: Area = $\dfrac{1}{2}bh$

Complex Geometry Questions:

- If you find yourself stuck, look for hidden information.
- Pencil in additions to the given diagrams.
- Figureless problems: Draw your own diagram.
- Multistep problems: Break down complex problems into simpler steps.

STEP TEN SUMMARY

The key is to read very quickly but actively, getting a sense of the "main idea" of the passage.

Know Where You're Going:

- Pay careful attention to "structural clues."
- *But*, *nevertheless*, and *moreover* help you get a sense of where a piece of writing is going.
- *Clearly*, *as a result*, or *no one can deny that* helps determine the logic of the passage.

Kaplan's Five-Step Method for ACT Reading:

Step 1. Preread the passage quickly.
- Underline, jot down notes, circle clues; don't get bogged down by details.

Step 2. Consider the question stem.
- Don't let answer choices direct your thinking.

Step 3. Refer to the passage.
— Always refer back to the passages before choosing an answer.

Step 4. Answer the question in your own words.
— Formulate an answer to the question before reading the answer choices.

Step 5. Match your answer to one of the choices.
— Find the answer choice that most closely matches your formulated answer.

The Fiction and Science Passages:

- The Prose Fiction passage:
  — This passage will not break down into an orderly outline, so do not try to organize the passage by the function of each paragraph; instead, focus on the story itself and its characters.
  — Prose Fiction passage strategy:
    - Who are these people?
    - What is their state of mind?
    - What's really going on?
- The Natural Sciences passage:
  — It is especially important not to get distracted by detail in the science passage.

The Kaplan Method for Paired Passages:

Step 1: Read Passage A and answer the questions about it.
Step 2: Read Passage B and answer the questions about it.
Step 3: Answer questions asking about both passages.

STEP ELEVEN SUMMARY

There are three main types of Reading questions on the test:

- Detail questions:
  — Look for the answer in the passage.
  — When given a specific line reference, always read a few sentences before and after the cited lines to understand the context.
- Inference questions:
  — Combine ideas logically to make an inference.
  — Keep inferences as close to the passage as possible.
- Big Picture questions:
  — Test your understanding of the theme, purpose, and organization of the passage.
  — Focus on the main point or purpose of the passage, author's attitude or tone, logic underlying the author's argument, how ideas in different parts of the passage relate to each other, and the difference between fact and opinion.
  — It's a good idea to do the Detail and Inference questions first, which will then help you complete the Big Picture questions.

Proven Reading Strategies:

- Your task is to "find and paraphrase," not "comprehend and remember."
- Skipping questions: Answer the easy questions for each passage first. Skip the hard ones and come back to them later.

STEP TWELVE SUMMARY

Reading Skills for Science Reasoning:

- Learn to "read" graphs, tables, and research summaries.
- Learn to look for patterns in the numbers that appear.

Kaplan's Three-Step Method for ACT Science:

Step 1. Map the passage, identifying and marking the purpose, method, and results of the experiment.
— Take notes so you can easily find information once you tackle the questions.

Step 2. Scan figures, identifying variables and patterns.
— Don't forget to take a look at the figures and observe how they relate to the passage.

Step 3. Find support for the answer in the passage.
— Always look back at the passage and the question stem before choosing your answer so that you don't mix up units and/or words such as *not* and *except*.

Reading Tables and Graphs:

- Determine what is being represented.
- Determine what the axes (or columns and rows) represent.
- Take note of the units of measurement.
- Look for trends in the data. When you first examine the graph or table, don't focus on exact numbers; instead, look for patterns.

Three Characteristic Patterns in Graphs and Tables:

- *Extremes* (maximums and minimums): The highest and the lowest points that things reach
- *Critical points*: Points of change; values at which something dramatic happens
- *Variation* (proportionality): The way two different things change in relation to each other
- *Direct variation*: Two things vary in the same way
- *Inverse variation*: Two things vary in opposite ways

When You're Running Out of Time:

- Don't preread the passage. Instead, glance over the questions without reading the passage, and do as many Data Representation questions as possible.

STEP THIRTEEN SUMMARY

How Scientists Think: Two Different Kinds of Logic:

- *General-to-specific thinking*: Scientists use a general rule to find a specific fact.
- *Specific-to-general thinking*: Scientists look at something specific to develop a general rule. This conclusion is called a hypothesis because the scientist has not checked this general rule on everything.

How Experiments Work:

- Experiments help scientists do specific-to-general thinking efficiently by forming and then testing a hypothesis.

A Controlled Situation:

- An experiment will contain only a single variable that changes from test to test or group to group.
- All other factors (diet, temperatures, space, etc.) remain the same.
- There must be a control group for comparison purposes.

Find What Varies:

- You can tell what a researcher is trying to find out about by checking to see what he/she allows to vary.
- When you see an experiment, ask yourself three things:
  — What is the varying factor?
  — What is the control group?
  — What do the results show?

STEP FOURTEEN SUMMARY

Prereading the Conflicting Viewpoints Passage:

- Don't waste time trying to decide which scientist's viewpoint is "correct," just make sure to understand the differing opinions.
  — Remember the Five-Step Method for ACT Science:
    – Step 1. Map the passage, identifying and marking the purpose, method, and results of the experiment.
    – Step 2. Scan figures, identifying variables and patterns.
    – Step 3. Find support for the answer in the passage.
- A scientific viewpoint on the ACT usually consists of two parts:
  — A statement of the general theory; it is important to see how each theory opposes the other.

— A summary of the data behind the theory; there are two kinds of data: data that weakens the opposing scientist's theory and data that supports the scientist's own theory.

Key Strategies:

- Identifying the conflict
- Attacking the questions

STEP FIFTEEN SUMMARY

Essay Scoring:

- Graded on a scale of 1–6 along four domains
- Skills tested in the Writing test:
  — Stating a clear perspective on an issue; answering the question being asked in the prompt
  — Providing supporting evidence and logical reasoning
  — Maintaining focus and organizing your ideas logically
  — Writing clearly

Kaplan's Four-Step Method for the ACT Essay:

Step 1. Prompt
— There is no right or wrong answer to the essay. Just choose your position and then support your opinion with examples.

Step 2. Plan
— Take five minutes or less to build a plan for your essay.
— *Subject matter*: Avoid emotional and offensive examples.
— *Controlled brainstorming*: Come up with workable examples and arguments as quickly as possible.
— *Information banks*: Refresh your memory about your favorite books, school subjects, historical events, personal experiences, and so on so that you can use them as examples in your essays.
— *Structure your essay*: Create a clear introduction with a hook, a body with transitions, and a conclusion that ends with a bang.

Step 3. Produce
— *Appearances count*: Write 3–5 paragraphs, and write neatly.
— *Stick with the plan:* Don't introduce any new ideas other than the ones from your outline.
— *Write carefully:* Low scores can result from misspellings and grammatical errors.
— *Stay on task:* Make your writing direct and persuasive.

Last-Minute Tips

Testing Time Frame
- The Night before the Test
- The Morning of the Test
- During the Test
- After the Test

Is it starting to feel like your whole life is a buildup to the ACT? You've known about it for years, you've worried about it for months, and now you've spent at least a few hours in solid preparation for it. As the test gets closer, you may find your anxiety is on the rise. But you really shouldn't worry. After the preparation you've received from this book, you're in good shape for test day.

To calm any pre-test jitters you may have (and assuming you've left yourself at least some breathing time before your ACT), let's go over a few last-minute tips.

THE NIGHT BEFORE THE TEST

Don't study!

Get together an "ACT survival kit" containing the following items:

- A calculator
- A watch
- At least three sharpened No. 2 pencils
- A pencil sharpener
- Two erasers
- Photo ID card
- Your admission ticket
- A snack—there's a break, and you'll probably get hungry

Know exactly where you're going and how you're getting there. It's probably a good idea to visit your test center sometime before test day, so that you know what to expect on the big day.

Read a good book, take a bubble bath, watch TV. Exercise can be a good idea early in the afternoon. Working out makes it easier to sleep when you're nervous, and it also makes many people feel better.

Take It Easy

Don't study the night before the test. Relax!

Get a good night's sleep. Go to bed early and allow for some extra time to get ready in the morning.

THE MORNING OF THE TEST

- Dress in layers so that you can adjust to the temperature of the test room.
- Eat breakfast. Make it something substantial, but not anything too heavy or greasy. Don't drink a lot of coffee if you're not used to it; bathroom breaks cut into your time, and too much caffeine—or any other kind of drug—is a bad idea.
- Read something. Warm up your brain with a newspaper or a magazine. Don't let the ACT be the first thing you read that day.

- Be sure to get there early. Allow yourself extra time for traffic, mass-transit delays, and any other possible problems. If you can, go to the test with a friend (even if he or she isn't taking the test). It's nice to have somebody supporting you right up to the last minute.

DURING THE TEST

Don't get rattled. If you find your confidence slipping, remind yourself that you know the test; you know the strategies; you know the material tested. You're in great shape, as long as you relax!

Even if something goes really wrong, don't panic. If the test booklet is defective, try to stay calm. Raise your hand, and tell the proctor you need a new book. If you accidentally misgrid your answer page or put the answers in the wrong section, again don't panic. Raise your hand, and tell the proctor. He or she might be able to arrange for you to re-grid your test after it's over, when it won't cost you any time.

AFTER THE TEST

Once the test is over, put it out of your mind. If you don't plan to take the ACT again, shelve this book and start thinking about more interesting things.

You might walk out of the ACT thinking that you blew it. This is a normal reaction. Lots of people—even the highest scorers—feel that way. You tend to remember the questions that stumped you, not the many that you knew.

If you really did blow the test, you can take it again and no admissions officer will be the wiser. Odds are, though, you didn't really blow it. Most people only remember their disasters on the test; they don't remember the numerous small victories that kept piling up the points. And no test experience is going to be perfect. If you were distracted by the proctor's hacking cough this time around, next time you may be even more distracted by construction noise, or a cold, or the hideous lime-green sweater of the person sitting in front of you.

Canceling Your Score

Don't cancel your score unless you have a good, solid reason. But if you have a good reason, do it.

Finishing the ACT is an accomplishment. Celebrate!

Stress Management

Managing Your Stress

- Identify the sources of stress.
- Take stock of your strengths and weaknesses.
- Imagine yourself succeeding.
- Exercise your frustrations away.
- Take a deep breath . . .
- . . . and keep breathing.
- Quick tips for the days just before the exam
- Stress tips
- Handling stress during the test

The countdown has begun. Your date with *the test* is looming on the horizon. Anxiety is on the rise. Butterflies in your stomach have gone ballistic. Perhaps you feel as if the last thing you ate has turned into a lead ball. Your thinking is getting cloudy. Maybe you think you won't be ready. Maybe you already know your stuff, but you're going into panic mode anyway. Worst of all, you're not sure of what to do about it.

Don't worry! It is possible to tame that anxiety and stress—before and during the ACT or any other test. We'll show you how. You won't believe how quickly and easily you can deal with that anxiety.

Lack of control is one of the prime causes of stress. A ton of research shows that if you don't have a sense of control over what's happening in your life, you can easily end up feeling helpless and hopeless. So just having concrete things to do and to think about—taking control—will help reduce your stress. This resource shows you how to take control during the days leading up to the test.

Identify the Sources of Stress

In the space provided, jot down anything you identify as a source of your test-related stress. The idea is to pin down any sources of anxiety so that you can take control of them. Here are some common examples to get you started.

- I always freeze up on tests.
- I'm nervous about the math (or the grammar or reading comp, etc.).
- I need a good/great score to go to my top choice school.
- My older brother/sister/best friend/girl- or boyfriend did really well. I must match their scores or do better.
- My parents, who are paying for school, will be really disappointed if I don't test well.
- I'm afraid of losing my focus and concentration.
- I'm afraid I'm not spending enough time preparing.
- I study like crazy, but nothing seems to stick in my mind.
- I always run out of time and get panicky.
- I feel as though thinking is becoming like wading through thick mud.

My Sources of Stress

_____

_____

_____

_____

_____

Take a few minutes to think about the things you've just written down. Then put them in some sort of order. List the statements you most associate with your stress and anxiety first, and put the least disturbing items last. Chances are, the top of the list is a fairly accurate description of exactly how you react to test anxiety, both physically and mentally. The later items usually describe your fears (disappointing mom and dad, looking bad, etc.). As you write the list, you're forming a hierarchy of items so you can deal first with the anxiety-provokers that bug you most. Very often, taking care of the major items from the top of the list goes a long way toward relieving overall testing anxiety. You probably won't have to bother with the stuff you placed last.

My Strengths and Weaknesses

Take one minute to list the areas of the ACT or any other test that you are good at. They can be general ("world history") or specific ("Nevada from 1850 to 1875"). Put down as many as you can think of, and if possible, time yourself. Write for the entire time; don't stop writing until you've reached the one-minute stopping point.

Strong Test Subjects

_____

_____

_____

_____

_____

Next, take one minute to list areas of the test you're not so good at, just plain bad at, have failed at, or keep failing at. Again, keep it to one minute, and continue writing until you reach the cutoff. Don't be afraid to identify and write down your weak spots. In all probability, as you do both lists, you'll find you are strong in some areas and not so strong in others. Taking stock of your strengths and weaknesses lets you know the areas you don't have to worry about and the ones that will demand extra attention and effort.

Weak Test Subjects

_____

_____

_____

_____

_____

Facing your weaknesses gives you some distinct advantages. It helps a lot to find out where you need to spend extra effort. Increased exposure to tough material makes it more familiar and less intimidating. (After all, we mostly fear what we don't know and are probably afraid to face.) You'll feel better about yourself because you're dealing directly with areas of the test that bring on your anxiety. You can't help feeling more confident when you know you're actively strengthening your chances of earning a higher overall score.

Now, go back to the "good" list, and expand it for two minutes. Take the general items on that first list and make them more specific; take the specific items and expand them into more general conclusions. Naturally, if anything new comes to mind, jot it down. Focus all of your attention and effort on your strengths. Don't underestimate yourself or your abilities. Give yourself full credit. At the same time, don't list strengths you don't really have; you'll only be fooling yourself.

Expanding from general to specific might go as follows: If you listed "world history" as a broad topic you feel strong in, you would then narrow your focus to include areas of this subject about which you are particularly knowledgeable. Your areas of strength might include modern European history, the events leading up to World War I, the Bolshevik revolution, etc.

Whatever you know comfortably (that is, almost as well as you know the back of your hand) goes on your "good" list. Okay. You've got the picture. Now, get ready, check your starting time, and start writing down items on your expanded "good" list.

Strong Test Subjects: An Expanded List

_____

_____

_____

_____

After you've stopped, check your time. Did you find yourself going beyond the two minutes allotted? Did you write down more things than you thought you knew? Is it possible you know more than you've given yourself credit for? Could that mean you've found a number of areas in which you feel strong?

You just took an active step toward helping yourself. Notice any increased feelings of confidence? Enjoy them.

Here's another way to think about your writing exercise. Every area of strength and confidence you can identify is much like having a reserve of solid gold at Fort Knox. You'll be able to draw on your reserves as you need them, and you can use your reserves to solve difficult questions, maintain confidence, and keep test stress and anxiety at a distance. The encouraging thing is that every time you recognize another area of strength, succeed at coming up with a solution, or get a good score on a test, you increase your reserves. And there is absolutely no limit to how much self-confidence you can have or how good you can feel about yourself.

Imagine Yourself Succeeding

This next little group of exercises is both physical and mental. It's a natural follow-up to what you've just accomplished with your lists.

First, get yourself into a comfortable sitting position in a quiet setting. Wear loose clothes. If you wear glasses, take them off. Then, close your eyes and breathe in a deep, satisfying breath of air. Really fill your lungs until your rib cage is fully expanded and you can't take in any more. Then, exhale the air completely. Imagine you're blowing out a candle with your last little puff of air. Do this two or three more times, filling your lungs to their maximum and emptying them totally. Keep your eyes closed, comfortably but not tightly. Let your body sink deeper into the chair as you become even more comfortable.

Strategy

Forcing relaxation is like asking yourself to flap your arms and fly. You can't do it, and every push and prod only gets you more frustrated. Relaxation is something you don't work at. You simply let it happen. Think about it. When was the last time you tried to force yourself to go to sleep and it worked?

With your eyes shut, you can notice something very interesting. You're no longer dealing with the worrisome stuff going on in the world outside of you. Now you can concentrate on what happens *inside* you. The more you recognize your own physical reactions to stress and anxiety, the more you can do about them. You may not realize it, but you've begun to regain a sense of being in control.

Let images begin to form on the "viewing screens" on the back of your eyelids. You're experiencing visualizations from the place in your mind that makes pictures. Allow the images to come easily and naturally; don't force them. Imagine yourself in a relaxing situation. It might be in a special place you've visited before or one you've read about. It can be a fictional location that you create in your imagination, but a real-life memory of a place or situation you know is usually better. Make it as detailed as possible and notice as much as you can.

Stay focused on the images as you sink farther back into your chair. Breathe easily and naturally. You might have the sensations of any stress or tension draining from your muscles and flowing downward, out your feet and away from you.

Take a moment to check how you're feeling. Notice how comfortable you've become. Imagine how much easier it would be if you could take the test feeling this relaxed and in this state of ease. You've coupled the images of your special place with sensations of comfort and relaxation. You've also found a way to become relaxed simply by visualizing your own safe, special place.

Now, close your eyes and start remembering a real-life situation in which you did well on a test. If you can't come up with one, remember a situation in which you did something (academic or otherwise) that you were really proud of—a genuine accomplishment. Make the memory as detailed as possible. Think about the sights, the sounds, the smells, even the tastes associated with this experience. Remember how confident you felt as you accomplished your goal. Now start thinking about the upcoming test. Keep your thoughts and feelings in line with that prior successful experience. Don't make comparisons between them. Just imagine taking the upcoming test with the same feelings of confidence and relaxed control.

This exercise is a great way to bring the test down to earth. You should practice this exercise often, especially when the prospect of taking the exam starts to bum you out. The more you practice it, the more effective the exercise will be for you.

Exercise Your Frustrations Away

Whether it is jogging, walking, biking, mild aerobics, push-ups, or a pickup basketball game, physical exercise is a very effective way to stimulate both your mind and body and to improve your ability to think and concentrate. A surprising number of students get out of the habit of regular exercise, ironically because they're spending so much time prepping for the exam. Also, sedentary people—this is medical fact—get less oxygen to the blood and hence to the head than active people. You can live fine with a little less oxygen; you just can't think as well.

Any big test is a bit like a race. Thinking clearly at the end is just as important as having a quick mind early on. If you can't sustain your energy level in the last sections of the exam, there's too good a chance you could blow it. You need a fit body that can weather the demands any big exam puts on you. Along with a good diet and adequate sleep, exercise is an important part of keeping yourself in shape and thinking clearly for the long haul.

There's another thing that happens when you don't make exercise an integral part of your test preparation. Like any organism in nature, you operate best if all your "energy systems" are in balance. Studying uses a lot of energy, but it's all mental. When you take a study break, do something active instead of raiding the fridge or vegging-out in front of the TV. Take a 5- to 10-minute activity break for every 50 or 60 minutes that you study. The physical exertion gets your body into the act which helps to keep your mind and body in sync. Then, when you finish studying for the night and hit the sack you won't lie there, tense and unable to sleep, because your head is overtired and your body wants to pump iron or run a marathon.

One warning about exercise, however: it's not a good idea to exercise vigorously right before you go to bed. This could easily cause sleep onset problems. For the same reason, it's also not a good idea to study right up to bedtime. Make time for a "buffer period" before you go to bed: for 30 to 60 minutes, just take a hot shower, meditate, or simply veg out.

Take a Deep Breath . . .

Here's another natural route to relaxation and invigoration. It's a classic isometric exercise that you can do whenever you get stressed out—just before the test begins, even *during* the test. It's very simple and takes just a few minutes.

Close your eyes. Starting with your eyes and—without holding your breath—gradually tighten every muscle in your body (but not to the point of pain) in the following sequence:

1. Close your eyes tightly.
2. Squeeze your nose and mouth together so that your whole face is scrunched up. (If it makes you self-conscious to do this in the test room, skip the face-scrunching part.)
3. Pull your chin into your chest, and pull your shoulders together.
4. Tighten your arms to your body, then clench your fists.
5. Pull in your stomach.
6. Squeeze your thighs and buttocks together, and tighten your calves.
7. Stretch your feet, then curl your toes (watch out for cramping in this part).

At this point, every muscle should be tightened. Now, relax your body, one part at a time, *in reverse order*, starting with your toes. Let the tension drop out of each muscle. The entire process might take five minutes from start to finish (maybe a couple of minutes during the test). This clenching and unclenching exercise should help you to feel very relaxed.

. . . and Keep Breathing

Conscious attention to breathing is an excellent way of managing that ACT test stress (or any stress, for that matter). The majority of people who get into trouble during tests take shallow breaths. They breathe using only their upper chests and shoulder muscles and may even hold their breath for long periods of time. Conversely, the test taker who by accident or design keeps breathing normally and rhythmically is likely to be more relaxed and in better control during the entire test experience.

So now is the time to get into the habit of relaxed breathing. Do the next exercise to learn to breathe in a natural, easy rhythm. By the way, this is another technique you can use during the test to collect your thoughts and ward off excess stress. The entire exercise should take no more than three to five minutes.

With your eyes still closed, breathe in slowly and deeply through your nose. Hold the breath for a bit, and then release it through your mouth. The key is to breathe slowly and deeply by using your diaphragm (the big band of muscle that spans your body just above your waist) to draw air in and out naturally and effortlessly. Breathing with your diaphragm encourages relaxation and helps minimize tension. Try it and notice how relaxed and comfortable you feel.

Quick Tips for the Days Just before the Exam

- The best test takers do less and less as exam day approaches. Taper off on your study schedule and take it easy on yourself. You want to be relaxed and ready on test day. Give yourself time off, especially the evening before the exam. By that time, if you've

studied well, everything you need to know is firmly stored in your memory banks.
- Positive self-talk can be extremely liberating and invigorating, especially as the test looms closer. Tell yourself things such as, "I *choose* to take this test" rather than "I *have* to"; "I *will* do well" rather than "I *hope* things go well"; "I *can*" rather than, "I *cannot.*" Be aware of negative, self-defeating thoughts and images and immediately counter any you become aware of. Replace them with affirming statements that encourage your self-esteem and confidence. Create and practice doing visualizations that build on your positive statements.
- Get your act together sooner rather than later. Have everything (including choice of clothing) laid out days in advance. Most importantly, *know where the test will be held and the easiest, quickest way to get there.* You will gain great peace of mind if you know that all the little details—gas in the car, directions, etc.—are firmly in your control before test day.
- Experience the test site a few days in advance. This is very helpful if you are especially anxious. If at all possible, find out what room your part of the alphabet is assigned to, and try to sit there (by yourself) for a while. Better yet, bring some practice material and do at least a section or two, if not an entire practice test, in that room. In this case, familiarity doesn't breed contempt; it generates comfort and confidence.
- Forgo any practice on the day before the test. It's in your best interest to marshal your physical and psychological resources for 24 hours or so. Even race horses are kept in the paddock and treated like princes the day before a race. Keep the upcoming test out of your consciousness; go to a movie, take a pleasant hike, or just relax. Don't eat junk food or tons of sugar. And—of course—get plenty of rest the night before. Just don't go to bed too early. It's hard to fall asleep earlier than you're used to, and you don't want to lie there thinking about the test.
- When you dress on test day, do it in loose layers. That way you'll be prepared no matter what the temperature of the room is. (An uncomfortable temperature will just distract you from the job at hand.) And if you have an item of clothing that you tend to feel "lucky" or confident in—a shirt, a pair of jeans, whatever—wear it.

Study Tips

- Don't work in a messy or cramped area. Before you sit down to study, clear yourself a nice, open space. And make sure you have books, paper, pencils—whatever tools you will need—within easy reach.
- Don't study on your bed, especially if you have problems with insomnia. Your mind may start to associate the bed with work and make it even harder for you to fall asleep.
- A lamp with a 75-watt bulb is optimal for studying. But don't keep it so close that you create a glare.
- If you want to play music, keep it low and in the background. Music with a regular, mathematical rhythm—reggae, for example—aids the learning process. A recording of ocean waves is also soothing.

Handling Stress during the Test

The biggest stress will be test day itself. Fear not; there are methods of quelling your stress during the test.

- Keep moving forward instead of getting bogged down in a difficult question. You don't have to get everything right to achieve a fine score. The best test takers skip difficult material in search of the easier stuff. They mark the ones that require extra time and thought. This strategy buys time and builds confidence so you can handle the tough stuff later.
- Don't be thrown if other test takers seem to be working more busily and furiously than you are. Continue to spend your time patiently but doggedly thinking through your answers; it's going to lead to better results. Don't mistake the other people's sheer activity for progress and higher scores.
- *Keep breathing!* Weak test takers forget to breathe properly as the test proceeds. They start holding their breath without realizing it, or they breathe erratically or arrhythmically. Improper breathing interferes with clear thinking.
- Some quick isometrics during the test—especially if concentration is wandering or energy is waning—can help. Try this: Put your palms together and press intensely for a few seconds. Concentrate on the tension you feel through your palms, wrists, forearms, and up into your biceps and shoulders. Then, quickly release the pressure. Feel the difference as you let go. Focus on the warm relaxation that floods through the muscles. Now you're ready to return to the task.
- Here's another isometric exercise that will relieve tension in both your neck and eye muscles. Slowly rotate your head from side to side, turning your head and eyes to look as far back over each shoulder as you can. Feel the muscles stretch on one side of your neck as they contract on the other. Repeat five times in each direction.

With what you've just learned here, you're armed and ready to do battle with the ACT—or any other test. This book and your studies will give you the information you'll need to answer the questions. It's all firmly planted in your mind. You also know how to deal with any excess tension that might come along, both when you're studying for and taking the exam. You've experienced everything you need to tame your test anxiety and stress. You *are* going to get a great score.

100 Essential Math Concepts

The math on the ACT covers a lot of ground—from arithmetic to algebra to geometry.

Don't let yourself be intimidated. We've highlighted the 100 most important concepts that you'll need for ACT Math and listed them in this chapter.

Use this list to remind yourself of the key areas you'll need to know. Do four concepts a day, and you'll be ready within a month. If a concept continually causes you trouble, circle it and refer to it as you try to do the questions.

You've probably been taught most of these concepts in school already, so this list is a great way to refresh your memory.

NUMBER PROPERTIES

1. Number Categories

Integers are **whole numbers**; they include negative whole numbers and zero.

A **rational number** is a number that can be expressed as a **ratio of two integers**. **Irrational numbers** are real numbers—they have locations on the number line—but they can't be expressed precisely as a fraction or decimal. The most important irrational numbers are $\sqrt{2}, \sqrt{3}$, and π.

2. Adding/Subtracting Signed Numbers

To **add a positive and a negative number**, first ignore the signs and find the positive difference between the number parts. Then attach the sign of the original number with the larger number part. For example, to add 23 and −34, first ignore the minus sign and find the positive difference between 23 and 34—that's 11. Then attach the sign of the number with the larger number part—in this case, it's the minus sign from the −34. So 23 + (−34) = −11.

Make **subtraction** situations simpler by turning them into addition. For example, you can think of −17 − (−21) as −17 + (+21) or −17 −21 as −17 + (−21).

To **add or subtract a string of positives and negatives**, first turn everything into addition. Then combine the positives and negatives so that the string is reduced to the sum of a single positive number and a single negative number.

3. Multiplying/Dividing Signed Numbers

To multiply and/or divide positives and negatives, treat the number parts as usual, and **attach a minus sign if there were originally an odd number of negatives**. For example, to multiply −2, −3, and −5, first multiply the number parts: 2 × 3 × 5 = 30. Then go back and note that there were *three*—an *odd* number—negatives, so the product is negative: (−2) × (−3) × (−5) = −30.

4. PEMDAS

When performing multiple operations, remember to perform them in the right order.

PEMDAS, which means **Parentheses** first, then **Exponents**, then **Multiplication** and **Division** (left to right), and lastly **Addition** and **Subtraction** (left to right). In the expression 9 − 2 × (5 − 3)² + 6 ÷ 3, begin with the parentheses: (5 − 3) = 2. Then do the exponent: 2^2 = 4. Now the expression is: 9 − 2 × 4 + 6 ÷ 3. Next do the multiplication and division to get 9 − 8 + 2, which equals 3. If you have difficulty remembering PEMDAS, use this sentence to recall it: Please Excuse My Dear Aunt Sally.

5. Counting Consecutive Integers

To count consecutive integers, **subtract the smallest from the largest and add 1**. To count the number of integers from 13 through 31, subtract: 31 − 13 = 18. Then add 1: 18 + 1 = 19.

NUMBER OPERATIONS AND CONCEPTS

6. Exponential Growth

If r is the ratio between consecutive terms, a_1 is the first term, a_n is the nth term, and S_n is the sum of the first n terms, then $a_n = a_1 r^{n-1}$ and $S_n = \dfrac{a_1 - a_1 r^n}{1 - r}$.

7. Union and Intersection of Sets

The things in a set are called elements or members. The **union** of Set A and Set B, sometimes expressed as $A \cup B$, is the set of elements that are in either or both Set A and Set B. If Set $A = \{1, 2\}$ and Set $B = \{3, 4\}$, then $A \cup B = \{1, 2, 3, 4\}$. The **intersection** of Set A and Set B, sometimes expressed as $A \cap B$, is the set of elements common to both Set A and Set B. If Set $A = \{1, 2, 3\}$ and Set $B = \{3, 4, 5\}$, then $A \cap B = \{3\}$.

DIVISIBILITY

8. Factor/Multiple

The **factors** of integer n are the positive integers that divide into n with no remainder. The **multiples** of n are the integers that n divides into with no remainder. For example, 6 is a factor of 12, and 24 is a multiple of 12. 12 is both a factor and a multiple of itself, since 12 × 1 = 12 and 12 ÷ 1 = 12.

9. Prime Factorization

To find the prime factorization of an integer, continue factoring until **all the factors are prime**. For example, to factor 36: 36 = 9 × 4 = 3 × 3 × 2 × 2.

10. Relative Primes

Relative primes are integers that have no common factor other than 1. To determine whether two integers are relative primes, break them both down to their prime factorizations. For example: 35 = 5 × 7, and 54 = 2 × 3 × 3 × 3. They have **no prime factors in common**, so 35 and 54 are relative primes.

11. Common Multiple

A common multiple is a number that is a multiple of two or more integers. You can always get a common multiple of two integers by **multiplying** them, but unless the two numbers are relative primes, the product will not be the *least* common multiple. For example, to find a common multiple for 12 and 15, you could just multiply: $12 \times 15 = 180$.

To find the **least common multiple (LCM)**, check out the **multiples of the larger integer** until you find one that's **also a multiple of the smaller**. To find the LCM of 12 and 15, begin by taking the multiples of 15: 15 is not divisible by 12; 30 is not; nor is 45. But the next multiple of 15, 60, *is* divisible by 12, so it's the LCM.

12. Greatest Common Factor (GCF)

To find the greatest common factor, break down the integers into their prime factorizations and multiply **all the prime factors they have in common**. For example: $36 = 2 \times 2 \times 3 \times 3$ and $48 = 2 \times 2 \times 2 \times 2 \times 3$. These integers have a 2×2 and a 3 in common, so the GCF is $2 \times 2 \times 3 = 12$.

13. Even/Odd

To predict whether a sum, difference, or product will be even or odd, just **take simple numbers like 1 and 2 and see what happens**. There are rules—"odd times even is even," for example—but there's no need to memorize them. What happens with one set of numbers generally happens with all similar sets.

14. Multiples of 2 and 4

An integer is divisible by 2 (even) if the **last digit** is even. An integer is divisible by 4 if the **last two digits form a multiple of 4**. The last digit of 562 is 2, which is even, so 562 is a multiple of 2. The last two digits form 62, which is *not* divisible by 4, so 562 is not a multiple of 4. The integer 512, however, is divisible by 4 because the last two digits form 12, which is a multiple of 4.

15. Multiples of 3 and 9

An integer is divisible by 3 if the **sum of its digits is divisible by 3**. An integer is divisible by 9 if the **sum of its digits is divisible by 9**. The sum of the digits in 957 is 21, which is divisible by 3 but not by 9, so 957 is divisible by 3 but not by 9.

16. Multiples of 5 and 10

An integer is divisible by 5 if the **last digit is 5 or 0**. An integer is divisible by 10 if the **last digit is 0**. The last digit of 665 is 5, so 665 is a multiple of 5 but *not* a multiple of 10.

17. Remainders

The remainder is the **whole number left over after division**. 487 is 2 more than 485, which is a multiple of 5, so when 487 is divided by 5, the remainder is 2.

FRACTIONS AND DECIMALS

18. Reducing Fractions

To reduce a fraction to lowest terms, **factor out and cancel** all factors the numerator and denominator have in common.

$$\frac{28}{36} = \frac{4 \times 7}{4 \times 9} = \frac{7}{9}$$

19. Adding/Subtracting Fractions

To add or subtract fractions, first find a **common denominator**, then add or subtract the numerators.

$$\frac{2}{15} + \frac{3}{10} = \frac{4}{30} + \frac{9}{30} = \frac{4+9}{30} = \frac{13}{30}$$

20. Multiplying Fractions

To multiply fractions, **multiply** the numerators and **multiply** the denominators.

21. Dividing Fractions

To divide fractions, **invert** the second one and **multiply**.

$$\frac{1}{2} \div \frac{3}{5} = \frac{1}{2} \times \frac{5}{3} = \frac{1 \times 5}{2 \times 3} = \frac{5}{6}$$

22. Mixed Numbers and Improper Fractions

To convert a mixed number to an improper fraction, **multiply** the whole number part by the denominator, then **add** the numerator. The result is the new numerator (over the same denominator). To convert $7\frac{1}{3}$, first multiply 7 by 3, then add 1, to get the new numerator of 22. Put that over the same denominator, 3, to get $\frac{22}{3}$.

To convert an improper fraction to a mixed number, divide the denominator into the numerator to get a **whole number quotient with a remainder**. The quotient becomes the whole number part of the mixed number, and the remainder becomes the new numerator—with the same denominator. For example, to convert $\frac{108}{5}$, first divide 5 into 108, which yields 21 with a remainder of 3. Therefore, $\frac{108}{5} = 21\frac{3}{5}$.

23. Reciprocal

To find the reciprocal of a fraction, **switch the numerator and the denominator**. The reciprocal of $\frac{3}{7}$ is $\frac{7}{3}$. The reciprocal of 5 is $\frac{1}{5}$. The product of reciprocals is 1.

24. Comparing Fractions

One way to compare fractions is to **reexpress them with a common denominator**. $\frac{3}{4} = \frac{21}{28}$ and $\frac{5}{7} = \frac{20}{28}$. $\frac{21}{28}$ is greater than $\frac{20}{28}$, so $\frac{3}{4}$ is greater than $\frac{5}{7}$. Another method is to **convert them both to decimals**. $\frac{3}{4}$ converts to 0.75, and $\frac{5}{7}$ converts to approximately 0.714.

25. Converting Fractions and Decimals

To convert a fraction to a decimal, **divide the bottom into the top**. To convert $\frac{5}{8}$, divide 8 into 5, yielding 0.625.

To convert a decimal to a fraction, set the decimal over 1 and **multiply the numerator and denominator by 10** raised to the number of digits which are to the right of the decimal point.

To convert 0.625 to a fraction, you would multiply $\frac{0.625}{1}$ by $\frac{10^3}{10^3}$ or $\frac{1,000}{1,000}$. Then simplify: $\frac{625}{1,000} = \frac{5 \times 125}{8 \times 125} = \frac{5}{8}$.

26. Repeating Decimal

To find a particular digit in a repeating decimal, note the **number of digits in the cluster that repeats**. If there are two digits in that cluster, then every second digit is the same. If there are three digits in that cluster, then every third digit is the same. And so on. For example, the decimal equivalent of $\frac{1}{27}$ is 0.037037037..., which is best written $0.\overline{037}$. There are three digits in the repeating cluster, so every third digit is the same: 7. To find the 50th digit, look for the multiple of 3 just less than 50—that's 48. The 48th digit is 7, and with the 49th digit the pattern repeats with 0. The 50th digit is 3.

27. Identifying the Parts and the Whole

The key to solving most fraction and percent word problems is to identify the **part** and the **whole**. Usually you'll find the **part** associated with the verb *is/are* and the **whole** associated with the word *of*. In the sentence "Half of the boys are blonds," the whole is the boys ("*of* the boys"), and the part is the blonds ("*are* blonds").

PERCENTS

28. Percent Formula

Whether you need to find the part, the whole, or the percent, use the same formula:

$$\text{Part} = \text{Percent} \times \text{Whole}$$

Example:	What is 12 percent of 25?
Setup:	Part = 0.12 × 25
Example:	15 is 3 percent of what number?
Setup:	15 = 0.03 × Whole
Example:	45 is what percent of 9?
Setup:	45 = Percent × 9

29. Percent Increase and Decrease

To increase a number by a percent, **add the percent to 100 percent**, convert to a decimal, and multiply. To increase 40 by 25 percent, add 25 percent to 100 percent, convert 125 percent to 1.25, and multiply by 40. 1.25 × 40 = 50.

30. Finding the Original Whole

To find the **original whole before a percent increase or decrease**, set up an equation. Think of the result of a 15 percent increase over *x* as 1.15*x*.

Example:	After a 5 percent increase, the population was 59,346. What was the population before the increase?
Setup:	1.05*x* = 59,346

31. Combined Percent Increase and Decrease

To determine the combined effect of multiple percent increases and/or decreases, **start with 100 and see what happens**.

Example: A price went up 10 percent one year, and the new price went up 20 percent the next year. What was the combined percent increase?

Setup: First year: 100 + (10 percent of 100) = 110. Second year: 110 + (20 percent of 110) = 132. That's a combined 32 percent increase.

RATIOS, PROPORTIONS, AND RATES

32. Setting Up a Ratio

To find a ratio, put the number associated with the word **of on top** and the quantity associated with the word **to on the bottom**, and reduce. The ratio of 20 oranges to 12 apples is $\frac{20}{12}$, which reduces to $\frac{5}{3}$.

33. Part-to-Part Ratios and Part-to-Whole Ratios

If the parts add up to the whole, a part-to-part ratio can be turned into two part-to-whole ratios by putting **each number in the original ratio over the sum of the numbers**. If the ratio of males to females is 1 to 2, then the males-to-people ratio is $\frac{1}{1+2} = \frac{1}{3}$ and the females-to-people ratio is $\frac{2}{1+2} = \frac{2}{3}$. In other words, $\frac{2}{3}$ of all the people are female.

34. Solving a Proportion

To solve a proportion, cross multiply:

$$\frac{x}{5} = \frac{3}{4}$$
$$4x = 3 \times 5$$
$$x = \frac{15}{4} = 3.75$$

35. Rate

To solve a rate problem, **use the units** to keep things straight.

Example: If snow is falling at the rate of one foot every four hours, how many inches of snow will fall in seven hours?

Setup:
$$\frac{1 \text{ foot}}{4 \text{ hours}} = \frac{x \text{ inches}}{7 \text{ hours}}$$

$$\frac{12 \text{ inches}}{4 \text{ hours}} = \frac{x \text{ inches}}{7 \text{ hours}}$$

$$4x = 12 \times 7$$

$$x = 21$$

36. Average Rate

Average rate is *not* simply the average of the rates.

$$\text{Average } A \text{ per } B = \frac{\text{Total } A}{\text{Total } B}$$

$$\text{Average Speed} = \frac{\text{Total distance}}{\text{Total time}}$$

To find the average speed for 120 miles at 40 mph and 120 miles at 60 mph, **don't just average the two speeds**. First, figure out the total distance and the total time. The total distance is 120 + 120 = 240 miles. The times are three hours for the first leg and two hours for the second leg, or five hours total. The average speed, then, is $\frac{240}{5}$ = 48 miles per hour.

AVERAGES

37. Average Formula

To find the average of a set of numbers, **add them up and divide by the number of numbers**.

$$\text{Average} = \frac{\text{Sum of the terms}}{\text{Number of terms}}$$

To find the average of the five numbers 12, 15, 23, 40, and 40, first add them: 12 + 15 + 23 + 40 + 40 = 130. Then, divide the sum by 5: 130 ÷ 5 = 26.

38. Average of Evenly Spaced Numbers

To find the average of evenly spaced numbers, just **average the smallest and the largest**. The average of all the integers from 13 through 77 is the same as the average of 13 and 77:

$$\frac{13 + 77}{2} = \frac{90}{2} = 45$$

39. Using the Average to Find the Sum

$$\text{Sum} = (\text{Average}) \times (\text{Number of terms})$$

If the average of 10 numbers is 50, then they add up to 10×50, or 500.

40. Finding the Missing Number

To find a missing number when you're given the average, **use the sum**. If the average of four numbers is 7, then the sum of those four numbers is 4×7, or 28. Suppose that three of the numbers are 3, 5, and 8. These three numbers add up to 16 of that 28, which leaves 12 for the fourth number.

41. Median and Mode

The median of a set of numbers is the **value that falls in the middle of the set**. If you have five test scores, and they are 88, 86, 57, 94, and 73, you must first list the scores in increasing or decreasing order: 57, 73, 86, 88, 94.

The median is the middle number, or 86. If there is an even number of values in a set (six test scores, for instance), simply take the average of the two middle numbers.

The mode of a set of numbers is the **value that appears most often**. If your test scores were 88, 57, 68, 85, 99, 93, 93, 84, and 81, the mode of the scores would be 93 because it appears more often than any other score. If there is a tie for the most common value in a set, the set has more than one mode.

POSSIBILITIES AND PROBABILITY

42. Counting the Possibilities

The fundamental counting principle: If there are ***m* ways** one event can happen and ***n* ways** a second event can happen, then there are ***m* × *n* ways** for the two events to happen. For example, with five shirts and seven pairs of pants to choose from, you can have $5 \times 7 = 35$ different outfits.

43. Probability

$$\text{Probability} = \frac{\text{Favorable Outcomes}}{\text{Total Possible Outcomes}}$$

For example, if you have 12 shirts in a drawer and 9 of them are white, the probability of picking a white shirt at random is $\frac{9}{12} = \frac{3}{4}$. This probability can also be expressed as 0.75 or 75%.

POWERS AND ROOTS

44. Multiplying and Dividing Powers

To multiply powers with the same base, **add the exponents and keep the same base**:

$$x^3 \times x^4 = x^{3+4} = x^7$$

To divide powers with the same base, **subtract the exponents and keep the same base**:

$$y^{13} \div y^8 = y^{13-8} = y^5$$

45. Raising Powers to Powers

To raise a power to a power, **multiply the exponents**:

$$(x^3)^4 = x^{3 \times 4} = x^{12}$$

46. Simplifying Square Roots

To simplify a square root, **factor out the perfect squares** under the radical, unsquare them, and put the result in front:

$$\sqrt{12} = \sqrt{4 \times 3} = \sqrt{4} \times \sqrt{3} = 2\sqrt{3}$$

47. Adding and Subtracting Roots

You can add or subtract radical expressions **when the part under the radicals is the same**:

$$2\sqrt{3} + 3\sqrt{3} = 5\sqrt{3}$$

Don't try to add or subtract when the radical parts are different. There's not much you can do with an expression like:

$$3\sqrt{5} + 3\sqrt{7}$$

48. Multiplying and Dividing Roots

The product of square roots is equal to the **square root of the product**:

$$\sqrt{3} \times \sqrt{5} = \sqrt{3 \times 5} = \sqrt{15}$$

The quotient of square roots is equal to the **square root of the quotient**:

$$\frac{\sqrt{6}}{\sqrt{3}} = \sqrt{\frac{6}{3}} = \sqrt{2}$$

49. Negative Exponent and Rational Exponent

To find the value of a number raised to a negative exponent, simply rewrite the number, without the negative sign, as the bottom of a fraction with 1 as the numerator of the fraction: $3^{-2} = \frac{1}{3^2} = \frac{1}{9}$. If x is a positive number and a is a nonzero number, then $x^{\frac{1}{a}} = \sqrt[a]{x}$. So $4^{\frac{1}{2}} = \sqrt[2]{4} =$. If p and q are integers, then $x^{\frac{p}{q}} = \sqrt[q]{x^p}$. So $4^{\frac{3}{2}} = \sqrt[2]{4^3} = \sqrt{64} = 8$.

ABSOLUTE VALUE

50. Determining Absolute Value

The absolute value of a number is the distance of the number from zero on the number line. Because absolute value is a distance, it is always positive. The absolute value of 7 is 7; this is expressed |7| = 7. Similarly, the absolute value of −7 is 7: |7| = 7. Every positive number is the absolute value of two numbers: itself and its negative.

ALGEBRAIC EXPRESSIONS

51. Evaluating an Expression

To evaluate an algebraic expression, **plug in** the given values for the unknowns and calculate according to **PEMDAS**. To find the value of $x^2 + 5x - 6$ when $x = -2$, plug in −2 for x: $(-2)^2 + 5(-2) - 6 = -12$.

52. Adding and Subtracting Monomials

To combine like terms, **keep the variable part unchanged while adding or subtracting the coefficients**:

$$2a + 3a = (2 + 3)a = 5a$$

53. Adding and Subtracting Polynomials

To add or subtract polynomials, **combine like terms**.

$$(3x^2 + 5x - 7) - (x^2 + 12) =$$
$$(3x^2 - x^2) + 5x + (-7 - 12) =$$
$$2x^2 + 5x - 19$$

54. Multiplying Monomials

To multiply monomials, **multiply the coefficients and the variables separately**:

$$2a \times 3a = (2 \times 3)(a \times a) = 6a^2$$

55. Multiplying Binomials—FOIL

To multiply binomials, use **FOIL**. To multiply $(x + 3)$ by $(x + 4)$, first multiply the **F**irst terms: $x \times x = x^2$. Next the **O**uter terms: $x \times 4 = 4x$. Then the **I**nner terms: $3 \times x = 3x$. And finally the **L**ast terms: $3 \times 4 = 12$. Then add and combine like terms:

$$x^2 + 4x + 3x + 12 = x^2 + 7x + 12$$

56. Multiplying Other Polynomials

FOIL works only when you want to multiply two binomials. If you want to multiply polynomials with more than two terms, make sure you **multiply each term in the first polynomial by each term in the second**:

$$(x^2 + 3x + 4)(x + 5)$$
$$x^2(x+5) + 3x(x+5) + 4(x+5)$$
$$x^3 + 5x^2 + 3x^2 + 15x + 4x + 20 =$$
$$x^3 + 8x^2 + 19x + 20$$

After multiplying two polynomials together, the number of terms in your expression before simplifying should equal the number of terms in one polynomial multiplied by the number of terms in the second. In the example, you should have $3 \times 2 = 6$ terms in the product before you simplify like terms.

FACTORING ALGEBRAIC EXPRESSIONS

57. Factoring Out a Common Divisor

A factor common to all terms of a polynomial can be **factored out**. All three terms in the polynomial $3x^3 + 12x^2 - 6x$ contain a factor of $3x$. Pulling out the common factor yields $3x(x^2 + 4x - 2)$.

58. Factoring the Difference of Squares

One of the test maker's favorite factorables is the **difference of squares**.

$$a^2 - b^2 = (a - b)(a + b)$$

$x^2 - 9$, for example, factors to $(x - 3)(x + 3)$.

59. Factoring the Square of a Binomial

Recognize polynomials that are squares of binomials:

$$a^2 + 2ab + b^2 = (a + b)^2$$
$$a^2 - 2ab + b^2 = (a - b)^2$$

For example, $4x^2 + 12x + 9$ factors to $(2x + 3)^2$, and $n^2 - 10n + 25$ factors to $(n - 5)^2$.

60. Factoring Other Polynomials—FOIL in Reverse

To factor a quadratic expression, **think about what binomials you could use FOIL on to get that quadratic expression**. To factor $x^2 - 5x + 6$, think about what First terms will produce x^2, what Last terms will produce $+6$, and what Outer and Inner terms will produce $-5x$. Some common sense—and a little trial and error—lead you to $(x - 2)(x - 3)$.

61. Simplifying an Algebraic Fraction

Simplifying an algebraic fraction is a lot like simplifying a numerical fraction. The general idea is to **find factors common to the numerator and denominator and cancel them**. Thus, simplifying an algebraic fraction begins with factoring.

For example, to simplify $\dfrac{x^2 - x - 12}{x^2 - 9}$, first factor the numerator and denominator:

$$\frac{x^2 - x - 12}{x^2 - 9} = \frac{(x-4)(x+3)}{(x-3)(x+3)}$$

Canceling $x + 3$ from the numerator and denominator leaves you with $\dfrac{x-4}{x-3}$.

SOLVING EQUATIONS

62. Solving a Linear Equation

To solve an equation, do whatever is necessary to both sides to **isolate the variable**. To solve the equation $5x - 12 = -2x + 9$, first get all the *x*'s on one side by adding $2x$ to both sides: $7x - 12 = 9$. Then add 12 to both sides: $7x = 21$. Then divide both sides by 7: $x = 3$.

63. Solving "In Terms Of"

To solve an equation for one variable **in terms of** another means to **isolate the one variable on one side of the equation**, leaving an expression containing the other variable on the other side of the equation. To solve the equation $3x - 10y = -5x + 6y$ for *x* in terms of *y*, isolate *x*:

$$3x - 10y = -5x + 6y$$
$$3x + 5x = 6y + 10y$$
$$8x = 16y$$
$$x = 2y$$

64. Translating from English into Algebra

To translate from English into algebra, look for the key words and systematically turn phrases into algebraic expressions and sentences into equations. Be careful about order, especially when subtraction is called for.

Example: Celine and Remi play tennis. Last year, Celine won 3 more than twice the number of matches that Remi won. If Celine won 11 more matches than Remi, how many matches did Celine win?

Setup: You are given two sets of information. One way to solve this is to write a system of equations—one equation for each set of information. Use variables that relate well with what they represent. For example, use *r* to represent Remi's winning matches. Use *c* to represent Celine's winning matches. The phrase "Celine won 3 more than twice Remi" can be written as $c = 2r + 3$. The phrase "Celine won 11 more matches than Remi" can be written as $c = r + 11$.

65. Solving a Quadratic Equation

To solve a quadratic equation, put it in the "$ax^2 + bx + c = 0$" form, **factor** the left side (if you can), and set each factor equal to 0 separately to get the two solutions. To solve $x^2 + 12 = 7x$, first rewrite it as $x^2 - 7x + 12 = 0$. Then factor the left side:

$$(x-3)(x-4) = 0$$
$$x - 3 = 0 \text{ or } x - 4 = 0$$
$$x = 3 \text{ or } 4$$

66. Solving a System of Equations

You can solve for two variables only if you have two distinct equations. Two forms of the same equation will not be adequate. **Combine the equations** in such a way that **one of the variables adds or subtracts out**. To solve the two equations $4x + 3y = 8$ and $x + y = 3$, multiply both sides of the second equation by -3 to get: $-3x - 3y = -9$. Now add the two equations; the $3y$ and the $-3y$ cancel out, leaving: $x = -1$. Plug that back into either one of the original equations and you'll find that $y = 4$.

67. Solving an Inequality

To solve an inequality, do whatever is necessary to both sides to **isolate the variable**. Just remember that when you **multiply or divide both sides by a negative number**, you must **reverse the sign**. To solve $-5x + 7 < -3$, subtract 7 from both sides to get: $-5x < -10$. Now divide both sides by -5, remembering to reverse the sign: $x > 2$.

68. Radical Equations

A radical equation contains at least one radical expression. Solve radical equations by using standard rules of algebra. If $5\sqrt{x} - 2 = 13$, then $5\sqrt{x} = 15$ and $\sqrt{x} = 3$, so $x = 9$.

FUNCTIONS

69. Function Notation and Evaluation

Standard function notation is written $f(x)$ and read "f of 4." To evaluate the function $f(x) = 2x + 3$ for $f(4)$, replace x with 4 and simplify: $f(4) = 2(4) + 3 = 11$.

70. Direct and Inverse Variation

In direct variation, $y = kx$, where k is a nonzero constant. In direct variation, the variable y changes directly as x does. If a unit of Currency A is worth 2 units of Currency B, then $A = 2B$. If the number of units of B were to double, the number of units of A would double, and so on for halving, tripling, etc. In inverse variation, $xy = k$, where x and y are variables and k is a constant. A famous inverse relationship is *rate × time = distance*, where distance is constant. Imagine having to cover a distance of 24 miles. If you were to travel at 12 miles per hour, you'd need two hours. But if you were to halve your rate, you would have to double your time. This is just another way of saying that rate and time vary inversely.

71. Domain and Range of a Function

The domain of a function is the set of values for which the function is defined. For example, the domain of $f(x) = \dfrac{1}{1-x^2}$ is all values of x except 1 and −1, because for those values the denominator has a value of 0 and is therefore undefined. The range of a function is the set of outputs or results of the function. For example, the range of $f(x) = x^2$ is all numbers greater than or equal to zero, because x^2 cannot be negative.

COORDINATE GEOMETRY

72. Finding the Distance between Two Points

To find the distance between points, **use the Pythagorean theorem** or **special right triangles**. The difference between the *x*'s is one leg and the difference between the *y*'s is the other.

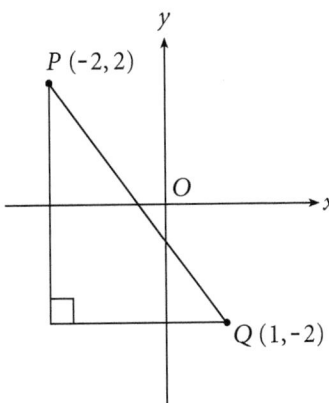

In the figure above, *PQ* is the hypotenuse of a 3-4-5 triangle, so *PQ* = 5.

You can also use the **distance formula**:

$$d = \sqrt{(x_1 - x_2)^2 + (y_1 - y_2)^2}$$

To find the distance between $R(3,6)$ and $S(5,-2)$:

$$d = \sqrt{(3-5)^2 + [6-(-2)]^2}$$
$$= \sqrt{(-2)^2 + (8)^2}$$
$$= \sqrt{68} = 2\sqrt{17}$$

73. Using Two Points to Find the Slope

$$\text{Slope} = \frac{\text{Change in } y}{\text{Change in } x} = \frac{\text{Rise}}{\text{Run}}$$

The slope of the line that contains the points $A(2,3)$ and $B(0,-1)$ is:

$$\frac{y_A - y_B}{x_A - x_B} = \frac{3-(-1)}{2-0} = \frac{4}{2} = 2$$

74. Using an Equation to Find the Slope

To find the slope of a line from an equation, put the equation into the **slope-intercept** form:

$$y = mx + b$$

The **slope is m**. To find the slope of the equation $3x + 2y = 4$, rearrange it:

$$3x + 2y = 4$$
$$2y = -3x + 4$$
$$y = -\frac{3}{2}x + 2$$

The slope is $-\frac{3}{2}$.

75. Using an Equation to Find an Intercept

To find the y-intercept, you can either put the equation into **y = mx + b (slope-intercept)** form—in which case **b is the y-intercept**—or you can just **plug x = 0** into the equation and **solve for y**. To find the x-intercept, plug **y = 0** into the equation and **solve for x**.

76. Finding the Midpoint

The midpoint of two points on a line segment is the average of the x-coordinates of the endpoints and the average of the y-coordinates of the endpoints. If the endpoints are (x_1, y_1) and (x_2, y_2), the midpoint is $\frac{x_1 + x_2}{2}, \frac{y_1 + y_2}{2}$. The midpoint of (3,5) and (9,1) is $\frac{3+9}{2}, \frac{5+1}{2}$ or (6,3).

LINES AND ANGLES

77. Intersecting Lines

When two lines intersect, **adjacent angles are supplementary and vertical angles are equal**.

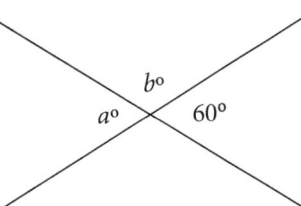

In the figure above, the angles marked a° and b° are adjacent and supplementary, so a + b = 180. Furthermore, the angles marked a° and 60° are vertical and equal, so a = 60.

78. Parallel Lines and Transversals

A transversal across parallel lines forms **four equal acute angles and four equal obtuse angles**. If the transversal meets the lines at a right angle, then all eight angles are right angles.

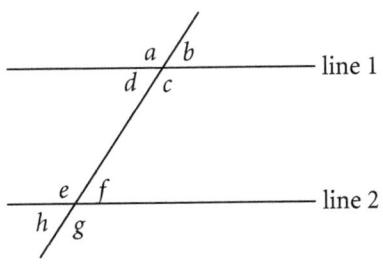

In the previous figure, line 1 is parallel to line 2. Angles *a*, *c*, *e*, and *g* are obtuse, so they are all equal. Angles *b*, *d*, *f*, and *h* are acute, so they are all equal.

Furthermore, **any of the acute angles is supplementary to any of the obtuse angles**. Angles *a* and *h* are supplementary, as are *b* and *e*, *c* and *f*, and so on.

TRIANGLES—GENERAL

79. Interior and Exterior Angles of a Triangle

The three angles of any triangle **add up to 180 degrees**.

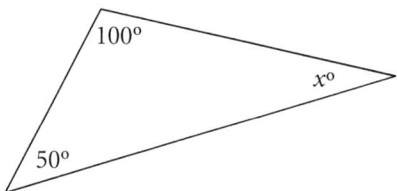

In the figure above, $x + 50 + 100 = 180$, so $x = 30$.

An exterior angle of a triangle is equal to the **sum of the remote interior angles**.

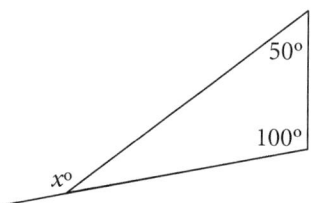

In the figure above, the exterior angle labeled $x°$ is equal to the sum of the remote angles: $x = 50 + 100 = 150$.

The three exterior angles of a triangle **add up to 360 degrees**.

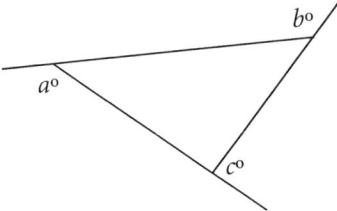

In the figure above, $a + b + c = 360$.

80. Similar Triangles

Similar triangles have the same shape: **corresponding angles are equal, and corresponding sides are proportional**.

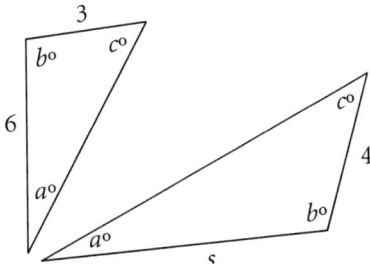

The triangles above are similar because they have the same angles. The side of length 3 corresponds to the side of length 4, and the side of length 6 corresponds to the side of length s.

$$\frac{3}{4} = \frac{6}{s}$$
$$3s = 24$$
$$s = 8$$

81. Area of a Triangle

Area of Triangle = $\frac{1}{2}$ (base)(height)

The height is the perpendicular distance between the side that's chosen as the base and the opposite vertex.

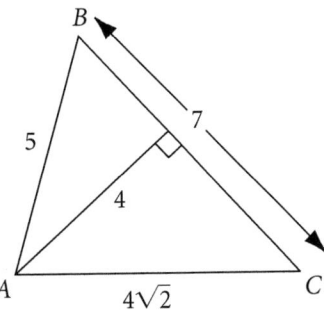

In the triangle above, 4 is the height when 7 is chosen as the base.

$$\text{Area} = \frac{1}{2}bh = \frac{1}{2}(7)(4) = 14$$

82. Triangle Inequality Theorem

The length of one side of a triangle must be **greater than the difference and less than the sum** of the lengths of the other two sides. For example, if it is given that the length of one side is 3 and the length of another side is 7, then you know that the length of the third side must be greater than 7 − 3 = 4 and less than 7 + 3 = 10.

83. Isosceles and Equilateral Triangles

An isosceles triangle is a triangle that has **two equal sides**. Not only are two sides equal, but the angles opposite the equal sides, called **base angles**, are also equal.

Equilateral triangles are triangles in which **all three sides are equal**. Since all the sides are equal, all the angles are also equal. All three angles in an equilateral triangle measure 60 degrees, regardless of the lengths of sides.

RIGHT TRIANGLES

84. Pythagorean Theorem

For all right triangles:

$$(\text{leg}_1)^2 + (\text{leg}_2)^2 = (\text{hypotenuse})^2$$

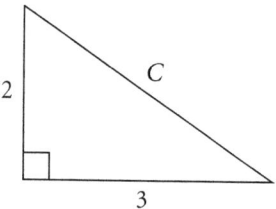

If one leg is 2 and the other leg is 3, then:

$$2^2 + 3^2 = c^2$$
$$c^2 = 4 + 9$$
$$c = \sqrt{13}$$

85. The 3-4-5 Triangle

If a right triangle's leg-to-leg ratio is 3:4, or if the leg-to-hypotenuse ratio is 3:5 or 4:5, it's a 3-4-5 triangle and you don't need to use the Pythagorean theorem to find the third side. Just figure out what multiple of 3-4-5 it is.

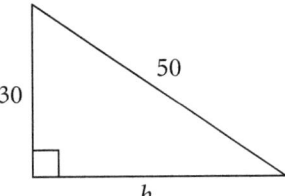

In the right triangle shown, one leg is 30 and the hypotenuse is 50. This is 10 times 3-4-5. The other leg is 40.

86. The 5-12-13 Triangle

If a right triangle's leg-to-leg ratio is 5:12, or if the leg-to-hypotenuse ratio is 5:13 or 12:13, then it's a 5-12-13 triangle and you don't need to use the Pythagorean theorem to find the third side. Just figure out what multiple of 5-12-13 it is.

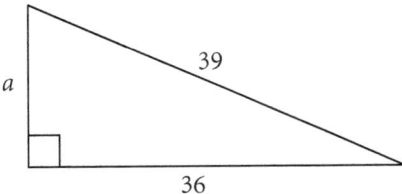

Here, one leg is 36 and the hypotenuse is 39. This is 3 times 5-12-13. The other leg is 15.

87. The 30-60-90 Triangle

The sides of a 30-60-90 triangle are in a ratio of $x:x\sqrt{3}:2x$. You don't need the Pythagorean theorem.

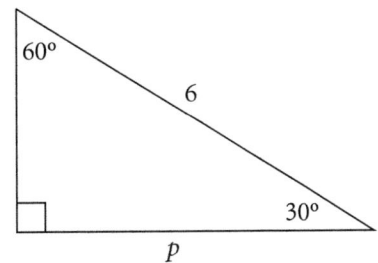

If the hypotenuse is 6, then the shorter leg is half that, or 3; and then the longer leg is equal to the short leg times $\sqrt{3}$, or $p = 3\sqrt{3}$.

88. The 45-45-90 Triangle

The sides of a 45-45-90 triangle are in a ratio of **x:x:x$\sqrt{2}$**.

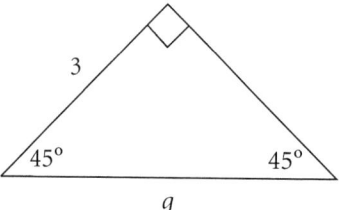

If one leg has a length of 3, then the other leg also has a length of 3, and the hypotenuse is equal to a leg times $\sqrt{2}$, or $q = 3\sqrt{2}$.

OTHER POLYGONS

89. Characteristics of a Rectangle

A rectangle is a **four-sided figure with four right angles**. Opposite sides are equal. Diagonals are equal.

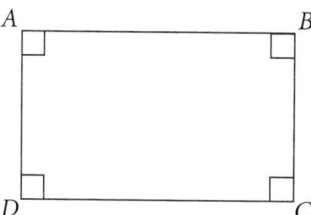

Quadrilateral *ABCD* above is shown to have three right angles. The fourth angle therefore also measures 90 degrees, and *ABCD* is a rectangle. The **perimeter** of a rectangle is equal to the sum of the lengths of the four sides, which is equivalent to 2(length + width).

Area of Rectangle = length × width

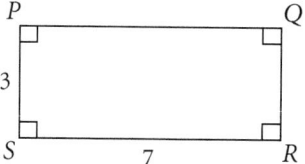

The area of a 7-by-3 rectangle is 7 × 3 = 21.

90. Characteristics of a Parallelogram

A parallelogram has **two pairs of parallel sides**. Opposite sides are equal. Opposite angles are equal. Consecutive angles add up to 180 degrees.

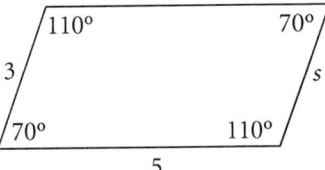

In the figure above, s is the length of the side opposite the 3, so s = 3.

Area of Parallelogram = base × height

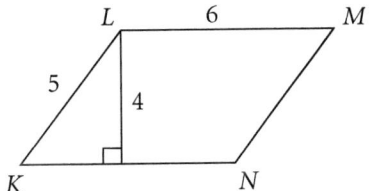

In parallelogram KLMN above, 4 is the height when LM or KN is used as the base.

Base × height = 6 × 4 = 24.

91. Characteristics of a Square

A square is a **rectangle with four equal sides**.

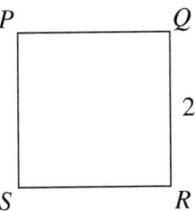

If PQRS is a square, all sides are the same length as QR. The **perimeter** of a square is equal to four times the length of one side.

Area of Square = (side)^2

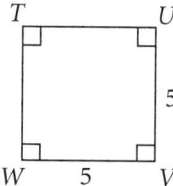

The square above, with sides of length 5, has an area of $5^2 = 25$.

92. Interior Angles of a Polygon

The **sum of the measures of the interior angles of a polygon = $(n - 2) \times 180$**, where n is the number of sides.

$$\text{Sum of the Angles} = (n - 2) \times 180$$

The eight angles of an octagon, for example, add up to $(8 - 2) \times 180 = 1{,}080$.

CIRCLES

93. Circumference of a Circle

$$\text{Circumference} = 2\pi r$$

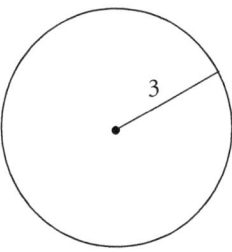

In the circle above, the radius has a length of 3, and so the circumference is $2\pi(3) = 6\pi$.

94. Length of an Arc

An arc is a piece of the circumference. If n is the degree measure of the arc's central angle, then the formula is:

$$\text{Length of an Arc} = \left(\frac{n}{360}\right)(2\pi r)$$

Busy Resources: 100 Essential Math Concepts

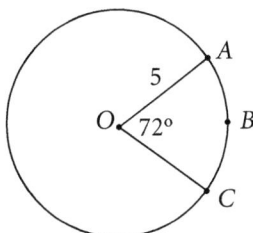

In the previous figure, the radius has a length of 5 and the measure of the central angle is 72 degrees. The arc length is $\frac{72}{360}$ or $\frac{1}{5}$ of the circumference:

$$\frac{72}{360}(2\pi)(5) = \frac{1}{5}(10\pi) = 2\pi$$

95. Area of a Circle

$$\text{Area of a Circle} = \pi r^2$$

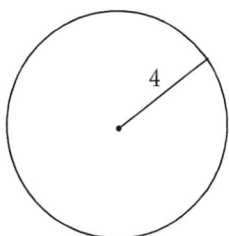

The area of the circle is $\pi(4)^2 = 16\pi$.

96. Area of a Sector

A sector is a piece of the area of a circle. If *n* is the degree measure of the sector's central angle, then the formula is:

$$\text{Area of a Sector} = \left(\frac{n}{360}\right)(\pi r^2)$$

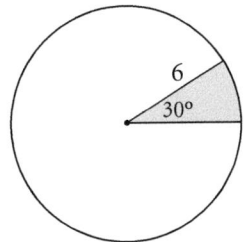

In the figure above, the radius has a length of 6 and the measure of the sector's central angle is 30 degrees. The sector has $\frac{30}{360}$ or $\frac{1}{12}$ of the area of the circle:

$$\frac{30}{360}(\pi)(6^2) = \frac{1}{12}(36\pi) = 3\pi$$

97. Tangency

When a line is tangent to a circle, the radius of the circle is perpendicular to the line at the point of contact.

SOLIDS

98. Surface Area of a Rectangular Solid

The surface of a rectangular solid consists of three pairs of identical faces. To find the surface area, find the area of each face and add them up. If the length is l, the width is w, and the height is h, the formula is:

$$\text{Surface Area} = 2lw + 2wh + 2lh$$

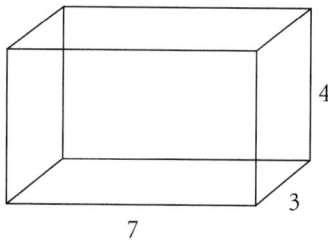

The surface area of the box above is: $(2 \times 7 \times 3) + (2 \times 3 \times 4) + (2 \times 7 \times 4) = 42 + 24 + 56 = 122$

99. Volume of a Rectangular Solid

$$\text{Volume of a Rectangular Solid} = lwh$$

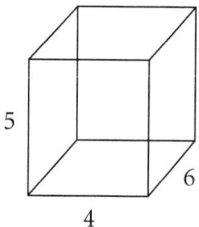

The volume of a 4-by-5-by-6 box is:

$$4 \times 5 \times 6 = 120$$

A cube is a rectangular solid with length, width, and height all equal. If s is the length of an edge of a cube, the volume formula is:

Volume of a Cube = s^3

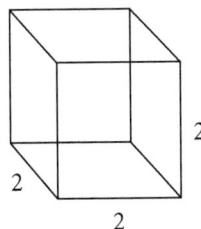

The volume of this cube is $2^3 = 8$.

100. Volume of a Cylinder

Volume of a Cylinder = $\pi r^2 h$

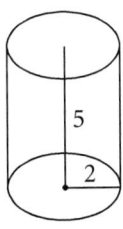

In the cylinder above, r = 2, h = 5, so:

$$\text{Volume} = \pi(2^2)(5) = 20\pi$$

Building Your Vocabulary

Both the ACT English and Reading tests depend on your ability to work with unfamiliar words. You won't be asked to actually define any words on the ACT, but you will often need to have a sense of their meaning to answer both types of questions.

TOUGH ACT WORDS

There are two types of tough ACT words:

- Unfamiliar words
- Familiar words with secondary meanings

Some words are hard because you haven't seen them before. The words *scintilla* or *circumlocution*, for instance, are probably not part of your everyday vocabulary, but they might pop up on your ACT. Easy words, such as *recognize* or *appreciation*, can also trip you up on the test because they have secondary meanings that you aren't used to.

KAPLAN'S THREE-STEP METHOD FOR VOCABULARY BUILDING

A great vocabulary can't be built overnight, but you can develop a better ACT vocabulary in a relatively short period of time. But you need to study wisely. Be strategic. How well you use your time between now and the day of the test is just as important as how much time you spend prepping.

Here's our Three-Step Method for building your vocabulary for the ACT:

Step 1. Learn words strategically.
Step 2. Learn word roots and prefixes.
Step 3. Personalize your study method.

Step 1. Learn Words Strategically

The best words to learn are words that have appeared often on the ACT. The test makers are not very creative in their choice of words for each test, so words that have appeared frequently are likely to show up again.

Step 2. Learn Word Roots and Prefixes

Most ACT words are made up of prefixes and roots that can get you at least partway to a definition. Often, that's all you need to get a right answer. Use the Word Root list to learn the most valuable ACT word roots. Target these words in your vocabulary review. Learn a few new roots a day, then familiarize yourself with meanings and sample words.

Step 3. Personalize Your Study Method

There's not just one *right* way to study vocabulary. Figure out a study method that works best for you, and stick to it. Here are some proven strategies:

- Use flashcards. Write down new words or word groups, and run through them whenever you have a few spare minutes. Put one new word or word group on one side of a 3 × 5 index card and a short definition on the back.
- Make a vocabulary notebook. List words in one column and their meanings in another. Test yourself. Cover up the meanings, and see what words you can define from memory. Make a sample sentence using each word in context.
- Make a vocabulary playlist. Record unknown words and their definitions. Pause for a moment before you read the definition. This will give you time to define the word in your head when you play the track back. Quiz yourself. Listen to your recording on your mp3 player. Play it in the car, on the bus, or whenever you have a few spare moments.
- Think of hooks that lodge a new word in your mind: create visual images of words. For example, to remember the verb form of *flag*, you can picture a flag drooping or losing energy as the wind dies down.
- Use rhymes and other devices that help you remember the words. For example, you might remember that a *verbose* person uses a lot of verbs.

It doesn't matter which techniques you use, as long as you learn words steadily and methodically. Doing so over several months with regular reviews is ideal.

DECODING STRANGE WORDS ON THE TEST

Trying to learn every word that could possibly appear on the ACT is like trying to memorize the license plate number of every car on the freeway. There are just too many to commit to memory.

No matter how much time you spend with flashcards, vocabulary playlists, or word lists, you're bound to face some mystery words on your ACT. No big deal. Just as you can use your basic multiplication skills to find the product of even the largest numbers, you can use what you know about words to focus on likely meanings of tough vocabulary words.

Go with Your Hunches

When you look at an unfamiliar word, your first reaction may be to say, "Don't know it. Gotta skip it." Not so fast. Vocabulary knowledge on the ACT is not an all-or-nothing proposition.

- Some words you know so well you can rattle off a dictionary definition of them.
- Some words you "sort of" know. You understand them when you see them in context but don't feel confident using them yourself.
- Some words are vaguely familiar. You know you've heard them somewhere before.

If you think you recognize a word, go with your hunch!

Use Your Foreign Language Skills

Many of the roots you'll encounter in ACT words come from Latin. Spanish, French, and Italian also come from Latin and have retained much of it in their modern forms. English is also a cousin to German and Greek. That means that if you don't recognize a word, try to remember if you know a similar word in another language. Look at the word *carnal*. Unfamiliar? What about *carne*, as in *chili con carne*? *Carn* means *meat* or *flesh*, which leads you straight to the meaning of *carnal*—pertaining to the flesh.

You could decode *carnivorous* (meat eating) in the same way. You can almost always figure out something about strange words on the test because ACT words are never all that strange. Chances are that few words on the ACT will be totally new to you, even if your recollection is more subliminal than vivid.

When All Else Fails

If you feel totally at a loss, eliminate choices that are clearly wrong and make an educated guess from the remaining choices. A wrong answer won't hurt you, but a right answer will help you a lot.

Word Root List

Most ACT words are made up of prefixes and roots that can get you at least partway to a definition. Often, that's all you need to get a right answer. Knowing roots can help you in others ways as well. First, instead of learning one word at a time, you can learn a whole group of words that contain a certain root. They'll be related in meaning, so if you remember one, it will be easier for you to remember others. Second, roots can often help you decode an unknown ACT word. If you recognize a familiar root, you could get a good enough idea of the word to answer the question.

Use the root list that follows to pick up the most valuable ACT roots. Target these words in your vocabulary preparation.

A, AN—not, without
amoral, atrophy, asymmetrical, anarchy, anesthetic

AB, A—from, away, apart
abnormal, abdicate, ablution, abnegate, absolve, abstemious, abstruse, annul, avert

AC, ACR—sour, sharp
acid, acerbic, exacerbate, acute, acrimony

AD, A—to, toward
adhere, adjacent, adjunct, admonish, adroit, adumbrate, accretion, accertion, alleviate, aspire, assail, assonance, attest

ALI, ALTR—another
alias, alienate, inalienable, altruism

AM, AMI—love
amorous, amicable, amiable, amity

AMBI, AMPHI—both
ambiguous, ambivalent, ambidextrous, amphibious

AMBL, AMBUL—walk
amble, ambulatory, perambulator, somnambulist

ANIM—mind, spirit, breath
animal, animosity, unanimous, magnanimous

ANN, ENN—year
annual, annuity, biennial, perennial

ANTE, ANT—before
antecedent, antediluvian, antiquated, anticipate

ANTHROP—human
anthropology, philanthropy

ANTI, ANT—against, opposite
antidote, antithesis, antacid, antagonist, antonym

AUD—hear
audio, audience, audition

AUTO—self
autobiography, autocrat, autonomous

BELLI, BELL—war
belligerent, bellicose, antebellum, rebellion

BENE, BEN—good
benevolent, benefactor, beneficent, benign

BI—two
bicycle, bisect, bilateral, bilingual, biped

BIBLIO—book
bibliography, bibliophile

BIO—life
biography, biology, amphibious, symbiotic, macrobiotics

BURS—money, purse
reimburse, disburse, bursar

CAD, CAS, CID—happen, fall
accident, cadence, cascade, deciduous

CAP, CIP—head
captain, decapitate, precipitate, recapitulate, accident

CARN—flesh
carnal, carnage, incarnate

CAP, CAPT, CEPT, CIP—take, hold, seize
capable, capacious, captivate, deception, intercept, inception, anticipate, emancipation

CED, CESS—yield, go
cede, precede, accede, cease, cessation, incessant

CHROM—color
chrome, chromatic, monochrome

CHRON—time
chronology, chronic, anachronism

CIDE—murder
suicide, homicide, regicide, patricide

CIRCUM—around
circumference, circumlocution, circumspect, circumvent

CLIN, CLIV—slope
incline, declivity, proclivity

CLUD, CLUS, CLAUS, CLOIS—shut, close
conclude, reclusive, claustrophobia, cloister, preclude, occlude

CO, COM, CON—with, together
coeducation, coagulate, coalesce, coerce, collateral, commodious, complaint, concord, congenial, congenital

COGN, GNO—know
recognize, cognition, diagnosis, agnostic, prognosis

CONTRA—against
controversy, incontrovertible, contravene

CORP—body
corpse, corporeal, corpulence

COSMO, COSM—world
cosmopolitan, cosmos, microcosm, macrocosm

CRAC, CRAT—rule, power
democracy, bureaucracy, autocrat, aristocrat

CRED—trust, believe
incredible, credulous, credence

CRESC, CRET—grow
crescent, crescendo, accretion

CULP—blame, fault
culprit, culpable, inculpate, exculpate

CURR, CURS—run
current, concur, cursory, precursor, incursion

DE—down, out, apart
depart, debase, debilitate, defamatory, demur

DEC—ten, tenth
decade, decimal, decathlon, decimate

DEMO, DEM—people
democrat, demographics, demagogue, epidemic

DI, DIURN—day
diary, quotidian, diurnal

DIA—across
diagonal, diatribe, diaphanous

DIC, DICT—speak
abdicate, diction, indict, verdict

DIS, DIF, DI—not, apart, away
disaffected, disband, disbar, distend, differentiate, diffidence, diffuse, digress, divert

DOC, DOCT—teach
docile, doctrine, doctrinaire

DOL—pain
condolence, doleful, dolorous, indolent

DUC, DUCT—lead
seduce, induce, conduct, viaduct, induct

EGO—self
ego, egoist, egocentric

EN, EM—in, into
enter, entice, encumber, embroil, empathy

ERR—wander
erratic, aberration, errant

EU—well, good
eulogy, euphemism, eurythmics, euthanasia

EX, E—out, out of
exit, exacerbate, excerpt, excommunicate, elicit, egress, egregious

FAC, FIC, FECT, FY, FEA—make, do
factory, facility, benefactor, malefactor, fiction, fictive, rectify, vilify, feasible

FAL, FALS—deceive
infallible, fallacious, false

FERV—boil
fervent, fervid, effervescent

FID—faith, trust
confident, diffidence, perfidious, fidelity

FLU, FLUX—flow
fluent, affluent, superfluous, flux

FORE—before
forecast, foreboding, forestall

FRAG, FRAC—break
fragment, fracture, refract

FUS—pour
profuse, infusion, effusive, diffuse

GEN—birth, class, kin
generation, congenital, homogeneous, ingenious, engender

GRAD, GRESS—step
graduate, gradual, retrograde, ingress, egress

GRAPH, GRAM—writing
biography, bibliography, epigram

GRAT—pleasing
grateful, gratitude, gratuitous, gratuity

GRAV, GRIEV—heavy
grave, gravity, aggrieve, grievous

GREG—crowd, flock
segregate, gregarious, aggregate

HABIT, HIBIT—have, hold
habit, cohabit, habitat, inhibit

HAP—by chance
happen, haphazard, hapless, mishap

HELIO, HELI—sun
heliocentric, heliotrope, aphelion, perihelion, helium

HETERO—other
heterosexual, heterogeneous, heterodox

HOL—whole
holocaust, catholic, holistic

HOMO—same
homogenize, homogeneous, homonym

HOMO—man
homo sapiens, homicide, bonhomie

HYDR—water
hydrant, hydrate, dehydration

HYPER—too much, excess
hyperactive, hyperbole, hyperventilate

HYPO—too little, under
hypodermic, hypothermia, hypochondria

IN, IG, IL, IM, IR—not
incorrigible, insomnia, interminable, incessant, ignorant, ignominious, ignoble, illicit, illimitable, immaculate, immutable, impertinent, improvident, irregular

IN, IL, IM, IR—in, on, into
invade, inaugurate, incandescent, illustrate, imbue, immerse, implicate, irrigate, irritate

INTER—between, among
intercede, intercept, interdiction, interject

INTRA, INTR—within
intrastate, intravenous, intramural, intrinsic

IT, ITER—between, among
transit, itinerant, transitory, reiterate

JECT, JET—throw
eject, interject, abject, trajectory, jettison

JOUR—day
journal, adjourn, sojourn

JUD—judge
judge, judicious, prejudice, adjudicate

JUNCT, JUG—join
junction, adjunct, injunction

JUR—swear, law
jury, abjure, perjure, jurisprudence

LAT—side
lateral, collateral, unilateral

LAV, LAU, LU—wash
lavatory, laundry, ablution, antediluvian

LEG, LEC, LEX—read, speak
legible, lecture, lexicon

LEV—light
elevate, levitate, levity, alleviate

LIBER—free
liberty, liberal, libertarian, libertine

LIG, LECT—choose, gather
eligible, elect, select

LIG, LI, LY—bind
ligament, oblige, religion, liable, liaison, lien, ally

LING, LANG—tongue
lingo, linguistics, bilingual, language

LITER—letter
literate, alliteration, literal

LITH—stone
monolith, lithograph, megalith

LOQU, LOC, LOG—speech, thought
eloquent, loquacious, colloquial, circumlocution, monologue, dialogue

LUC, LUM—light
lucid, elucidate, pellucid, translucent, illuminate

LUD, LUS—play
ludicrous, allude, delusion

MACRO—great
macrocosm, macrobiotics

MAG, MAJ, MAS, MAX—great
magnify, magnanimous, magnate, magnitude, majesty, master, maximum

MAL—bad
malady, maladroit, malevolent, malodorous

MAN—hand
manual, manuscript, manifest

MAR—sea
submarine, marine, maritime

MATER, MATR—mother
maternal, matron, matrilineal

MEDI—middle
intermediary, medieval, mediate

MEGA—great
megaphone, megalomania, megaton, megalith

MEM, MEN—remember
memory, memento, memorabilia, reminisce

METER, METR, MENS—measure
meter, thermometer, commensurate

MICRO—small
microscope, microorganism, microcosm, microbe

MIS—wrong, bad, hate
misunderstand, misapprehension, misconstrue, mishap

MIT, MISS—send
transmit, emit, missive

MOLL—soft
mollify, emollient, mollusk

MON, MONIT—warn
admonish, monitor, premonition

MONO—one
monologue, monotonous, monogamy

MOR—custom, manner
moral, mores, morose

MOR, MORT—dead
morbid, moribund, mortal, amortize

MORPH—shape
amorphous, anthropomorphic, morphology

MOV, MOT, MOB, MOM—move
remove, motion, mobile, momentum, momentous

MUT—change
mutate, mutability, immutable, commute

NAT, NASC—born
native, nativity, cognate, nascent, renascent, renaissance

NAU, NAV—ship, sailor
nautical, nauseous, navy, circumnavigate

NEG—not, deny
negative, abnegate, renege

NEO—new
neoclassical, neophyte, neologism, neonate

NIHIL—none, nothing
annihilation, nihilism

NOM, NYM—name
nominate, nomenclature, nominal, synonym, anonymity

NOX, NIC, NEC, NOC—harm
obnoxious, internecine, innocuous

NOV—new
novelty, innovation, novitiate

NUMER—number
numeral, numerous, innumerable, enumerate

OB—against
obstruct, obdurate, obsequious, obtrusive

OMNI—all
omnipresent, omnipotent, omniscient, omnivorous

ONER—burden
onerous, exonerate

OPER—work
operate, cooperate, inoperable

PAC—peace
pacify, pacifist, pacific

PALP—feel
palpable, palpitation

PAN—all
panorama, panacea, pandemic, panoply

PATER, PATR—father
paternal, paternity, patriot, compatriot, expatriate

PATH, PASS—feel, suffer
sympathy, antipathy, pathos, impassioned

PEC—money
pecuniary, impecunious, peculation

PED, POD—foot
pedestrian, pediment, quadruped, tripod

PEL, PULS—drive
compel, compelling, expel, propel, compulsion

PEN—almost
peninsula, penultimate, penumbra

PEND, PENS—hang
pendant, pendulous, suspense, propensity

PER—through, by, for, throughout
perambulator, percipient, perfunctory, pertinacious

PER—against, destruction
perfidious, pernicious, perjure

PERI—around
perimeter, periphery, perihelion, peripatetic

PET—seek, go toward
petition, impetus, impetuous, petulant, centripetal

PHIL—love
philosopher, philanderer, philanthropy, philology

PHOB—fear
phobia, claustrophobia, xenophobia

PHON—sound
phonograph, megaphone, phonics

PLAC—calm, please
placate, implacable, placid, complacent

PON, POS—put, place
postpone, proponent, juxtaposition, depose

PORT—carry
portable, deportment, rapport

POT—drink
potion, potable

POT—power
potential, potent, impotent, potentate, omnipotence

PRE—before
precede, precipitate, premonition, preposition

PRIM, PRI—first
prime, primary, primordial, pristine

PRO—ahead, forth
proceed, proclivity, protestation, provoke

PROTO—first
prototype, protagonist, protocol

PROX, PROP—near
approximate, propinquity, proximity

PSEUDO—false
pseudoscientific, pseudonym

PYR—fire
pyre, pyrotechnics, pyromania

QUAD, QUAR, QUAT—four
quadrilateral, quadrant, quarter, quarantine

QUES, QUER, QUIS, QUIR—question
quest, inquest, query, querulous, inquisitive, inquiry

QUIE—quiet
disquiet, acquiesce, quiescent, requiem

QUINT, QUIN—five
quintuplets, quintessence

RADI, RAMI—branch
radiate, radiant, eradicate, ramification

RECT, REG—straight, rule
rectangle, rectitude, rectify, regular

REG—king, rule
regal, regent, interregnum

RETRO—backward
retrospective, retroactive, retrograde

RID, RIS—laugh
ridiculous, deride, derision

ROG—ask
interrogate, derogatory, arrogant

RUD—rough, crude
rude, erudite, rudimentary

RUPT—break
disrupt, interrupt, rupture

SACR, SANCT—holy
sacred, sacrilege, sanction, sacrosanct

SCRIB, SCRIPT, SCRIV—write
scribe, ascribe, script, manuscript, scrivener

SE—apart, away
separate, segregate, secede, sedition

SEC, SECT, SEG—cut
secant, sector, dissect, bisect, intersect, segment

SED, SID—sit
sedate, sedentary, supersede, reside, residence

SEM—seed, sow
seminar, seminal, disseminate

SEN—old
senior, senile, senescent

SENT, SENS—feel, think
sentiment, nonsense, consensus, sensual

SEQU, SECU—follow
sequence, sequel, subsequent, consecutive

SIGN—mark, sign
signal, designation, assignation

SIM, SEM—similar, same
similar, verisimilitude, semblance, dissemble

SIN—curve
sinuous, insinuate

SOL—sun
solar, parasol, solarium, solstice

SOL—alone
solo, solitude, soliloquy, solipsism

SOMN—sleep
insomnia, somnolent, somnambulist

SON—sound
sonic, consonance, sonorous, resonate

SOPH—wisdom
philosopher, sophistry, sophisticated, sophomoric

SPEC, SPIC—see, look
spectator, retrospective, perspective, perspicacious

SPER—hope
prosper, prosperous, despair, desperate

SPERS, SPAR—scatter
disperse, aspersion, sparse, disparate

SPIR—breathe
respire, inspire, spiritual, aspire, transpire

STRICT, STRING—bind
stricture, constrict, stringent, astringent

STRUCT, STRU—build
structure, obstruct, construe

SUB—under
subconscious, subjugate, subliminal, subpoena

SUMM—highest
summit, summary, consummate

SUPER, SUR—above
supervise, supercilious, superfluous, insurmountable, surfeit

SURGE, SURRECT—rise
surge, resurgent, insurgent, insurrection

SYN, SYM—together
synthesis, sympathy, symposium, symbiosis

TACIT, TIC—silent
tacit, taciturn, reticent

TACT, TAG, TANG—touch
tact, tactile, contagious, tangent, tangential, tangible

TEN, TIN, TAIN—hold, twist
detention, tenable, pertinacious, retinue, retain

TEND, TENS, TENT—stretch
intend, distend, tension, tensile, ostensible, contentious

TERM—end
terminal, terminus, terminate, interminable

TERR—earth, land
terrain, terrestrial, extraterrestrial, subterranean

TEST—witness
testify, attest, testimonial, protestation

THE—god
atheist, theology, apotheosis, theocracy

THERM—heat
thermometer, thermal, thermonuclear, hypothermia

TIM—fear, frightened
timid, intimidate, timorous

TOP—place
topic, topography, utopia

TORP—stiff, numb
torpedo, torpid, torpor

TORT—twist
distort, extort, tortuous

TOX—poison
toxic, toxin, intoxication

TRACT—draw
tractor, intractable, protract

TRANS—across, over, through, beyond
transport, transgress, transient, transitory, translucent

TREM, TREP—shake
tremble, tremor, trepidation, intrepid

TURB—shake
disturb, turbulent, perturbation

UMBR—shadow
umbrella, umbrage, adumbrate, penumbra

UNI, UN—one
unify, unilateral, unanimous

URB—city
urban, suburban, urbane

VAC—empty
vacant, evacuate, vacuous

VAL, VAIL—value, strength
valid, valor, ambivalent, convalescence, avail

VEN, VENT—come
convene, intervene, venue, convention, adventitious

VER—true
verify, verity, verisimilitude, verdict

VERB—word
verbal, verbose, verbiage, verbatim

VERT, VERS—turn
avert, convert, revert, incontrovertible, divert, aversion

VICT, VINC—conquer
victory, conviction, evict, evince, invincible

VID, VIS—see
evident, vision, visage, supervise

VIL—base, mean
vile, vilify, revile

VIV, VIT—life
vivid, convivial, vivacious, vital

VOC, VOK, VOW—call, voice
vocal, equivocate, invoke, avow

VOL—wish
voluntary, malevolent, benevolent, volition

VOLV, VOLUT—turn, roll
revolve, evolve, convoluted

VOR—eat
devour, carnivore, omnivorous, voracious

Printed by Libri Plureos GmbH in Hamburg, Germany